Practice Book

McGraw Hill

mheducation.com/prek-12

Copyright © 2023 McGraw Hill

All rights reserved. The contents, or parts thereof, may be
reproduced in print form for non-profit educational use with
Wonders, provided such reproductions bear copyright notice,
but may not be reproduced in any form for any other purpose
without the prior written consent of McGraw Hill, including,
but not limited to, network storage or transmission, or broadcast
for distance learning.

Send all inquiries to:
McGraw Hill
1325 Avenue of the Americas
New York, NY 10121

ISBN: 978-1-26-580827-3
MHID: 1-26-580827-9

Printed in the United States of America.

6 7 8 9 10 LHN 27 26 25 24 23

C

Contents

Copyright © McGraw Hill. Permission is granted to reproduce for classroom use.

Copyright © McGraw Hill. Permission is granted to reproduce for classroom use.

Copyright © McGraw Hill. Permission is granted to reproduce for classroom use.

Copyright © McGraw Hill. Permission is granted to reproduce for classroom use.

Copyright © McGraw Hill. Permission is granted to reproduce for classroom use.

Copyright © McGraw Hill. Permission is granted to reproduce for classroom use.

Name _____

> - A **sentence** is a group of words that shows a complete thought. *The cat played with string.*
> - A **sentence fragment** is a group of words that does not show a complete thought: *Drove the car.*
> - Every sentence begins with a **capital letter** and ends with a **punctuation mark**. *The pencils are sharpened.*

Read each group of words. On the lines provided, write *sentence* **if the group of words forms a sentence. Write** *fragment* **if it does not form a sentence.**

1. There are many stars in the sky. _____

2. Brought it into the kitchen. _____

3. My classroom at school. _____

4. Did you see the rabbit? _____

5. I can jump very high. _____

6. Great day! _____

7. The student was late. _____

8. Laughing loudly at the joke. _____

9. Do you want to play a game? _____

10. I think we won! _____

 **In your writer's notebook, write about the last time you won a game or a prize. Make sure each sentence expresses a complete thought and ends with a punctuation mark.**

Copyright © McGraw Hill. Permission is granted to reproduce for classroom use.

Name _____

- A **sentence** shows a complete thought. A **sentence fragment** does not.
- A **statement** is a sentence that tells something. *We went to the store.*
- A **question** is a sentence that asks something. *Are we there yet?*
- A **command** is a sentence that tells someone to do something. *Wash your hands.*
- An **exclamation** is a sentence that expresses surprise, excitement, or a strong feeling. *I can't believe you're here!*

Read each group of words. Underline the group of words that is a sentence. Then write *statement, question, command,* or *exclamation* to name the type of sentence it is.

1. Live far away from me. / You live far away. _____

2. Is it in here? / The book in here? _____

3. This is the best gift ever! / Best gift I ever got! _____

4. The button when the light comes on. / Push the button quickly. _____

5. How old is your cousin? / Your cousin's age? _____

6. The tallest building in the world! / That is the tallest building! _____

7. Red backpack today. / My backpack ripped. _____

8. The name of your teacher? / Who is your teacher? _____

 **Read this paragraph from "A World of Change." Underline the exclamation. In your writer's notebook, explain why you think the author used an exclamation in the paragraph.**

> The surface of Earth constantly changes through natural processes. These processes can be gradual or swift. They help to make Earth the amazing planet that it is!

Copyright © McGraw Hill. Permission is granted to reproduce for classroom use.

Name _____

> - Every sentence begins with a **capital letter**.
> - A **statement** ends with a **period**. (.)
> - A **question** ends with a **question mark**. (?)
> - A **command** ends with a **period** or an **exclamation mark**. (. or !)
> - An **exclamation** ends with an **exclamation mark**. (!)

Write each sentence correctly using capital letters and end punctuation. Label each sentence as a *statement,* *question,* *command,* **or** *exclamation.*

1. put the bottle in the bin outside _____

_____

2. who is your favorite actor _____

_____

3. the snow sticks to the tree branches _____

_____

4. how many push-ups can you do in a row _____

_____

Writing Connection — **Think about a person you admire. Write two sentences about that person. Include an exclamation sentence. Remember that punctuation can be used for effect. It can show the reader how you feel about something.**

_____

_____

_____

Copyright © McGraw Hill. Permission is granted to reproduce for classroom use.

Name _____

- A **sentence** shows a complete thought. A **sentence fragment** does not.

- A **statement** is a sentence that tells something. A **question** is a sentence that asks something.

- A **command** is a sentence that tells someone to do something. An **exclamation** is a sentence that expresses a strong feeling.

- Every sentence begins with a **capital letter** and ends with a **period, question mark,** or **exclamation mark.**

Rewrite the paragraphs below, correcting any mistakes you might find.

HANDWRITING CONNECTION

Be sure to write legibly. Use proper cursive and remember to leave spaces between words.

1. today was the best day ever? woke up to find that it snowed last night. Was no school! I made a snowman. then I went sledding?

_____

_____

_____

2. Have you ever made a peanut butter and jelly sandwich. is really easy. Spread peanut butter on one slice of bread? then spread jelly on the other slice. The two slices together. now you have a delicious sandwich!

_____

_____

3. I wrote a science report about the desert! Wrote about the weather and the animals that live there. now I want to visit the desert to see it in person? what place would you like to see?

_____

_____

_____

Copyright © McGraw Hill. Permission is granted to reproduce for classroom use.

Name _____

Read the student draft that follows. Then answer the questions.

(1) Amy and Leta are at the library. (2) "What kind of book do you want to read, Amy?" Leta asks.

(3) "I love mysteries!" Amy answers.

(4) "Me too," Leta says.

(5) The girls look at the books on the shelves. (6) "Take a look at this," Leta says, and she reads out a title, *Clues from the Cat's Claws.*

(7) Then Amy reads aloud text from the book. (8) "How does a cat claw itself out of trouble? (9) Only Cleo the clever cat can do that! (10) Read on to find out how Cleo the cat leaves clues to be rescued."

(11) "This is *purrfect*! (12) We can read the mystery with our cats!" says Leta.

1. Which of the following is a statement?

   A Sentence 1
   B Sentence 8
   C Sentence 9
   D Sentence 11

2. Which of the following is a question?

   F Sentence 3
   G Sentence 5
   H Sentence 8
   J Sentence 12

3. Which of the following is a command?

   A Sentence 3
   B Sentence 5
   C Sentence 10
   D Sentence 12

4. Which of the following is an exclamation?

   F Sentence 7
   G Sentence 8
   H Sentence 10
   J Sentence 11

Copyright © McGraw Hill. Permission is granted to reproduce for classroom use.

Name _____

Fold back the paper along the dotted line. Use the blanks to write each word as it is read aloud. When you finish the test, unfold the paper. Use the list at the right to correct any spelling mistakes.	1. _____	1.	flat
	2. _____	2.	cash
	3. _____	3.	band
	4. _____	4.	bell
	5. _____	5.	left
	6. _____	6.	shelf
	7. _____	7.	wealth
	8. _____	8.	grim
	9. _____	9.	mill
	10. _____	10.	hint
	11. _____	11.	plot
	12. _____	12.	dock
	13. _____	13.	blot
	14. _____	14.	odd
	15. _____	15.	sum
	16. _____	16.	plum
	17. _____	17.	bluff
	18. _____	18.	crunch
	19. _____	19.	build
	20. _____	20.	gym
Review Words	21. _____	21.	snack
	22. _____	22.	step
	23. _____	23.	pond
Challenge Words	24. _____	24.	heavy
	25. _____	25.	shovel

Copyright © McGraw Hill. Permission is granted to reproduce for classroom use.

Name _____

Words with the same short vowel sound can be spelled in different ways.
- The words *ink*, *build*, and *gym* each have a short *i* sound.
- The words *egg* and *head* each have a short *e* sound.

Copyright © McGraw Hill. Permission is granted to reproduce for classroom use.

SPELLING TIP

Short *a* words are usually spelled using the vowel *a* (*flap, tap, clap*). Short *o* words are usually spelled using the vowel *o* (*lot, stop, plod*).

Write the spelling words that contain each short vowel sound.

flat	left	mill	blot	bluff
grim	shelf	gym	wealth	band
plot	plum	crunch	bell	build
sum	cash	dock	odd	hint

short *a* as in *splat*

1. _____
2. _____
3. _____

short *e* spelled *e* as in *tell*

4. _____
5. _____
6. _____

short *e* spelled *ea* as in *health*

7. _____

short *i* spelled *i* as in *flick*

8. _____
9. _____
10. _____

short *i* spelled *ui* as in *guilt*

11. _____

short *i* spelled *y* as in *myth*

12. _____

short *o* as in *stock*

13. _____
14. _____
15. _____
16. _____

short *u* as in *nuts*

17. _____
18. _____
19. _____
20. _____

 **Look through this week's selection for more words to sort. Read the words aloud and create a word sort for a partner in your writer's notebook.**

Name _____

Words with the same short vowel sound can be spelled in different ways.
- The words *ink*, *build*, and *gym* each have a short *i* sound.
- The words *egg* and *head* each have a short *e* sound.

SPELLING TIP

Short *a* words are usually spelled using the vowel *a* (*flap, tap, clap*). Short *o* words are usually spelled using the vowel *o* (*lot, stop, plod*).

Write the spelling words that contain each short vowel sound.

flat	left	mill	blot	past
list	smell	gym	tax	band
plot	plum	lunch	bell	when
mud	cash	rot	odd	hint

short *a* as in *splat*

1. _____
2. _____
3. _____
4. _____
5. _____

short *i* spelled *y* as in *myth*

6. _____

short *e* spelled *e* as in *tell*

7. _____
8. _____
9. _____
10. _____

short *i* spelled *i* as in *flick*

11. _____
12. _____
13. _____

short *o* as in *stock*

14. _____
15. _____
16. _____
17. _____

short *u* as in *nuts*

18. _____
19. _____
20. _____

 **Look through this week's selection for more words to sort. Read the words aloud and create a word sort for a partner in your writer's notebook.**

Copyright © McGraw Hill. Permission is granted to reproduce for classroom use.

Name _____

Write the spelling words that contain each short vowel sound. If a word has two different short vowel sounds, include it in both columns and underline the appropriate vowel sound.

sandwich	skimming	miller	blot	bluff
alibi	shelves	culprit	wealthy	heavy
plots	plum	crunches	sketches	slipped
smudge	clamped	dock	typical	grimace

short _a_ as in _splat_

1. _____

2. _____

3. _____

short _e_ spelled _e_ as in _tell_

4. _____

5. _____

6. _____

short _i_ spelled _y_ as in _myth_

7. _____

short _i_ spelled _i_ as in _flick_

8. _____

9. _____

10. _____

11. _____

12. _____

13. _____

14. _____

short _e_ spelled _ea_ as in _health_

15. _____

16. _____

short _o_ as in _stock_

17. _____

18. _____

19. _____

short _u_ as in _nuts_

20. _____

21. _____

22. _____

23. _____

24. _____

 **Look through this week's selection for more words to sort. Read the words aloud and create a word sort for a partner in your writer's notebook.**

Copyright © McGraw Hill. Permission is granted to reproduce for classroom use.

Name _____

flat	left	mill	blot	bluff
cash	shelf	hint	odd	crunch
band	wealth	plot	sum	build
bell	grim	dock	plum	gym

A. Write the spelling word that best completes each sentence.

1. She is the drum player in a _____.

2. Did you tell the truth or was that a _____?

3. I did not have enough _____ on me to pay for it.

4. He brought the ball to _____ class.

5. The car tires will _____ the can on the street.

6. I did not know that flour was made at this _____.

7. My favorite fruit is the _____.

8. This _____ chimes at noon every day.

9. We got on the boat from the _____.

10. He _____ his glasses at home today.

B. Write the spelling word that matches each definition below.

11. soak up _____

12. gloomy _____

13. clue _____

14. make _____

15. story line _____

16. not even _____

17. ledge _____

18. a lot of money _____

19. not round _____

20. total _____

Copyright © McGraw Hill. Permission is granted to reproduce for classroom use.

Name _____

Underline the six misspelled words in the paragraphs below. Write the words correctly on the lines.

The classroom was quiet. Books sat closed and flatt on the desks. The class hamster was missing! The class liked Biscuit. The students had helped to bild the hamster's cage. They liked to watch Biscuit krunch food and run on the wheel.

Chad looked very grimm. He had taken Biscuit home last night. He planned to bring the hamster back, but he had leeft it at home. Chad raised his hand. No one needed another hent. The class knew who had taken Biscuit.

1. _____ 4. _____

2. _____ 5. _____

3. _____ 6. _____

Write about something that happened in your classroom. Use at least four words from the spelling list. Review the spelling rules for words with short vowels before you write.

_____

_____

_____

_____

_____

_____

_____

Copyright © McGraw Hill. Permission is granted to reproduce for classroom use.

Name _____

Copyright © McGraw Hill. Permission is granted to reproduce for classroom use.

Remember

Words with the same short vowel sound are not always spelled the same way. The short vowel sound *i* can be spelled with *i, ui,* or *y*. The short *e* sound can be spelled with *e* or *ea*.

A. Circle the word that rhymes with the word in bold. Read the correct word aloud and write it on the line provided.

1. **clock**   deck   dock   poke   _____
2. **dash**   cash   floss   cost   _____
3. **rod**   add   odd   told   _____
4. **stuff**   stung   stiff   bluff   _____
5. **bat**   flat   plot   float   _____
6. **pill**   mile   mill   mall   _____
7. **stand**   bond   ban   band   _____
8. **shot**   shout   plot   plate   _____
9. **trim**   gym   groom   time   _____
10. **health**   wheat   wealth   weather   _____
11. **tell**   toll   stall   bell   _____
12. **drum**   elm   plum   room   _____
13. **glint**   hint   gate   light   _____
14. **theft**   left   last   foot   _____
15. **bunch**   clinch   crank   crunch   _____

B. Write these words in alphabetical order. Alphabetize them to the second letter.   *grim, blot, sum, build, shelf*

16. _____   18. _____   20. _____

17. _____   19. _____

Name _____

> **Content words** are words related to a particular field of study. For example, words such as *magma*, *crust*, and *igneous rock* are earth science content words.
>
> Authors use content words to explain or describe specific concepts, processes, events, people, animals, places, and objects. Sometimes context clues will help you figure out what a content word means. You can also use a dictionary to find the meaning of content words.

With a partner, find as many content words related to changes in Earth's surface as you can. Write them in the cloud and raindrops.

Earth Science Words

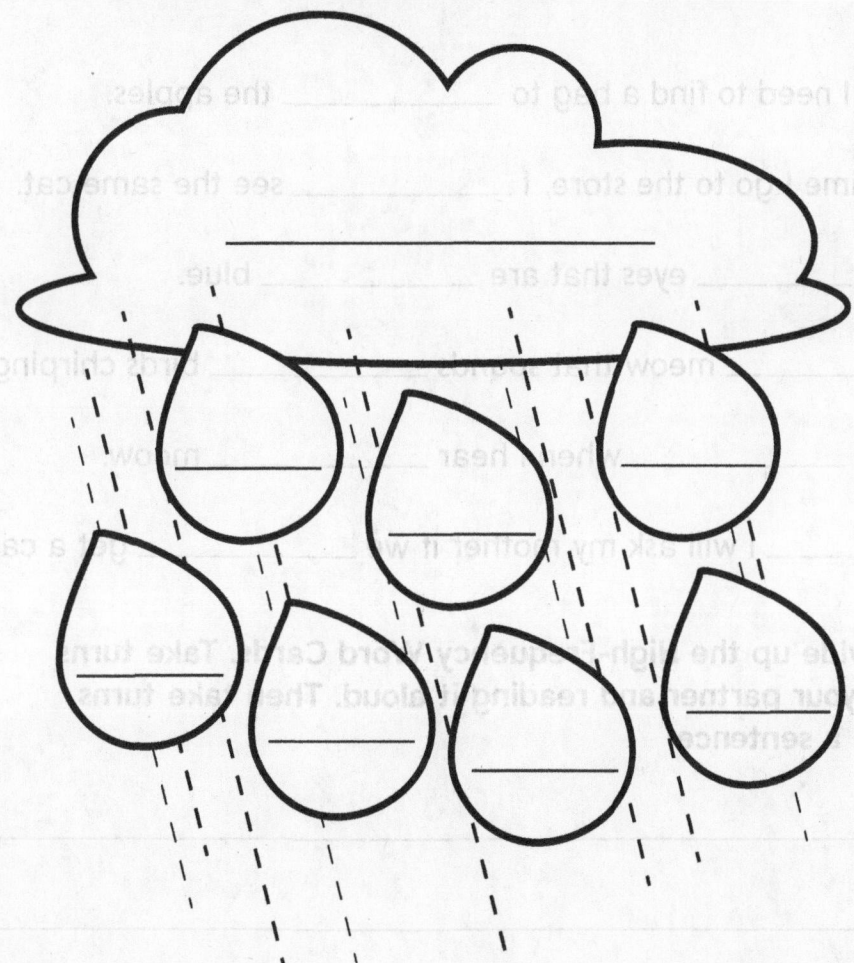

Copyright © McGraw Hill. Permission is granted to reproduce for classroom use.

Name _____

High-frequency words are the most common words in the English language. They do not follow regular sound or spelling patterns. The more you read and write them, the easier they are to remember. Read these high-frequency words out loud. Then complete the sentences using the words from the box.

because	carry	very	her
every	laugh	like	first
pretty	funny	walk	could
don't	today	always	green

1. I will _____ to the store _____ it is nearby.

2. At the store, I will buy _____ apples since I _____ like red ones.

3. _____ , I need to find a bag to _____ the apples.

4. _____ time I go to the store, I _____ see the same cat.

5. The cat has _____ eyes that are _____ blue.

6. She has a _____ meow that sounds _____ birds chirping.

7. I always start to _____ when I hear _____ meow.

8. Maybe _____ I will ask my mother if we _____ get a cat.

With a partner, divide up the High-Frequency Word Cards. Take turns showing a card to your partner and reading it aloud. Then take turns using each word in a sentence.

_____

_____

Copyright © McGraw Hill. Permission is granted to reproduce for classroom use.

Name _____

> • The **subject** names the person or thing the sentence is about. The **simple subject** is the main noun or pronoun in the **complete subject**.
>
> *(The blue bird) flew out of the nest.*
>
> • The **predicate** tells what the subject is or does. The **simple predicate** is the main verb or verb phrase in the **complete predicate**.
>
> *The man (swam to the side of the pool.)*

A. Read each sentence and circle the complete subject. Then write the simple subject on the line provided.

1. The young boy rode the bus to school. _____

2. Curious Mrs. Hill likes museums. _____

3. The two playful children made up a new game. _____

4. Sports-loving Ana plays soccer. _____

5. Jan's friendly dog ran very fast. _____

B. Read each sentence and circle the complete predicate. Then write the simple predicate on the line provided.

6. We walked to the park. _____

7. My brother Ken collects old stamps. _____

8. I cooked a delicious dinner. _____

9. Mom works hard all day. _____

10. The shy rabbit hopped away quickly. _____

 **In your writer's notebook, write about your favorite holiday. Underline two simple subjects and circle two complete predicates.**

Copyright © McGraw Hill. Permission is granted to reproduce for classroom use.

Name _____

> • The **subject** names the person or thing the sentence is about.
> The **predicate** tells what the subject is or does.
>
> • A **compound subject** is two or more subjects with the same predicate.
> The subjects are usually joined by **and** or **or**. _Jamie and Andrea_ run.
>
> • A **compound predicate** is two or more predicates with the same
> subject. The simple predicates in a compound predicate are usually
> joined by **and, but,** or **or**. Mom and Dad _wash and dry_ the car.

**Read each sentence. Underline the compound subject or compound
predicate. Then write** compound subject **or** compound predicate **on the
line provided.**

1. The cat and dog get along very well. _____

2. Mom and Dad rented a car for the vacation. _____

3. We could drive or walk to school. _____

4. My little sisters whine, fuss, and cry at bedtime. _____

5. Aunt Eileen and Uncle Will live down the block. _____

**Talk to a parent or trusted adult about a food from
a different culture you would like to try. Then write a
paragraph about the food and why you want to try it.
Use compound subjects and compound predicates in your
writing. Underline the compound subjects and predicates.**

_____

_____

_____

_____

Copyright © McGraw Hill. Permission is granted to reproduce for classroom use.

Name _____

- If a **compound subject** has two subjects, the subjects are not separated by a comma. If it has three or more subjects, they are separated by commas. *Mom, Dad, and I had so much fun at the park today!*
- If a **compound predicate** has two predicates, the predicates are not separated by a comma. If it has three or more predicates, they are separated by commas. *Today I planned, wrote, and turned in my essay.*

Read each sentence. Decide if the compound subject or compound predicate needs commas. If it does, rewrite the sentence correctly on the line provided. If it does not, write *No change needed* **on the line.**

1. My mother my cousin and I went to the store together.

   _____

2. We all sat ate and drank at the dinner table.

   _____

3. Miguel dove off the diving board and swam across the pool.

   _____

4. The gray horse brown horse or black horse will win the race.

   _____

5. She was hungry but found nothing in the refrigerator.

   _____

 **Reread this excerpt from "Tornado." Circle the compound subject. In your writer's notebook, write about the last time you saw a big storm. Use one compound subject and one compound predicate in your writing.**

When warm and cold air masses collide, the result can be a fast-moving, dangerous force of nature—a tornado. A tornado is a violent windstorm over land. Wind makes a rotating, funnel-shaped cloud that extends toward the ground. As it moves, it picks up debris and objects in its path.

Copyright © McGraw Hill. Permission is granted to reproduce for classroom use.

Name _____

> - The **subject** names the person or thing the sentence is about. The **simple subject** is the main noun or pronoun in the **complete subject**.
> - The **predicate** tells what the subject is or does. The **simple predicate** is the main verb or verb phrase in the **complete predicate**.
> - A **compound subject** is two or more subjects with the same predicate. If a compound subject has three or more subjects, the subjects are separated by commas.
> - A **compound predicate** is two or more predicates with the same subject. If a compound predicate has three or more subjects, the predicates are separated by commas.

Rewrite the sentences below, adding commas and correcting mistakes in punctuation.

> HANDWRITING CONNECTION
>
> As you write in cursive, make sure that your letters are slanted in the same way and joined with the correct stroke.

1. The flags banner or ribbons will blow away in the storm.

   _____

2. Did the ranger call in and record his status on the way up the trail.

   _____

3. The baby robins tweeted, cried and called for their mother.

   _____

4. Regan Katrina, and I watched the amazing sight above us.

   _____

5. How long can we continue to sit but not talk, during the movie!

   _____

6. The badger and the snake circled bit and fought with each other.

   _____

Copyright © McGraw Hill. Permission is granted to reproduce for classroom use.

Name _____

Read the paragraph. Then answer the questions.

(1) <u>I</u> had a lot of homework last night. (2) Our teacher, Mr. Rye, gave us a Spanish assignment. (3) <u>My classmates and I</u> had to write in Spanish. (4) My pencil broke halfway through a sentence. (5) I had to <u>sharpen the pencil</u>. (6) My <u>dad</u> checked my homework later that night.

1. Which sentence shows a simple subject underlined?

  A Sentence 1

  B Sentence 3

  C Sentence 5

  D Sentence 6

2. Which sentence shows a complete subject underlined?

  F Sentence 1

  G Sentence 3

  H Sentence 5

  J Sentence 6

3. What is the simple predicate in sentence 2?

  A Mr. Rye

  B gave

  C gave us a Spanish assignment

  D Spanish assignment

4. What is the complete predicate in sentence 4?

  F pencil

  G broke halfway through a sentence

  H halfway through a sentence

  J broke

Read the student draft. Then answer the questions.

(1) The rain falls heavily on the roof. (2) My bicycle is still out in the driveway. (3) The storm might rust or break my bicycle. (4) My dad and I just bought a new horn for my bike last weekend. (5) The bike and horn sparkle when the sun shines.

5. Which sentences have a compound subject?

  A Sentences 1 and 2

  B Sentences 2 and 5

  C Sentences 2 and 3

  D Sentences 4 and 5

6. Which sentence has a compound predicate?

  F Sentence 1

  G Sentence 2

  H Sentence 3

  J Sentence 4

Copyright © McGraw Hill. Permission is granted to reproduce for classroom use.

Name _____

Fold back the paper along the dotted line. Use the blanks to write each word as it is read aloud. When you finish the test, unfold the paper. Use the list at the right to correct any spelling mistakes.

1. _____
2. _____
3. _____
4. _____
5. _____
6. _____
7. _____
8. _____
9. _____
10. _____
11. _____
12. _____
13. _____
14. _____
15. _____
16. _____
17. _____
18. _____
19. _____
20. _____

Review Words
21. _____
22. _____
23. _____

Challenge Words
24. _____
25. _____

1. major
2. clay
3. stray
4. today
5. bail
6. rail
7. drain
8. faint
9. claim
10. pale
11. face
12. graze
13. cane
14. slate
15. ache
16. steak
17. break
18. eight
19. they
20. obey
21. grim
22. plum
23. cash
24. neighbor
25. railway

Copyright © McGraw Hill. Permission is granted to reproduce for classroom use.

Name_____

> Words with the /ā/ sound can be spelled in different ways.
> - *a* as in *apron*
> - *ay* as in *stay*
> - *ai* as in *train*
> - *a_e* as in *cake*
> - *ea* as in *great*
> - *ei* as in *reins*
> - *eigh* as in *sleigh*
> - *ey* as in *they*

SPELLING TIP

Some sounds have several different spelling patterns. See the box to the left for the different ways to spell the long *a* sound.

Write the spelling words that contain the matching spelling of the long *a* sound.

eight	claim	bail	cane	stray
pale	graze	clay	slate	obey
face	ache	steak	drain	major
today	faint	rail	they	break

long *a* spelled *a* as in *table*

1. _____

long *a* spelled *ay* as in *gray*

2. _____
3. _____
4. _____

long *a* spelled *ei* as in *weigh*

5. _____

long *a* spelled *ai* as in *aid*

6. _____
7. _____
8. _____
9. _____
10. _____

long *a* spelled *ea* as in *great*

11. _____
12. _____

long *a* spelled *ey* as in *prey*

13. _____
14. _____

long *a* spelled *a_e* as in *bake*

15. _____
16. _____
17. _____
18. _____
19. _____
20. _____

 **Use the spelling rules above to write a short rhyming poem. Include four words from the spelling list. Read the words aloud and check your work for errors.**

Copyright © McGraw Hill. Permission is granted to reproduce for classroom use.

Name _____

Words with the /ā/ sound can be spelled in different ways.
- *a* as in <u>a</u>pron
- *ea* as in gr<u>ea</u>t
- *ay* as in st<u>ay</u>
- *ei* as in r<u>ei</u>ns
- *ai* as in tr<u>ai</u>n
- *eigh* as in sl<u>eigh</u>
- *a_e* as in c<u>a</u>k<u>e</u>
- *ey* as in th<u>ey</u>

SPELLING TIP

Some sounds have several different spelling patterns. See the box to the left for the different ways to spell the long *a* sound.

Write the spelling words that contain the matching spelling of the long *a* sound.

rain	mane	clay	crate	aim
pale	late	save	drain	weigh
face	faint	rail	they	major
today	paid	cane	tray	break

long *a* spelled *a* as in *table*

1. _____

long *a* spelled *ay* as in *gray*

2. _____
3. _____
4. _____

long *a* spelled *ei* as in *eight*

5. _____

long *a* spelled *ea* as in *great*

6. _____

long *a* spelled *ai* as in *aid*

7. _____
8. _____
9. _____
10. _____
11. _____
12. _____

long *a* spelled *ey* as in *prey*

13. _____

long *a* spelled *a_e* as in *bake*

14. _____
15. _____
16. _____
17. _____
18. _____
19. _____
20. _____

 Use the spelling rules above to write a short rhyming poem. Include four words from the spelling list. Read the words aloud and check your work for errors.

Copyright © McGraw Hill. Permission is granted to reproduce for classroom use.

Name _____

Write the spelling words that contain the matching spelling of the long *a* sound. If a word has more than one spelling for the long *a* sound, write it under both sections.

eighteen	mistake	display	remain	obeyed
pale	ache	steak	frail	major
parade	fainting	wailing	nickname	break
railway	bail	relay	stray	claimed

long *a* spelled *a* as in *table*

1. _____

long *a* spelled *ay* as in *gray*

2. _____

3. _____

4. _____

5. _____

long *a* spelled *ea* as in *great*

6. _____

7. _____

long *a* spelled *ai* as in *aid*

8. _____

9. _____

10. _____

11. _____

12. _____

13. _____

14. _____

long *a* spelled *ei* as in *eight*

15. _____

long *a* spelled *ey* as in *prey*

16. _____

long *a* spelled *a_e* as in *bake*

17. _____

18. _____

19. _____

20. _____

21. _____

Use the spelling rules above to write a short rhyming poem. Include four words from the spelling list. Read the words aloud and check your work for errors.

Name _____

major	bail	claim	cane	break
clay	rail	pale	slate	eight
stray	drain	face	ache	they
today	faint	graze	steak	obey

A. Write the spelling word that best completes each sentence.

1. Horses will _____ on this green grass all day if you let them.

2. The girls were best friends, and _____ went everywhere together.

3. The _____ ordered the troops to attack at sunrise.

4. He stood on the _____ of the fence to see better.

5. The lost hiker smiled when he saw the _____ glow of a house light.

6. The _____ in my back was getting worse, so I went to a doctor.

7. My grandfather uses a _____ to help him walk.

8. Did you see the smile on that girl's _____?

9. I added a chair so that there were _____ in all, not seven.

B. Write the spelling word that matches each definition below.

10. what pottery is made of _____

11. part of a fence _____

12. a type of meat _____

13. what water goes down _____

14. light or white _____

15. without a home _____

16. destroy _____

17. a flat, black stone _____

18. scoop out _____

19. to state _____

20. to eat grass _____

21. soft or slight _____

22. follow or listen to _____

23. day before tomorrow _____

Copyright © McGraw Hill. Permission is granted to reproduce for classroom use.

Name _____

**Circle the six misspelled words in the paragraphs
below. Write the words correctly on the lines.**

    Keisha bought a cactus at the plant sale todaye.
The seller said that it likes sandy soil, not clai soil.
She will keep the plant on her desk at home. She put
a piece of slayte under it to protect the wood.

    Jessie is Keisha's brother. He adopted a strai cat that pretends it
is in the jungle. Keisha is afraid that the cat will breke her plant.
Jessie says she should not worry. His cat knows how to obay!

1. _____   4. _____

2. _____   5. _____

3. _____   6. _____

Writing Connection

**Write about a pet you know that gets into trouble. It could
be your pet or someone else's pet. Use at least four words
from the spelling list. Then check over your work.**

_____

_____

_____

_____

_____

_____

_____

_____

_____

_____

Copyright © McGraw Hill. Permission is granted to reproduce for classroom use.

Name _____

Remember

> Words with the same long vowel sound are not always spelled the same
> way. These are some of the most common spelling patterns you will see
> for the long *a* vowel. Read them out loud:
>
> • *a* as in <u>a</u>corn   • *ai* as in cl<u>ai</u>m   • *ea* as in st<u>ea</u>k   • *eigh* as in n<u>eigh</u>
>
> • *ay* as in str<u>ay</u>   • *a_e* as in t<u>a</u>k<u>e</u>   • *ei* as in <u>ei</u>ght   • *ey* as in ob<u>ey</u>

Circle the word that rhymes with the word in bold type. Write the word.

1.	**gate**	strain	slate	that	_____
2.	**pail**	play	paid	bail	_____
3.	**shame**	claim	harm	slam	_____
4.	**stay**	why	my	they	_____
5.	**take**	tack	ache	act	_____
6.	**hooray**	clay	wait	star	_____
7.	**maze**	graze	jazz	daisy	_____
8.	**away**	yawn	today	toy	_____
9.	**tail**	fall	spill	pale	_____
10.	**snake**	break	seek	neck	_____
11.	**pain**	shine	drain	candle	_____
12.	**delay**	later	party	obey	_____
13.	**sail**	rail	seal	slant	_____
14.	**train**	ran	trace	cane	_____
15.	**wait**	part	eight	salt	_____
16.	**play**	plan	stray	any	_____
17.	**make**	steak	maid	tack	_____
18.	**case**	past	crack	face	_____
19.	**paint**	pain	faint	pant	_____
20.	**pager**	major	pay	judge	_____

Copyright © McGraw Hill. Permission is granted to reproduce for classroom use.

Name _____

Read each passage from "Rising Waters." Underline the context clues that help you figure out the meaning of each multiple-meaning word in bold. Then write the word's meaning on the line.

1. Have you ever been in an earthquake or a tornado? These terrible events may never happen where you live. But flooding is something that can happen in almost every **part** of the United States.

_____

_____

2. Not all floods are alike. Some floods happen over many days. A **flash** flood can happen in minutes. Learning about floods can help you stay safe.

_____

_____

3. The water in a river rises over the river's **banks**. This might happen because storms have caused too much rain to fall.

_____

_____

4. Floods also cause damage to buildings and bridges. They can even **wash** away entire roads! This can make it hard for rescue workers to help people who are trapped by the water.

_____

_____

Copyright © McGraw Hill. Permission is granted to reproduce for classroom use.

Name _____

> Like **homonyms, homographs** are words that are spelled the same but have different meanings and origins. Unlike homonyms, homographs sometimes have different pronunciations as well. When you see a homograph in a text, use context clues to figure out the meaning. Here are some examples:
>
> **bow   compact   console   entrance   fair   object   present   pupil**

Complete each sentence with a homograph from the box. You will use each word twice. Then write the letters from the boxes to solve the riddle at the bottom of the page.

record	well	content	hamper	desert

1. Alyssa is _____ to sit and read a book.

2. We packed a ☐ __ __ __ __ __ full of food for the picnic.

3. Theo was afraid we would __ ☐ __ __ __ __ him at the amusement park.

4. When the __ ☐ __ __ dried up, the family had no more water.

5. Hassan will __ ☐ __ __ __ __ his favorite show and watch it later.

6. The __ __ __ __ __ ☐ receives only one inch of rain a year.

7. Beans and whole grains are known for their high fiber __ __ __ ☐ __ __ __.

8. Will bad weather __ __ __ __ ☐ __ work on the house?

9. You just broke the world __ __ __ __ ☐ __ for the 100-meter dash!

10. Mara has a sore throat and is not feeling ☐ __ __ __ .

What do you find at the end of a rainbow?

__ __ __   __ __ __ __ __ __   __

Copyright © McGraw Hill. Permission is granted to reproduce for classroom use.

Name _____

> - A **clause** is a group of words that has a subject and a verb.
>
> - A **main,** or **independent, clause** can stand alone as a sentence. *I love playing video games.*
>
> - A **simple sentence** has one independent clause. *Devon played with the puppy.*
>
> - A **compound sentence** has two or more independent clauses. *I wanted to go to the mall, but I had to finish my chores.*

Read each sentence. On the lines provided, write *simple* **if it has one main, or independent, clause. Write** *compound* **if it has two or more main, or independent, clauses.**

1. I wanted to go to the concert, but my parents wouldn't let me. _____

2. Mrs. Gupta lives on a very busy road in the middle of the city. _____

3. He got a hot dog, she got a hamburger, and you got a salad. _____

4. Can we go to the movies later this evening? _____

5. There are too many stars in the sky to count all of them. _____

6. The little puppy was adopted quickly, for it was very sweet. _____

7. The balloon drifted up into the fluffy clouds above. _____

8. We left early, yet the traffic on the highway still made us late. _____

9. Do you want to read a book, or would you like to take a walk? _____

10. My cousin thinks he was lucky to get into his favorite college. _____

 **Use the sentences as a model. In your writer's notebook, write a short passage about a great dream you have had. Make sure to include simple and compound sentences. Then edit your work.**

Copyright © McGraw Hill. Permission is granted to reproduce for classroom use.

Name _____

> • A **clause** has a subject and a verb. A **main,** or **independent, clause** can stand alone as a sentence.
>
> • A **simple sentence** has one independent clause. A **compound sentence** has two or more independent clauses.
>
> • Independent clauses in a compound sentence are usually joined by a **coordinating conjunction,** such as *and, but, or, for, nor,* or *yet.* Conjunctions also join words and phrases in sentences.
>
>   *Alex had to wash the dog, but there was no more soap.*

Read each sentence. Circle the coordinating conjunction that best completes the sentence and write it on the line provided.

1. We can go to Florida for vacation, (or / nor) we can visit California. _____

2. My sister asked me to go with her, (for / but) I did not want to. _____

3. I brought a stool into the kitchen, (or / for) I could not reach the cabinet. _____

4. The ostrich has feathers and wings, (yet / nor) this bird cannot fly. _____

5. Haley is good at math, (but / for) Raul is better at science. _____

 **Think about your favorite season. Write two compound sentences and two simple sentences about why that time of year is your favorite. Then check that you used the best coordinating conjunctions in your sentences.**

_____

_____

_____

_____

Copyright © McGraw Hill. Permission is granted to reproduce for classroom use.

Name _____

> - Use a **comma** and a coordinating conjunction to join two independent clauses and form a compound sentence. *Haruto was hungry for lunch, but the food wasn't ready.*
> - You can also use a **semicolon** to join two independent clauses. *Anya loved baseball; she was the best pitcher in the league.*

A. Use a comma and a coordinating conjunction to combine each pair of independent clauses and form a compound sentence.

1. I am good at football. Luis is a better player than I am.

   _____

2. There is no milk left. My friends drank it all.

   _____

3. The class can take a trip to the zoo. We can visit the museum.

   _____

B. Use a semicolon to combine each pair of independent clauses and form a compound sentence.

4. Alligators have wide snouts. Crocodiles have narrow snouts.

   _____

5. I could not remember the answer. I had to take a guess.

   _____

 **Reread this paragraph from "The Talent Show." Underline the compound sentences and circle the conjunctions. In your writer's notebook, explain why you think the author used a compound sentence for each example instead of a simple sentence.**

"No," said my grandmother. "I said that you weren't respectful of your *own* ideas, or you would have spoken up. I understand that you're friends, but you're still accountable for your own actions."

Copyright © McGraw Hill. Permission is granted to reproduce for classroom use.

Name _____

- A **clause** has a subject and a verb. An **independent clause** can stand alone as a **sentence.**

- A **simple sentence** has one independent clause. A **compound sentence** has two or more independent clauses.

- Independent clauses in a compound sentence are usually joined by a **coordinating conjunction,** such as *and, but, or, for, nor,* or *yet.*

- Use a **comma** with a **coordinating conjunction** or a **semicolon** to join two independent clauses and form a compound sentence.

COMMON ERRORS

Connecting two sentences using a comma is an error called a **comma splice.** Either add a conjunction after the comma or replace the comma with a semicolon.

Rewrite the paragraph below, correcting any mistakes you find in the conjunctions and punctuation in compound sentences.

The mustang is America's symbol of the Wild West. These horses once roamed free; yet today there are few remaining. People are trying to save the mustangs that are left. And we should do what we can to help.

_____

_____

_____

 **Look back through your writer's notebook and find compound sentences you have written. Check that you used commas before coordinating conjunctions.**

Copyright © McGraw Hill. Permission is granted to reproduce for classroom use.

Name _____

Read the selection that follows. Then answer the questions.

(1) Everyone in my class is good at different things. (2) Aaron is the fastest runner in the entire school. (3) Shari, my best friend, can throw a ball farther than anyone I know. (4) What about me? (5) I am good at some things, and I am bad at others.

1. Which sentence is a compound sentence?

   A Sentence 1

   B Sentence 2

   C Sentence 4

   D Sentence 5

2. What word in sentence 5 is a coordinating conjunction?

   F am

   G at

   H and

   J bad

Read the student draft that follows. Then answer the questions.

(1) He does not play video games. (2) He does not watch television. (3) He goes to bed early. (4) He is still tired the next day.

3. Which conjunction best combines sentences 1 and 2?

   A He does not play video games, **for** he does not watch television.

   B He does not play video games, **but** he does not watch television.

   C He does not play video games, **and** he does not watch television.

   D He does not play video games, **or** he does not watch television.

4. Which conjunction best combines sentences 3 and 4?

   F He goes to bed early, **but** he is still tired the next day.

   G He goes to bed early, **or** he is still tired the next day.

   H He goes to bed early, **for** he is still tired the next day.

   J He goes to bed early, **nor** he is still tired the next day.

Copyright © McGraw Hill. Permission is granted to reproduce for classroom use.

Name _____

Fold back the
paper along the
dotted line. Use
the blanks to
write each word
as it is read aloud.
When you finish
the test, unfold
the paper. Use the
list at the right
to correct any
spelling mistakes.

1. _____
2. _____
3. _____
4. _____
5. _____
6. _____
7. _____
8. _____
9. _____
10. _____
11. _____
12. _____
13. _____
14. _____
15. _____
16. _____
17. _____
18. _____
19. _____
20. _____

Review Words 21. _____
22. _____
23. _____

Challenge Words 24. _____
25. _____

1. evening
2. zebra
3. breathe
4. league
5. squeaky
6. healer
7. sleek
8. indeed
9. reef
10. deed
11. speech
12. wheeze
13. concrete
14. scheme
15. belief
16. chief
17. honey
18. donkey
19. family
20. weary
21. bail
22. pale
23. eight
24. appeal
25. freedom

Copyright © McGraw Hill. Permission is granted to reproduce for classroom use.

Name _____

Words with the /ē/ sound can be spelled in different ways.
- *e* as in <u>we</u>
- *ie* as in *gri<u>e</u>f*
- *ea* as in *s<u>ea</u>t*
- *ei* as in *rec<u>ei</u>ve*
- *ee* as in *t<u>ee</u>th*
- *ey* as in *k<u>ey</u>*
- *e_e* as in *th<u>ese</u>*
- *y* as in *scar<u>y</u>*

SPELLING TIP

Some sounds have several different spelling patterns. See the box to the left for the different ways to spell the long *e* sound.

Write the spelling words that contain the matching long *e* spelling.

evening	indeed	honey	breathe	reef
deed	family	zebra	scheme	donkey
concrete	belief	speech	sleek	healer
league	squeaky	wheeze	chief	weary

long *e* spelled *ee*

1. _____
2. _____
3. _____
4. _____
5. _____
6. _____

long *e* spelled *e_e*

7. _____
8. _____
9. _____

long *e* spelled *y*

10. _____
11. _____

long *e* spelled *ea* and *y*

12. _____

long *e* spelled *ie*

13. _____
14. _____

long *e* spelled *ea*

15. _____
16. _____
17. _____

long *e* spelled *ey*

18. _____
19. _____

long *e* spelled *e*

20. _____

 **Look through this week's selection and pick out all the words that have a long *e* vowel. Read the words aloud, write them in a list, and sort them by their spelling patterns.**

Copyright © McGraw Hill. Permission is granted to reproduce for classroom use.

Name _____

Words with the /ē/ sound can be spelled in different ways.
- e as in w<u>e</u>
- ie as in gri<u>e</u>f
- ea as in s<u>ea</u>t
- ei as in rec<u>ei</u>ve
- ee as in t<u>ee</u>th
- ey as in k<u>ey</u>
- e_e as in th<u>e</u>se
- y as in scar<u>y</u>

SPELLING TIP

Some sounds have several different spelling patterns. See the box to the left for the different ways to spell the long e sound.

Write the spelling words that contain the matching long e spelling.

please	heal	weep	chief	reef
maybe	seem	gene	leak	key
deed	scene	speech	money	beam
feet	busy	zebra	either	only

long e spelled ee

1. _____
2. _____
3. _____
4. _____
5. _____
6. _____

long e spelled e_e

7. _____
8. _____

long e spelled y

9. _____
10. _____

long e spelled ey

11. _____
12. _____

long e spelled e

13. _____
14. _____

long e spelled ie

15. _____

long e spelled ei

16. _____

long e spelled ea

17. _____
18. _____
19. _____
20. _____

 Look through this week's selection and pick out all the words that have a long e vowel. Read the words aloud, write them in a list, and sort them by their spelling patterns.

Copyright © McGraw Hill. Permission is granted to reproduce for classroom use.

Name _____

Write the spelling words that contain the matching long *e* spelling. If a word has more than one spelling for the long *e* sound, write it under both sections.

evening	tea	honeybee	breathe	eerie
thirteen	mystery	feline	scheme	donkey
concrete	belief	succeed	appealing	creature
league	increased	wheeze	chief	weary

long *e* spelled *ee*

1. _____

2. _____

3. _____

4. _____

5. _____

long *e* spelled *e_e*

6. _____

7. _____

8. _____

long *e* spelled *y*

9. _____

10. _____

long *e* spelled *ie*

11. _____

12. _____

13. _____

long *e* spelled *ey*

14. _____

15. _____

long *e* spelled *ea*

16. _____

17. _____

18. _____

19. _____

20. _____

21. _____

long *e* spelled *e*

22. _____

 **Look through this week's selection and pick out all the words that have a long *e* vowel. Read the words aloud, write them in a list, and sort them by their spelling patterns.**

Copyright © McGraw Hill. Permission is granted to reproduce for classroom use.

Name _____

evening	squeaky	reef	concrete	honey
zebra	healer	deed	scheme	donkey
breathe	sleek	speech	belief	family
league	indeed	wheeze	chief	weary

A. An analogy is a statement that compares sets of words. Write the spelling word that best completes each analogy below.

1. *Happy* is to *glad* as *tired* is to _____.

2. *Colors* is to *rainbow* as *teams* is to _____.

3. *Song* is to *tune* as *plan* is to _____.

4. *Sun* is to *moon* as *morning* is to _____.

5. *Teacher* is to *instructor* as *leader* is to _____.

6. *Early* is to *late* as *low-pitched* is to _____.

7. *Promise* is to *vow* as *act* is to _____.

8. *Carpenter* is to *builder* as *doctor* is to _____.

9. *Dog* is to *wolf* as *horse* is to _____.

10. *Warm* is to *cool* as *dull* is to _____.

B. Write the spelling word that matches each definition below.

11. breathe roughly _____

12. way of thinking _____

13. something spoken
_____

14. brothers and sisters
_____

15. underwater ridge
_____

16. actually _____

17. take air into lungs
_____

18. cement mixture
_____

19. what bees make
_____

20. striped horse-like animal

Copyright © McGraw Hill. Permission is granted to reproduce for classroom use.

Name _____

**Underline the six misspelled words in the paragraphs below.
Write the words correctly on the lines.**

Being sick is not fun. A cold can give you a sore throat and a runny nose. Sometimes you may cough or wheze. A cold can be worse in the eavening, when you go to bed. It can even keep you up all night. This makes you feel fuzzy and wearie in the morning.

People do different things to get rid of a cold. Some people drink hot water or tea with hony. Others breethe steamy air to feel better. They may even see a doctor or other heler. Most of the time, rest is the best way to get rid of a cold.

1. _____ 4. _____

2. _____ 5. _____

3. _____ 6. _____

Writing Connection

Write about how you feel when you catch a cold. Review the spelling rules for words with long _e_ before you write. Use at least four words from the spelling list.

_____

_____

_____

_____

_____

_____

_____

Copyright © McGraw Hill. Permission is granted to reproduce for classroom use.

Name _____

Copyright © McGraw Hill. Permission is granted to reproduce for classroom use.

Remember

Words with the same long vowel sound are not always spelled the same way. These are some of the most common spelling patterns you will see for the long *e* vowel. Read these words aloud:

- *e* as in *f<u>e</u>line*
- *ea* as in *cr<u>ea</u>ture*
- *ee* as in *succ<u>ee</u>d*
- *e_e* as in *<u>eve</u>*
- *ie* as in *bel<u>ie</u>f*
- *ei* as in *conc<u>ei</u>ve*
- *ey* as in *monk<u>ey</u>*
- *y* as in *war<u>y</u>*

A. Circle the word that rhymes with the word in bold type. Write the word.

1. **reach**   rich   speech   patch   _____
2. **peeler**   parlor   seller   healer   _____
3. **dream**   rein   scheme   deep   _____
4. **teethe**   breathe   reed   with   _____
5. **mistreat**   concrete   reset   create   _____
6. **creaky**   shaky   funny   squeaky   _____
7. **leaf**   left   chief   stuff   _____
8. **reread**   indeed   complete   rounded   _____
9. **weak**   deck   sleek   sink   _____
10. **beef**   birth   feed   belief   _____
11. **money**   honey   many   penny   _____
12. **thief**   third   cliff   reef   _____
13. **cheery**   very   weary   chair   _____
14. **bead**   deed   lend   belt   _____
15. **please**   need   this   wheeze   _____

B. Write these spelling words in alphabetical order:
evening, donkey, league, zebra, family.

16. _____   18. _____   20. _____

17. _____   19. _____

Name_____

Expand your vocabulary by adding or removing inflectional endings, prefixes, or suffixes to a base word to create different forms of a word.

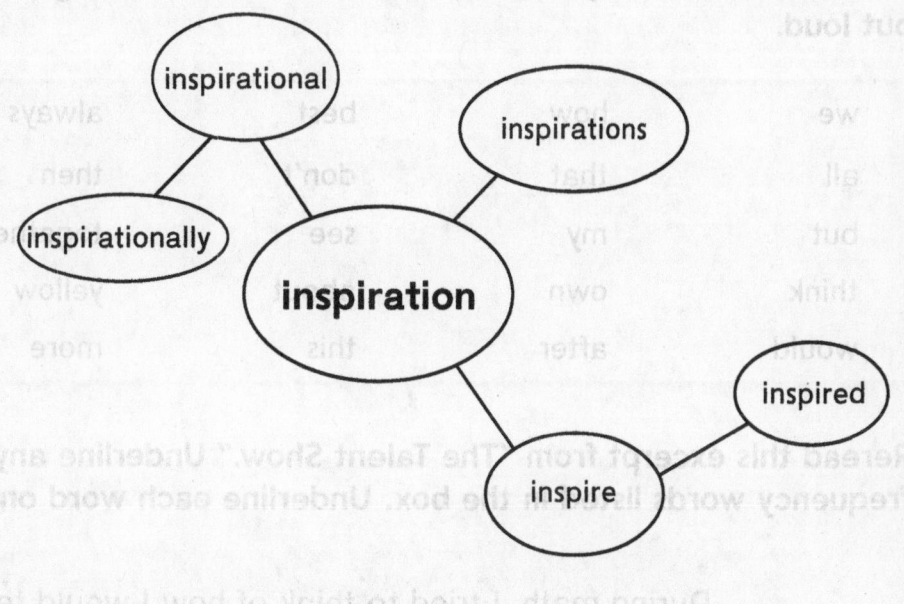

Write as many words related to *uncomfortably* as you can think of. Write them in the toes. Use a dictionary to help you.

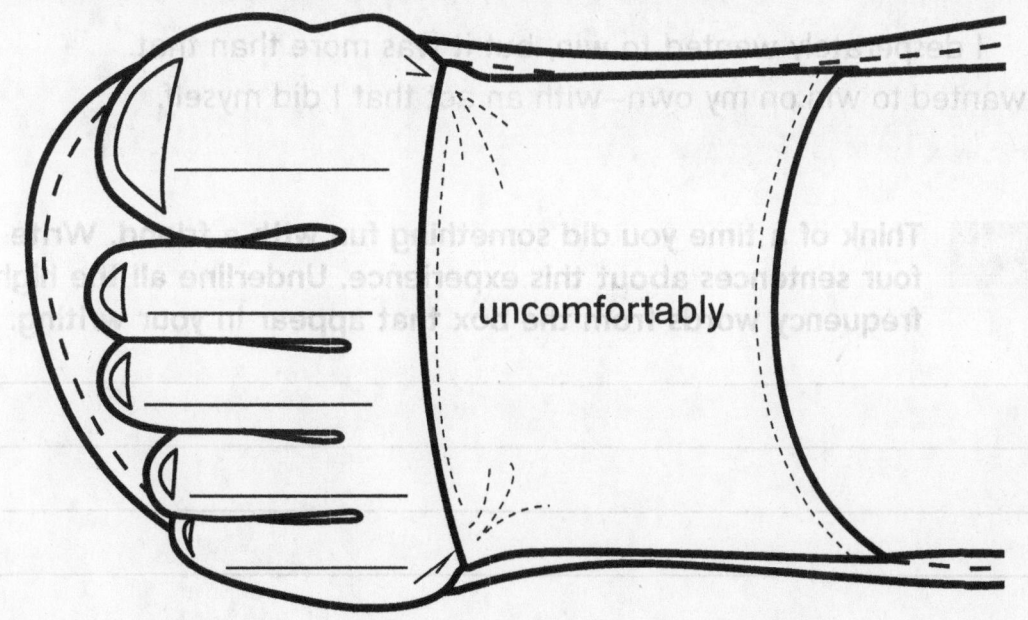

Copyright © McGraw Hill. Permission is granted to reproduce for classroom use.

Name _____

High-frequency words are the most common words in the English language. Many of them cannot be sounded out. They do not follow regular sound or spelling patterns. Most cannot be illustrated. The more you read and write them, the easier they are to remember. Read these high-frequency words out loud.

we	how	best	always	with
all	that	don't	then	could
but	my	see	together	was
think	own	about	yellow	up
would	after	this	more	myself

Reread this excerpt from "The Talent Show." Underline any high-frequency words listed in the box. Underline each word only once.

During math, I tried to think of how I would tell Tina that I wanted to do my own act. After all, we are best friends; we should be able to see eye to eye about this. The problem is Tina always takes charge, I don't speak up, and then I would end up feeling resentful about the whole situation.

I desperately wanted to win, but it was more than that. I wanted to win on my own—with an act that I did myself.

Reading/Writing Connection

Think of a time you did something fun with a friend. Write four sentences about this experience. Underline all the high-frequency words from the box that appear in your writing.

_____

_____

_____

_____

_____

Copyright © McGraw Hill. Permission is granted to reproduce for classroom use.

Name _____

> • A **clause** is a group of words that has a subject and a verb. A **main**, or **independent**, **clause** can stand alone as a sentence. *My dad flew on a plane to Texas.*
>
> • A **subordinate**, or **dependent**, **clause** usually begins with a **subordinating conjunction**, such as *before*, *when*, or *because*. A dependent clause cannot stand alone: *before the sun rose*. Conjunctions also join words and phrases in sentences.

Read each clause. On the lines provided, write *I* if the clause is independent and can stand alone as a sentence. Write *D* if it is dependent and cannot. Underline the subordinating conjunction in each dependent clause.

1. She got a perfect score. _____

2. Because she was so smart. _____

3. When it was time to go. _____

4. The school bell rang. _____

5. Because of the heat outside. _____

6. I felt very sleepy. _____

7. The doctor helped. _____

8. Before I could ask. _____

 **In your writer's notebook, write about a great adventure that you had. Include at least two sentences with dependent clauses. Circle the subordinating conjunctions.**

Copyright © McGraw Hill. Permission is granted to reproduce for classroom use.

Name _____

> - An **independent**, or **main, clause** can stand alone as a sentence, but a **dependent**, or **subordinate, clause** cannot. A dependent clause usually begins with a **subordinating conjunction**.
> - A **complex sentence** includes an independent clause and one or more dependent clauses. *I like to hang out with Sarah, who is my best friend.*
> - The subordinating conjunctions *who, whose, whom, which,* and *that* are called **relative pronouns**.
> - The subordinating conjunctions *where, when,* and *why* are called **relative adverbs**.

Read each sentence and circle the subordinating conjunction. Based on the conjunction, write *relative pronoun* or *relative adverb* on the line provided.

1. Call me when you arrive. _____

2. This is Harry, whom I met yesterday. _____

3. I fixed the lock, which wasn't easy! _____

4. This is the place where we had lunch. _____

5. I know the reason why we can't go. _____

Reading/Writing Connection

Read this sentence from "Speaking Out to Stop Bullying." Circle the subordinating conjunction and identify it as a relative pronoun or a relative adverb. Then rewrite the sentence so that the subordinating conjunction appears earlier in the sentence.

> Bullying occurs when a person uses aggressive behavior to hurt others on purpose.

_____

_____

Copyright © McGraw Hill. Permission is granted to reproduce for classroom use.

Name _____

> • When an **independent,** or **main, clause** begins a complex sentence, it is usually not followed by a comma. *I like to walk in the park when I exercise.*
>
> • When a **dependent,** or **subordinate, clause** begins a complex sentence, it is usually followed by a comma. *When I exercise, I like to walk in the park.*

Read each sentence. Decide if a clause needs a comma. If it does, rewrite the sentence correctly on the line provided. If it does not, write *No change needed* on the line.

1. When I get up in the morning I am hungry.

_____

2. Before the clock struck twelve Cinderella had to be home.

_____

_____

3. Camille closes her eyes before going underwater.

_____

_____

4. Ants are amazing because they work together to complete a task.

_____

_____

Writing Connection **Write two complex sentences including relative adverbs about your favorite outdoor activity. Then edit your work.**

_____

_____

_____

_____

_____

Copyright © McGraw Hill. Permission is granted to reproduce for classroom use.

Name _____

- A **complex sentence** includes an **independent clause** and one or more **dependent clauses**. An independent clause can stand alone as a sentence, but a dependent clause cannot.

- Dependent clauses use **subordinating conjunctions**, including **relative pronouns** and **relative adverbs**.

- When an independent clause begins a complex sentence, it usually is not followed by a comma.

- When a dependent clause begins a complex sentence, it usually is followed by a comma.

Rewrite the sentences below, adding commas and correcting mistakes in punctuation.

1. Because of the wind did the power lines come down.

_____

2. I was four years old, when my brother was born.

_____

3. She welcomed the people who just moved in?

_____

4. When a year has passed Earth has revolved once around the sun.

_____

5. Turn off the timer, that is buzzing in the kitchen.

_____

6. Before I got my shoes I put on my socks.

_____

Copyright © McGraw Hill. Permission is granted to reproduce for classroom use.

Name _____

Read the selection that follows. Then answer the questions.

(1) Because it was fall, the leaves were falling off the trees. (2) My dad made soup for dinner because the nights were getting so cold. (3) Dad invited someone over for dinner. (4) I didn't know who it was. (5) I hope they come before the soup gets cold!

1. Which part of sentence 1 is an independent clause?

   A Because it was fall

   B Because it was fall, the leaves

   C the leaves were falling off the trees

   D falling off the trees

2. Which word is the subordinating conjunction in sentence 4?

   F didn't

   G know

   H who

   J was

3. Which part of sentence 5 is a dependent clause?

   A I hope they come

   B they come before

   C the soup gets cold

   D before the soup gets cold

4. Which word is the subordinating conjunction in sentence 1?

   F Because

   G was

   H were

   J off

Read the student draft that follows. Then answer the questions.

(1) You left the room when the bell rang for lunch. (2) I watched where you went. (3) Did you see who was in the car? (4) Your dad said you could come home with me because we need to work on the project. (5) You should follow me because I go home.

5. What is the correct way to write sentence 5?

   A You should follow me who I go home.

   B You should follow me when I go home.

   C You should follow me, when I go home.

   D No change needs to be made.

Copyright © McGraw Hill. Permission is granted to reproduce for classroom use.

Name _____

Fold back the paper along the dotted line. Use the blanks to write each word as it is read aloud. When you finish the test, unfold the paper. Use the list at the right to correct any spelling mistakes.	1. _____	1. climb
	2. _____	2. minding
	3. _____	3. pies
	4. _____	4. die
	5. _____	5. height
	6. _____	6. sigh
	7. _____	7. fright
	8. _____	8. slight
	9. _____	9. drive
	10. _____	10. file
	11. _____	11. kite
	12. _____	12. prime
	13. _____	13. pride
	14. _____	14. slice
	15. _____	15. twice
	16. _____	16. wipe
	17. _____	17. pry
	18. _____	18. sly
	19. _____	19. shy
	20. _____	20. spy
Review Words	21. _____	21. chief
	22. _____	22. zebra
	23. _____	23. sleek
Challenge Words	24. _____	24. highway
	25. _____	25. wildlife

Copyright © McGraw Hill. Permission is granted to reproduce for classroom use.

Name _____

> Words with the / ī / sound can be spelled in different ways.
>
> - *i* as in *mind*
> - *ie* as in *pie*
> - *igh* as in *night*
> - *i_e* as in *pride*
> - *y* as in *fly*

SPELLING TIP

Some sounds have several different spelling patterns. See the box to the left for the different ways to spell the long *i* sound.

Write the spelling words that contain the matching spelling of the long *i* sound. Then read the words aloud.

climb	sly	drive	minding	pry
pride	kite	pies	slice	die
shy	twice	sigh	fright	file
height	slight	prime	wipe	spy

long *i* spelled i_e

1. _____
2. _____
3. _____
4. _____
5. _____
6. _____
7. _____
8. _____

long *i* spelled igh

9. _____
10. _____
11. _____
12. _____

long *i* spelled ie

13. _____
14. _____

long *i* spelled y

15. _____
16. _____
17. _____
18. _____

long *i* spelled i

19. _____
20. _____

Use the spelling rules above to write a short rhyming poem. Include four words from the spelling list. Check your work for errors.

Copyright © McGraw Hill. Permission is granted to reproduce for classroom use.

Name _____

Words with the / ī / sound can be spelled in different ways.

- *i* as in m*i*nd
- *ie* as in p*ie*
- *igh* as in n*igh*t
- *i_e* as in pr*i*d*e*
- *y* as in fl*y*

SPELLING TIP

Some sounds have several different spelling patterns. See the box to the left for the different ways to spell the long *i* sound.

Write the spelling words that contain the matching spelling of the long *i* sound. Then read the words aloud.

climb	sly	mind	minding	cry
pride	kite	pies	inside	die
shy	twice	sigh	flight	file
alike	time	line	wipe	spy

long *i* spelled *i_e*

1. _____
2. _____
3. _____
4. _____
5. _____
6. _____
7. _____
8. _____
9. _____

long *i* spelled *igh*

10. _____
11. _____

long *i* spelled *y*

12. _____
13. _____
14. _____
15. _____

long *i* spelled *ie*

16. _____
17. _____

long *i* spelled *i*

18. _____
19. _____
20. _____

 **Use the spelling rules above to write a short rhyming poem. Include four words from the spelling list. Check your work for errors.**

Copyright © McGraw Hill. Permission is granted to reproduce for classroom use.

Name _____

Write the spelling words that contain the matching spelling of the long *i* sound. Then read the words aloud.

climb	slyly	lightning	minding	pry
pride	reminded	tightly	likely	die
shiny	twice	sigh	frightened	filed
height	slightly	prime	wiping	spy

long *i* spelled *i_e*

1. _____

2. _____

3. _____

4. _____

5. _____

long *i* spelled *y*

6. _____

7. _____

8. _____

long *i* spelled *igh*

9. _____

10. _____

11. _____

12. _____

13. _____

14. _____

long *i* spelled *ie*

15. _____

long *i* spelled *i*

16. _____

17. _____

18. _____

19. _____

20. _____

 **Use the spelling rules above to write a short rhyming poem. Include four words from the spelling list. Check your work for errors.**

Copyright © McGraw Hill. Permission is granted to reproduce for classroom use.

Name _____

climb	height	drive	pride	pry
minding	sigh	file	slice	sly
pies	fright	kite	twice	shy
die	slight	prime	wipe	spy

A. Write the spelling word that is the antonym, or opposite, of each word below.

1. fearlessness _____

2. significant _____

3. secondary _____

4. live _____

5. bold _____

B. Write the spelling word that matches each definition below.

6. toy that flies _____

7. to force open _____

8. to go upward _____

9. two times _____

10. to watch secretly _____

11. self-respect _____

12. a release of breath _____

13. a folder of records _____

14. attending to _____

15. fruit and pastry desserts _____

16. how tall something is _____

17. clever or cunning _____

18. a piece that is cut _____

19. to dry or clean _____

20. to control a car _____

Copyright © McGraw Hill. Permission is granted to reproduce for classroom use.

Name _____

Circle the six misspelled words in the paragraphs below. Write the words correctly on the lines.

How many stars can you spie at night? The prighm time to see stars is when there is no moon in the sky. This is when it is very dark out. Even a slyce of moon can change what you see in the sky at night.

People leave the city to see the stars. They may clime a hill to get closer to the sky. Or they may driv to the top of a mountain. The hite of the place does not really matter. The darker it is, the more stars you will see.

1. _____   4. _____

2. _____   5. _____

3. _____   6. _____

Writing Connection

Write about something else you can see at night. Use at least four words from the spelling list.

_____

_____

_____

_____

_____

_____

_____

_____

_____

_____

_____

Copyright © McGraw Hill. Permission is granted to reproduce for classroom use.

Name _____

Copyright © McGraw Hill. Permission is granted to reproduce for classroom use.

Remember

Words with the same long vowel sound are not always spelled the same way. These are some of the most common spelling patterns you will see for the long *i* vowel. Read these words aloud:

- *i* as in *mind*
- *ie* as in *pie*
- *igh* as in *night*
- *i_e* as in *pride*
- *y* as in *fly*

A. Circle the word that rhymes with the word in bold type. Write the word.

1.	**time**	thin	came	prime	___
2.	**bite**	height	late	split	___
3.	**tie**	spy	fine	rim	___
4.	**while**	will	file	pail	___
5.	**guys**	pies	toys	breeze	___
6.	**nice**	race	wise	twice	___
7.	**chime**	find	sign	climb	___
8.	**lie**	glide	sly	lay	___
9.	**advice**	cries	voice	slice	___
10.	**might**	kite	wait	big	___
11.	**white**	hit	fright	what	___
12.	**bye**	kind	bait	die	___
13.	**right**	thigh	slight	grind	___
14.	**high**	shy	filled	night	___
15.	**my**	mine	rein	sigh	___

B. Write these spelling words in alphabetical order. Alphabetize them to the third letter. *pry, drive, pride, wipe, minding*

16. _____ 18. _____ 20. _____

17. _____ 19. _____

Name _____

A. Idioms are phrases that have a meaning different from the meaning of each word in the phrase. Read the idioms in the box. Find and underline an idiom in each sentence below. Then circle the context clues that help you understand the idiom.

---

butterflies in my stomach   between a rock and a hard place

right off the bat   get off on the wrong foot

---

1. Every time I got on the school bus, I felt sick, and got butterflies in my stomach. I had recently moved to a new school, and no one on the bus talked to me. I was certain I would never make any new friends.

2. Right off the bat, the very first week of school, I was in deep trouble.

3. I felt like I was stuck between a rock and a hard place. I wanted desperately to tell the truth, but that would mean getting Corey into trouble.

4. I didn't want to get off on the wrong foot or make a bad impression.

B. Read the sentences below. Underline each idiom. For each idiom, write a definition in your own words.

1. The test was a piece of cake because the questions were so easy.

   _____

   _____

2. He kept bothering me until I told him to cut it out.

   _____

   _____

Copyright © McGraw Hill. Permission is granted to reproduce for classroom use.

Name _____

> **Homophones** are words that sound the same but have different spellings and meanings. They are often commonly used words. Look at the examples below.
>
> break/brake   cent/scent   flour/flower   weather/whether
>
> When you write, make sure you use the correct spellings for any homophones.

These newspaper headlines need help! The reporters used the wrong homophones. Rewrite each headline so that it has all the correct words. Use a dictionary to check your work.

1. **Meteorologists Calling for Reign across the Dessert Southwest**

_____

2. **Local Teenager Already Board with Dad's Tail of Childhood**

_____

3. **Prior to Budget Cuts, Lawn of State Capital Building Was Moan Weakly**

_____

4. **Firefighters Lose There Hoses in Bazaar Feet of Forgetfulness**

_____

5. **Cowboy Goes Horse While Yelling to His Heard**

_____

Copyright © McGraw Hill. Permission is granted to reproduce for classroom use. Photo credit: Nicemonkey/Alamy Stock Photo

Name _____

> - A **run-on sentence** combines two or more independent clauses incorrectly. *I walked in the snow it was cold.*
>
> - A **comma splice** happens when two independent clauses are joined with a comma. *He ran in the street, the car stopped.*
>
> - Fix a **run-on sentence** by writing separate sentences or combining the sentences correctly. *I walked in the snow. It was cold. I walked in the snow; it was cold. I walked in the snow, and it was cold.*

Correct each run-on sentence and comma splice by separating it into two sentences or combining the clauses correctly.

1. We have a new car it is bright red.

   _____

2. I must hurry up, the store will close shortly.

   _____

3. The dog ran to meet its owner it was happy to see him.

   _____

4. The baby looked up the sun was shining but clouds were rolling in.

   _____

5. Snowflakes come in different sizes but I like big snowflakes best.

   _____

6. She was nervous when she got on stage there were so many people!

   _____

 In your writer's notebook, write about a day when things did not go your way. Include simple and compound sentences in your work. Check your work to make sure you avoided run-on sentences.

Copyright © McGraw Hill. Permission is granted to reproduce for classroom use.

Name _____

A **run-on sentence** combines two or more independent clauses incorrectly.

1. It may be missing a coordinating conjunction and comma.

   summer is coming I can't wait for summer break.

2. It may include a comma splice, but it does not include a coordinating conjunction or connecting word.

   Summer is coming, I can't wait for summer break.

3. It may include a comma and coordinating conjunction, but it has too many independent clauses.

   Summer is coming, and I can't wait for summer break, and I am excited to go swimming.

A **sentence fragment** may lack a subject or verb, or both; it can also be a dependent clause.

4. Missing a verb: 6. Missing a subject and a verb:

   A new blue car.   *From ten o'clock on.*

5. Missing a subject: 7. Dependent clause:

   Waited for you a long time.   *Before he had written.*

Read each sentence. Write C if the sentence is written correctly. If it is a run-on sentence or sentence fragment write the number from above that correctly describes the sentence.

1. We tried to catch the mouse, it got away. _____

2. The student was shy and did not make friends quickly. _____

3. The joke was funny everyone laughed at it. _____

4. You should bring an umbrella because it is raining outside. _____

5. I have a game, and my family plays it with me, and it is fun. _____

6. Only three of the gray and black kittens. _____

7. Goes faster and faster all the time. _____

Copyright © McGraw Hill. Permission is granted to reproduce for classroom use.

Name _____

> - A sentence has a subject and a predicate. A **fragment** is a group of words in a simple or compound sentence that is missing a subject, a predicate, or both. To correct a fragment, finish the thought. *Talk on the phone.* **We** *talk on the phone.*
> - To correct a **run-on sentence** or **comma splice**, rewrite it as separate sentences or combine the sentences correctly. *We talked we had a great conversation. We talked,* **and** *we had a great conversation. We talked; we had a great conversation.*

Rewrite the sentence correctly on the line provided.

1. Likes to eat oatmeal and waffles for dinner sometimes.

   _____

   _____

2. Told her to call me later, but she didn't.

   _____

3. They carried the bags, I held the door for them.

   _____

4. I practice hard but I'm still not the best player.

   _____

Writing Connection | Write two simple sentences and two compound sentences about an activity you wish your school had. Edit your sentences to avoid run-ons, comma splices, and fragments.

_____

_____

_____

_____

Copyright © McGraw Hill. Permission is granted to reproduce for classroom use.

Name _____

> • A **run-on sentence** combines two or more independent clauses incorrectly. To correct a run-on sentence, rewrite it as separate sentences or combine the sentences correctly.
>
> • A **fragment** is a group of words in a simple or compound sentence that is missing a subject, a predicate, or both. To correct a fragment, complete the thought.

Rewrite the paragraphs below, correcting any run-on sentences or fragments.

1. Venus is a planet in our solar system. It is about the same size as Earth, it is much hotter than Earth, is closer to the sun. Venus is too hot for people to live on it. There are many volcanoes there are also many mountains.

   _____

   _____

   _____

   _____

2. I live in Florida, but my Aunt Ana. I only see her a few times every year. Sometimes she visits me sometimes I visit her. Like going to Puerto Rico. It is warm, and it is sunny, and the markets have delicious foods. My favorite thing to do with Aunt Ana.

   _____

   _____

   _____

   _____

   _____

Copyright © McGraw Hill. Permission is granted to reproduce for classroom use.

Name _____

Read the selection that follows. Then answer the questions.

(1) It was night and my mom and I were out on a group hike. (2) The stars glittered in the sky; they were so far away. (3) The ground was soft in one spot, so we did not step there. (4) The group leader brought a map, she didn't need it. (5) We will visit more national parks, nature trails, and landmarks on vacation.

1. Which sentence is a run-on sentence?

   A Sentence 2

   B Sentence 3

   C Sentence 4

   D Sentence 5

2. Which sentences are NOT run-on sentences?

   F Sentences 1 and 3

   G Sentences 2 and 4

   H Sentences 3 and 4

   J Sentences 4 and 5

Read the student draft that follows. Then answer the questions.

(1) My brother likes to sleep late on Saturdays; he is very lazy. (2) Supposed to go shopping, and I am ready to go, but Mom can't find her shoes! (3) The shop is filled with items I am careful not to break anything. (4) I have enough money for the game; it's on sale.

3. What is the correct way to write sentence 2?

   A We are supposed to go shopping. I am ready to go, but Mom can't find her shoes!

   B We are supposed to go shopping, I am ready to go! But Mom can't find!

   C We are supposed to go shopping. I am ready to go! But can't find her shoes!

   D No change needs to be made.

4. What is the correct way to write sentence 3?

   A The shop is filled with items, I am careful not to break anything.

   B The shop is filled with items, but I am careful not to break anything.

   C The shop is filled with items because I am careful not to break anything.

   D No change needs to be made.

Copyright © McGraw Hill. Permission is granted to reproduce for classroom use.

Name _____

Fold back the paper along the dotted line. Use the blanks to write each word as it is read aloud. When you finish the test, unfold the paper. Use the list at the right to correct any spelling mistakes.

1. _____
2. _____
3. _____
4. _____
5. _____
6. _____
7. _____
8. _____
9. _____
10. _____
11. _____
12. _____
13. _____
14. _____
15. _____
16. _____
17. _____
18. _____
19. _____
20. _____

Review Words 21. _____
22. _____
23. _____

Challenge Words 24. _____
25. _____

1. bolt
2. mold
3. toll
4. shadow
5. flow
6. mows
7. lower
8. blown
9. quote
10. mole
11. stone
12. stove
13. chose
14. sole
15. stole
16. goal
17. groan
18. load
19. roasting
20. woe
21. kite
22. fright
23. climb
24. coaster
25. motor

Copyright © McGraw Hill. Permission is granted to reproduce for classroom use.

Name _____

> Words with the /ō/ sound can be spelled in different ways.
> - *o* as in c<u>o</u>ld
> - *ow* as in l<u>ow</u>
> - *o_e* as in n<u>o</u>te
> - *oa* as in b<u>oa</u>t
> - *oe* as in t<u>oe</u>

SPELLING TIP

Some sounds have several different spelling patterns. See the box to the left for the different ways to spell the long *o* sound.

Write the spelling words that contain the matching spelling of the long *o* sound. Then read the words aloud.

stone	woe	blown	stove	stole
quote	roasting	mold	sole	shadow
goal	flow	load	lower	toll
bolt	chose	groan	mows	mole

long *o* spelled *o_e*

1. _____
2. _____
3. _____
4. _____
5. _____
6. _____
7. _____

long *o* spelled *oe*

8. _____

long *o* spelled *ow*

9. _____
10. _____
11. _____
12. _____
13. _____

long *o* spelled *o*

14. _____
15. _____
16. _____

long *o* spelled *oa*

17. _____
18. _____
19. _____
20. _____

 **Look through this week's selection and pick out all the words that have a long *o* sound. Write them in a list and sort them by their spelling patterns.**

Copyright © McGraw Hill. Permission is granted to reproduce for classroom use.

Name _____

> Words with the /ō/ sound can be spelled in different ways.
>
> - *o* as in c<u>o</u>ld   · *oa* as in b<u>oa</u>t
> - *ow* as in l<u>ow</u>   · *oe* as in t<u>oe</u>
> - *o_e* as in n<u>o</u>t<u>e</u>

SPELLING TIP

Some sounds have several different spelling patterns. See the box to the left for the different ways to spell the long *o* sound.

Write the spelling words that contain the matching spelling of the long o sound. Then read the words aloud.

bolt	flow	know	tow	groan
mows	woke	mole	sole	chose
stole	lower	mold	most	foam
own	stone	stove	goal	woe

long o spelled o_e

1. _____
2. _____
3. _____
4. _____
5. _____
6. _____
7. _____

long o spelled o

8. _____
9. _____
10. _____

long o spelled oa

11. _____
12. _____
13. _____

long o spelled ow

14. _____
15. _____
16. _____
17. _____
18. _____
19. _____

long o spelled oe

20. _____

Look through this week's selection and pick out all the words that have a long o sound. Write them in a list and sort them by their spelling patterns.

Copyright © McGraw Hill. Permission is granted to reproduce for classroom use.

Name _____

Write the spelling words that contain the matching spelling of the long o sound. Then read the words aloud.

mole	floating	motionless	chosen	whole
groaned	quote	lonely	closer	mold
toll	lower	slowly	blown	poled
soaked	loading	coaster	goalie	woefully

long o spelled oa

1. _____

2. _____

3. _____

4. _____

5. _____

6. _____

long o spelled oe

7. _____

long o spelled ow

8. _____

9. _____

10. _____

long o spelled o_e

11. _____

12. _____

13. _____

14. _____

15. _____

16. _____

17. _____

long o spelled o

18. _____

19. _____

20. _____

 **Look through this week's selection and pick out all the words that have a long o sound. Write them in a list and sort them by their spelling patterns.**

Copyright © McGraw Hill. Permission is granted to reproduce for classroom use.

Name _____

bolt	flow	quote	chose	groan
mold	mows	mole	sole	load
toll	lower	stone	stole	roasting
shadow	blown	stove	goal	woe

A. Write the spelling word that best completes each sentence.

1. Be careful in the kitchen because the _____ is hot.

2. The windy storm has _____ away my umbrella!

3. I had a _____ of energy and cleaned my room.

4. Did the system restart and _____ up yet?

5. My _____ follows me when the sun is out.

6. I will be filled with _____ when summer is over.

7. The small boy could reach that shelf because it was _____.

8. The soccer player made a _____ right before the buzzer.

9. The rubber _____ of my sneaker keeps me from slipping.

10. There was _____ on the bathroom ceiling from all the humid air.

B. Write the spelling word that matches each definition below.

11. cuts down _____

12. cooking in an oven

_____

13. a rock _____

14. took without permission

15. a low sound of pain

_____

16. a payment or fee _____

17. move along _____

18. picked or selected

_____

19. something that was said

20. a small underground animal

_____

Copyright © McGraw Hill. Permission is granted to reproduce for classroom use.

Name _____

Find the three misspelled words in each paragraph below. Circle the misspelled words. Then write the words correctly on the lines.

There are many things to do in your home if your gole is to help. You can clean your room and sweep the floors. You can even rake the lawn. Rather than grone and act as if you are filled with wowe, why not have some fun while you do it?

One fun activity you can help with is cooking—just make sure you do it with an adult. You can start off small by preheating the stoav or getting things from loer shelves in the pantry. Helping out in the kitchen is a great way to get to know about food. One day you'll be rowsting dinner all by yourself!

1. _____   4. _____

2. _____   5. _____

3. _____   6. _____

Writing Connection

Write about something else you can do to help around your home. Use four words from the spelling list.

_____
_____
_____
_____
_____
_____
_____
_____

Copyright © McGraw Hill. Permission is granted to reproduce for classroom use.

Name _____

Remember

Words with the same long vowel sound are not always spelled the same way. These are some of the most common spelling patterns you will see for the long *o* vowel. Read the words aloud:

- *o* as in <u>bo</u>ld
- *o_e* as in sm<u>o</u>ke
- *oe* as in <u>foe</u>
- *ow* as in s<u>low</u>
- *oa* as in <u>oa</u>ts

A. Circle the spelling word in each row that rhymes with the word in bold type. Write the spelling word on the line.

1. **bowl**	goal	pond	house	_____
2. **rolled**	doll	found	mold	_____
3. **show**	woe	cow	saw	_____
4. **boat**	late	quote	spot	_____
5. **sowed**	feed	load	few	_____
6. **moan**	train	on	blown	_____
7. **grove**	give	save	stove	_____
8. **so**	flow	frog	sod	_____
9. **goes**	gold	chose	chop	_____
10. **foal**	poke	toll	rail	_____
11. **bowl**	stole	growl	told	_____
12. **own**	foul	groan	paw	_____
13. **loan**	lead	said	stone	_____
14. **coal**	mole	fall	clock	_____
15. **hose**	mows	shop	mope	_____

B. Write these spelling words in alphabetical order. Alphabetize them to the second letter. *bolt, shadow, roasting, sole, lower*

16. _____ 18. _____ 20. _____

17. _____ 19. _____

Copyright © McGraw Hill. Permission is granted to reproduce for classroom use.

Name _____

Expand your vocabulary by adding or removing inflectional endings, prefixes, or suffixes to a base word to create different forms of a word.

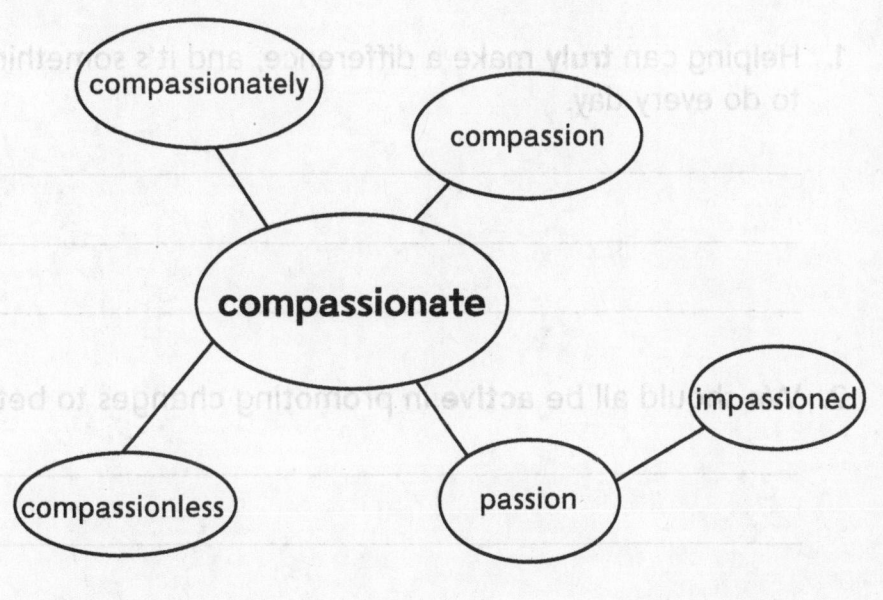

Write as many related words as you can to the word *funds* **in the piggy bank. Use a dictionary to help you.**

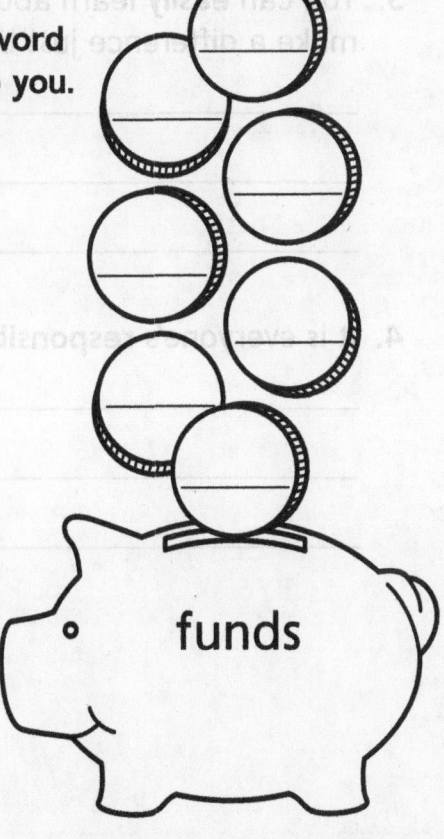

Copyright © McGraw Hill. Permission is granted to reproduce for classroom use.

Name _____

Read each sentence from "A Helping Hand" below. Underline the suffix of the word in bold and write the word's definition on the line. Then write your own sentence using the word in bold.

1. Helping can **truly** make a difference, and it's something you're able to do every day.

   _____
   _____
   _____

2. We should all be **active** in promoting changes to better our community.

   _____
   _____
   _____

3. You can **easily** learn about other people who live near you and make a difference just by talking to them.

   _____
   _____
   _____

4. It is everyone's **responsibility** to help people who are in need.

   _____
   _____
   _____

Copyright © McGraw Hill. Permission is granted to reproduce for classroom use.

Name _____

- A **noun** is a word that names a person, a place, or a thing.

- A **common noun** names any person, place, or thing: *teacher, market, kitten.*

- A **proper noun** is the name or title of a specific person, place, or organization: *Jack, Murray Middle School, Department of Education.*

- Proper nouns begin with capital letters. If a proper noun has more than one word, each important word begins with a capital letter.

Read each sentence and circle the nouns. Write *C* over each noun that is a common noun. Write *P* over each noun that is a proper noun.

1. The house is brown and white.

2. Mrs. LaRusso is my teacher.

3. My cousin is moving to New York City.

4. Does Ellie want to go to the carnival?

5. Uncle Pete is volunteering for the Peace Corps.

6. Dr. Grady was kind and helpful.

 **Read this paragraph from "Animal Adaptations." Underline the nouns. In your writer's notebook, identify each noun as common or proper.**

In Florida's vast Everglades ecosystem, the dry season is brutal for many plants and animals. Alligators have found a way to survive these dry conditions in the freshwater marshes. They use their feet and snouts to clear dirt from the holes in the limestone bedrock. When the ground dries up, the alligators can drink from their water holes.

Copyright © McGraw Hill. Permission is granted to reproduce for classroom use.

Name _____

- A **noun** is a word that names a person, a place, or a thing.

- A **common noun** names any person, place, or thing. A **proper noun** is the name or title of a specific person, place, or organization.

- A **concrete noun** names a person, place, or thing that can be identified with any of the five senses: sight, hearing, touch, smell, or taste: *house, laugh, gerbil, book, apple.*

- An **abstract noun** names a person, place, or thing that cannot be identified with any of the five senses. Abstract nouns usually name ideas: *justice, happiness, lie, cowardice.*

Read the list of nouns below. Decide whether each word is a concrete noun or an abstract noun. Sort the words in the correct columns.

paper	love	honesty	pride
trust	loyalty	animal	music
student	baseball	pain	perfume

CONCRETE

1. _____

2. _____

3. _____

4. _____

5. _____

6. _____

ABSTRACT

7. _____

8. _____

9. _____

10. _____

11. _____

12. _____

 **In your writer's notebook, write about a time you went somewhere with a friend or family member. Underline and label at least five common nouns and three proper nouns in your work. Then edit your work to make sure the correct nouns are capitalized.**

Copyright © McGraw Hill. Permission is granted to reproduce for classroom use.

Name _____

> • Capitalize each important word in a proper noun.
> • Capitalize names of days of the week, months, and holidays; important words in titles of books, stories, and essays; historical periods and documents; names of languages, races, nationalities, and historical events; and product and geographical names.

Write each sentence correctly using capital letters for proper nouns.

1. I will speak with mr. perry on friday about spanish class.

_____

2. I read an essay called "the kindness of a stranger."

_____

3. We will visit the grand canyon right after memorial day!

_____

4. I saw a painting of the signing of the declaration of independence.

_____

Write a paragraph about where you would like to go on your dream vacation. Underline at least three proper nouns in your paragraph. Then edit your work.

_____

_____

_____

_____

Copyright © McGraw Hill. Permission is granted to reproduce for classroom use.

Name _____

> - A **noun** names a person, place, or thing. **Common nouns** name any person, place, or thing. **Proper nouns** name a specific person, place, or organization.
> - **Concrete nouns** can be identified with the five senses. **Abstract nouns** cannot be identified with the senses; they are usually ideas, such as bravery or freedom.
> - Capitalize each important word in a proper noun, including days, months, and holidays; titles; languages; races and nationalities; historical events, periods, and documents; and product and geographical names.

Rewrite the sentences below, correcting mistakes in capitalization of nouns.

1. eli's favorite history topic is the renaissance.

   _____

HANDWRITING CONNECTION

How is your grip? Let your pencil rest at the base of your thumb. Then steady near the tip with your thumb, pointer, and middle fingers.

2. Does your Aunt have an appointment with the Dentist in January?

   _____

   _____

3. Next Week we will be learning about african american history.

   _____

4. Mom and dad have Faith that things will work out for the best.

   _____

5. World war I was also known as the great war.

   _____

   _____

Copyright © McGraw Hill. Permission is granted to reproduce for classroom use.

Name _____

Read the student draft and look for any corrections that need to be made. Then choose the best answer to each question.

(1) Mr. Barry talked to us in class today about different american holidays. (2) I could not contain my excitement because I knew a lot about this topic.

(3) I was born at noon on independence day. (4) This holiday celebrates independence in the United States. (5) My dad usually lets us go to my favorite Chinese restaurant for a birthday meal.

1. How should you write the phrase "american holidays" in sentence 1?

   A American Holidays

   B american Holidays

   C American holidays

   D american holidays

2. Which words are abstract nouns in sentence 2?

   F *I* and *contain*

   G *excitement* and *topic*

   H *because* and *topic*

   J There are no abstract nouns.

3. How should you write the phrase "independence day" in sentence 3?

   A Independence Day

   B independence Day

   C Independence day

   D independence day

4. Which nouns are abstract in sentence 4?

   F *holiday* and *independence*

   G *celebrates* and *United*

   H *this* and *holiday*

   J There are no abstract nouns.

Copyright © McGraw Hill. Permission is granted to reproduce for classroom use.

Name _____

Fold back the paper along the dotted line. Use the blanks to write each word as it is read aloud. When you finish the test, unfold the paper. Use the list at the right to correct any spelling mistakes.

1. _____
2. _____
3. _____
4. _____
5. _____
6. _____
7. _____
8. _____
9. _____
10. _____
11. _____
12. _____
13. _____
14. _____
15. _____
16. _____
17. _____
18. _____
19. _____
20. _____

Review Words
21. _____
22. _____
23. _____

Challenge Words
24. _____
25. _____

1. unblock
2. unborn
3. unchain
4. unload
5. unlock
6. recall
7. relearn
8. resell
9. rewash
10. rewind
11. imperfect
12. indirect
13. incorrect
14. illegal
15. overact
16. overheat
17. subway
18. premix
19. preplan
20. supersize
21. stone
22. blown
23. lower
24. interact
25. transmit

Copyright © McGraw Hill. Permission is granted to reproduce for classroom use.

Name _____

Prefixes are added to the beginnings of words to change a word's meaning. Each prefix has its own meaning.

- *over-* means "too much"
- *re-* means "again"
- *in-* means "not"
- *pre-* means "before"
- *un-* means "not"
- *super-* means "over"
- *im-* means "not"
- *sub-* means "under"
- *il-* means "not"

DECODING WORDS

Use your knowledge of prefixes to figure out the meaning of *premade*. The first syllable contains the open syllable /prē/. Blend the sounds and read the word aloud: /prē/ /mād/.

Write the spelling words that contain each prefix. Read each word aloud.

overact	premix	rewash	resell	relearn
unlock	unchain	rewind	illegal	unborn
incorrect	subway	supersize	unblock	preplan
recall	unload	indirect	overheat	imperfect

over-

1. _____

2. _____

re-

3. _____

4. _____

5. _____

6. _____

7. _____

in-

8. _____

9. _____

pre-

10. _____

11. _____

sub-

12. _____

il-

13. _____

un-

14. _____

15. _____

16. _____

17. _____

18. _____

super-

19. _____

im-

20. _____

Look through this week's selection for more words to sort and read the words aloud. Create a word sort for a partner in your writer's notebook.

Copyright © McGraw Hill. Permission is granted to reproduce for classroom use.

Name _____

Prefixes are added to the beginnings of words to change a word's meaning. Each prefix has its own meaning.

- *over-* means "too much"
- *re-* means "again"
- *in-* means "not"
- *pre-* means "before"
- *un-* means "not"
- *super-* means "over"
- *im-* means "not"
- *sub-* means "under"
- *il-* means "not"

DECODING WORDS

Use your knowledge of prefixes to figure out the meaning of *premade.* The first syllable contains the open syllable /prē/. Blend the sounds and read the word aloud: /prē/ /mād/.

Write the spelling words that contain each prefix.

overact	premix	rewash	resell	repay
unlock	unchain	rewind	illegal	unborn
incorrect	subway	supersize	unblock	preplan
recall	unload	indirect	overheat	retie

over-

1. _____

2. _____

re-

3. _____

4. _____

5. _____

6. _____

7. _____

8. _____

in-

9. _____

10. _____

pre-

11. _____

12. _____

sub-

13. _____

il-

14. _____

un-

15. _____

16. _____

17. _____

18. _____

19. _____

super-

20. _____

 **Look through this week's selection for more words to sort. Create a word sort for a partner in your writer's notebook.**

Copyright © McGraw Hill. Permission is granted to reproduce for classroom use.

Name _____

Write the spelling words that contain each prefix.

overacting	preseason	rewashed	reselling	relearned
unlocked	unchained	rewind	illegally	unborn
incorrectly	submarine	superpower	unblock	preplan
recalled	unloaded	indirectly	overheat	imperfect

over-

1. _____

2. _____

re-

3. _____

4. _____

5. _____

6. _____

7. _____

in-

8. _____

9. _____

pre-

10. _____

11. _____

un-

12. _____

13. _____

14. _____

15. _____

16. _____

super-

17. _____

im-

18. _____

sub-

19. _____

il-

20. _____

 **Look through this week's selection for more words to sort. Create a word sort for a partner in your writer's notebook.**

Copyright © McGraw Hill. Permission is granted to reproduce for classroom use.

Name _____

unblock	unlock	rewash	incorrect	subway
unborn	recall	rewind	illegal	premix
unchain	relearn	imperfect	overact	preplan
unload	resell	indirect	overheat	supersize

A. Write the spelling word that belongs with the other words in the group.

1. improper, impolite, _____

2. subtitle, submarine, _____

3. illogical, illegible, _____

4. indirect, inexact, _____

5. supermarket, superhighway, _____

6. overload, overeat, _____

B. Write the spelling word that matches each definition below.

7. not born _____

8. to wind again _____

9. to sell again _____

10. to heat too much _____

11. to learn again _____

12. opposite of lock _____

13. to think ahead of time

_____

14. not direct _____

15. opposite of load _____

16. to stir before _____

17. to wash again _____

18. to take the chain off _____

19. to call again _____

20. opposite of block _____

Copyright © McGraw Hill. Permission is granted to reproduce for classroom use.

Name _____

Underline the six misspelled words in the paragraphs below. Write the words correctly on the lines.

"It's so hot that I think I'm going to ovurheat!" said Elena to her friend Keisha. "Let's take the subbway instead of walking. We just need to make sure that we get on the right train so that we don't end up taking an undirect route."

The girls watched as the train pulled up and the doors began to inlock. Then they waited for the car to uneload. Once they were inside, they felt the air conditioning in the car. "I cannot reecall a better idea, Elena!" Keisha said with a huge smile.

1. _____   4. _____

2. _____   5. _____

3. _____   6. _____

Writing Connection

Write about a time when you had a great idea. Use at least four words from the spelling list.

_____

_____

_____

_____

_____

_____

_____

_____

_____

_____

Copyright © McGraw Hill. Permission is granted to reproduce for classroom use.

Name _____

Copyright © McGraw Hill. Permission is granted to reproduce for classroom use.

Remember

A prefix is added to the beginning of a word to change the word's meaning. The prefixes *in-, un-, im-,* and *il-* mean "not." The prefix *super-* means "over," and *sub-* means "under." The prefix *re-* means "again," *pre-* means "before," and *over-* means "too much."

Prefixes usually form their own syllables. For example, the prefix *sub-* forms the first syllable in *submarine*. To read a word with a prefix, first sound out the prefix, then sound out the rest of the word: *sub/ma/rine*.

Write a prefix to make a spelling word. Then write the spelling word on the line and read the word aloud. Choose from the prefixes above.

1. ____ ____ ____ ____ s i z e _____
2. ____ ____ b l o c k _____
3. ____ ____ l e a r n _____
4. ____ ____ ____ h e a t _____
5. ____ ____ c o r r e c t _____
6. ____ ____ p e r f e c t _____
7. ____ ____ ____ w a y _____
8. ____ ____ l e g a l _____
9. ____ ____ ____ m i x _____
10. ____ ____ c h a i n _____
11. ____ ____ w i n d _____
12. ____ ____ ____ ____ a c t _____
13. ____ ____ l o c k _____
14. ____ ____ s e l l _____
15. ____ ____ ____ p l a n _____
16. ____ ____ l o a d _____
17. ____ ____ d i r e c t _____
18. ____ ____ w a s h _____
19. ____ ____ b o r n _____
20. ____ ____ c a l l _____

Name _____

Writers use **content words** to explain concepts, events, or objects related to a particular field of study. In this unit, you will find words such as *ecosystem, predator,* and *prey.* These terms are often used in biology and ecology texts.

As you read, you may discover content words that are unfamiliar to you. Use context clues to figure out their meanings if possible. You can also consult a dictionary to confirm meanings and pronunciations.

With a partner, search science texts for content words related to ecology, or the study of how animals interact with each other and their environments. Write the words below.

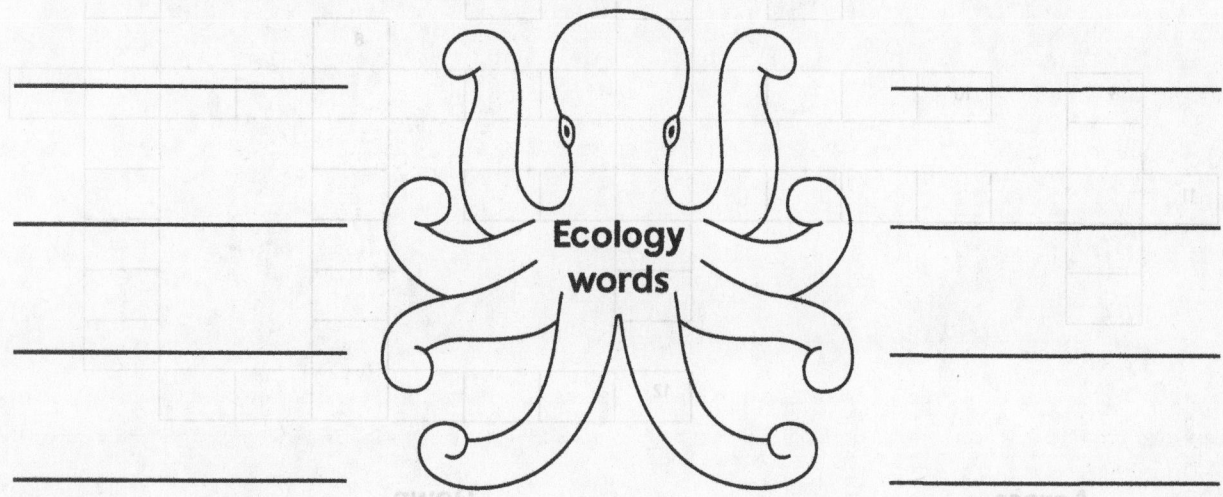

Ecology words

_____   _____

_____   _____

_____   _____

Circle two words that you were able to define by using context clues. Look within and beyond the sentence to find the meaning. Write the words and their meanings on the lines.

_____

_____

Copyright © McGraw Hill. Permission is granted to reproduce for classroom use.

Name _____

Use the words in the box and the clues below to help you solve the crossword puzzle. Then look up the meanings in a print or digital dictionary.

undertaking	crisis	compassionate	routine
exceptional	enterprise	innovative	funds
alter	collapse	process	advise

Across

5. Done in a new way
7. A daily habit
10. Kind and sympathetic
11. A business
12. A series of actions

Down

1. A dangerous situation
2. Give one's opinion
3. Change
4. A difficult thing you plan to do
6. Extraordinary
8. Fall down or cave in
9. Money ready for use

Copyright © McGraw Hill. Permission is granted to reproduce for classroom use.

Name _____

> • A **singular noun** names one person, place, or thing: *cow, house, toy.*
>
> • A **plural noun** names more than one person, place, or thing: *zebras, drinks, cars.*
>
> • Add *-s* to form the plural of most singular nouns.

Circle the nouns in each sentence. Write the plural noun on the line provided.

1. The boy has two pencils in his backpack. _____

2. Which trains have already arrived at the station? _____

3. Kelsey plays fun games at recess. _____

4. There were computers at every desk in the room. _____

5. The tree dropped a few nuts from its branch. _____

Connect to Community

Talk to a trusted adult about somewhere you want to visit. Then write a paragraph about why you want to visit there. After you finish, review your work and check that you have used singular and plural nouns correctly.

_____

_____

_____

_____

_____

Copyright © McGraw Hill. Permission is granted to reproduce for classroom use.

Name _____

> • A **singular noun** names one person, place, or thing. A **plural noun** names more than one person, place, or thing.
> • Add -**s** to form the plural of most singular nouns: *phones, desks, pencils.*
> • Add -**es** to form the plural of singular nouns that end in **s, sh, ch, x,** or **z**: *buses, bushes, screeches, axes, buzzes.*
> • To form the plural of nouns ending in a consonant followed by the letter **y**, change **y** to **i** and add -**es**: *grizzly* becomes *grizzlies.*

On the line provided, write the correct plural form of each noun in parentheses.

1. We saw baby (bear) _____ coming out of the den.

2. The (bush) _____ needed to be trimmed.

3. After the rain, the (match) _____ were useless.

4. How many (phone) _____ are in the house?

5. Name two (country) _____ that border the United States.

6. (Airplane) _____ make travel a lot easier.

 **Read this excerpt from "Anansi and the Birds." Circle the singular nouns and underline the plural nouns. In your writer's notebook, write about an event. Use three singular nouns and three plural nouns in your writing. Check that you have used the nouns correctly.**

Anansi always welcomed a challenge. His attempts to fool merchants out of their riches and lions from their jungle thrones made for exciting adventures. Today he would show those haughty birds that he could fly with the best of them.

He begged a feather from every bird he could find to create his own pair of wings, and then he began to practice flying. Anansi's wings camouflaged him well, and he looked just like a bird.

Copyright © McGraw Hill. Permission is granted to reproduce for classroom use.

Name _____

> • If three or more items are listed in a series, use commas to separate them: *carrots*, *peas*, and *celery*.
> • If only two items are listed in a sentence, do not use a comma to separate them: *apples and oranges.*

Read each sentence. If commas are needed, rewrite the sentence correctly on the line. If no commas are needed, write *No change needed* on the line.

1. The students with the highest scores were Ana Sarah and Jonathan.

_____

2. I need to get milk and eggs at the supermarket this afternoon.

_____

3. The girl wore a hat gloves and scarf when she went to play in the snow.

_____

_____

4. Cate plays tennis basketball and field hockey at her school.

_____

5. The horse trotted and cantered happily around the paddock.

_____

 **Use the sentences as a model. In your writer's notebook, write about what you want to be when you grow up. Talk about the different activities you will do in your job. Include one list of two things and one list of three things in your writing.**

Grammar • Proofreading

Name _____

- A **singular noun** names one person, place, or thing. A **plural noun** names more than one person, place, or thing.

- Nouns can be made plural by adding -**s**, by adding -**es**, or by changing the final **y** to **i** and adding -**es**. The plural rules depend on the letters at the end of the singular noun.

- Commas are used to separate three or more items in a series. If only two items are listed, do not use a comma to separate them.

Rewrite the paragraphs below, correcting mistakes in plural nouns and in punctuating items in a series.

1. My brotheres play football, and basketball at school. I'm not good at sports. Instead, I like to draw paint, and sculpt. My parentes say I don't have to be like my siblings. I'm special just the way I am.

HANDWRITING CONNECTION

Be sure that your capital letters are taller than your lowercase letters.

_____

_____

_____

2. Do you like to sing dance and laugh? Then Catch the Beat is the perfect game for you. Groups of playeres take turns singing and dancing for each other. The first one to make the other group laugh wins! Buy it today. You'll be sure to make girles boys, and even babys giggle with joy!

_____

_____

_____

_____

Copyright © McGraw Hill. Permission is granted to reproduce for classroom use.

Name _____

Read the paragraph and choose the best answer to each question.

(1) The hikers saw the fox trotting silently away. (2) One hiker put her identification guide in her backpack. (3) Both hikers headed toward the beach. (4) The beach was filled with seashells. (5) Should they collect some seashells as souvenirs?

1. Which noun is plural in sentence 1?

   A hikers

   B saw

   C fox

   D away

2. Which nouns are singular in sentence 2?

   F *hiker* and *guide*

   G *identification* and *backpack*

   H *put* and *backpack*

   J *hiker, guide,* and *backpack*

3. Which nouns are plural in sentence 5?

   A *should* and *collect*

   B *collect* and *seashells*

   C *seashells* and *souvenirs*

   D *collect* and *souvenirs*

4. Which noun is singular in sentence 4?

   F the

   G beach

   H filled

   J seashells

Read the student draft and look for any corrections that need to be made. Then choose the best answer to each question.

(1) How many seasones are in one year? (2) Winter is the time for building snowmen and wearing thick coats. (3) In spring, daisys sway in the breeze. (4) Summer is my favorite season because there is no school. (5) The leaves change color in the fall.

5. What change, if any, should be made to *seasones* in sentence 1?

   A seasonies

   B seasons

   C season

   D Make no change

6. What change, if any, should be made to *daisys* in sentence 3?

   F daisyes

   G daisies

   H daisis

   J Make no change

Copyright © McGraw Hill. Permission is granted to reproduce for classroom use.

Name _____

Fold back the paper along the dotted line. Use the blanks to write each word as it is read aloud. When you finish the test, unfold the paper. Use the list at the right to correct any spelling mistakes.

1. _____
2. _____
3. _____
4. _____
5. _____
6. _____
7. _____
8. _____
9. _____
10. _____
11. _____
12. _____
13. _____
14. _____
15. _____
16. _____
17. _____
18. _____
19. _____
20. _____

Review Words
21. _____
22. _____
23. _____

Challenge Words
24. _____
25. _____

1. thirty
2. width
3. northern
4. fifth
5. choose
6. touch
7. chef
8. chance
9. pitcher
10. kitchen
11. sketched
12. ketchup
13. snatch
14. stretching
15. rush
16. whine
17. whirl
18. bring
19. graph
20. photo
21. unload
22. relearn
23. subway
24. expression
25. theater

Copyright © McGraw Hill. Permission is granted to reproduce for classroom use.

Name _____

Sometimes single sounds are represented by certain letter combinations. **Digraphs** are two-letter combinations, and **trigraphs** are three-letter combinations.

- /th/ can be spelled *th*
- /ch/ can be spelled *ch* or *tch*
- /hw/ can be spelled *wh*
- /f/ can be spelled *ph*
- /ng/ can be spelled *ng*
- /sh/ can be spelled *sh, ch, s, ss,* or *sc*

DECODING WORDS

The first syllable of *charting* contains the digraph *ch* and the *r*-controlled vowel sound /är/. The second syllable contains the ending *-ing*. Blend the sounds and read the word aloud.

Read aloud and write the spelling words that contain each digraph or trigraph.

whine	photo	bring	width	whirl
fifth	rush	kitchen	stretching	pitcher
northern	chef	chance	touch	graph
snatch	sketched	ketchup	thirty	choose

ch

1. _____
2. _____
3. _____
4. _____

ng

5. _____

tch

6. _____
7. _____
8. _____
9. _____
10. _____
11. _____

ph

12. _____
13. _____

th

14. _____
15. _____
16. _____
17. _____

wh

18. _____
19. _____

sh

20. _____

 **Use the spelling patterns above to write a short fable. Include four words from the spelling list. Check your work for errors.**

Copyright © McGraw Hill. Permission is granted to reproduce for classroom use.

Name _____

Sometimes single sounds are represented by certain letter combinations, called **digraphs** or **trigraphs.**

- /th/ can be spelled *th*
- /ch/ can be spelled *ch* or *tch*
- /hw/ can be spelled *wh*
- /sh/ can be spelled *sh, ch, s, ss,* or *sc*

- /f/ can be spelled *ph*
- /ng/ can be spelled *ng*

DECODING WORDS

The first syllable of *charting* contains the digraph *ch* and the *r*-controlled vowel sound /är/. The second syllable contains the ending *-ing*. Blend the sounds and read the word aloud.

Read aloud and write the spelling words that contain each digraph or trigraph.

whine	photo	bring	shed	whirl
fifth	rush	kitchen	march	branch
north	chef	chance	touch	graph
patch	couch	ketchup	thanks	choose

ch

1. _____
2. _____
3. _____
4. _____
5. _____
6. _____
7. _____

ng

8. _____

tch

9. _____
10. _____
11. _____

wh

12. _____
13. _____

th

14. _____
15. _____
16. _____

sh

17. _____
18. _____

ph

19. _____
20. _____

Use the spelling patterns above to write a short fable. Include four words from the spelling list. Check your work for errors.

Copyright © McGraw Hill. Permission is granted to reproduce for classroom use.

Name _____

Read aloud and write the spelling words that contain each digraph or trigraph. If a word contains more than one digraph or trigraph, write it under both headings.

whine	photograph	bringing	width	whirl
cherish	physical	kitchen	nowhere	marshal
beach	chef	charade	touchdown	phase
finished	sketched	ketchup	bathtub	flinched

ch

1. _____

2. _____

3. _____

4. _____

5. _____

6. _____

ng

7. _____

tch

8. _____

9. _____

10. _____

th

11. _____

12. _____

wh

13. _____

14. _____

15. _____

sh

16. _____

17. _____

18. _____

ph

19. _____

20. _____

21. _____

 **Use the spelling patterns above to write a short fable. Include four words from the spelling list. Check your work for errors.**

Copyright © McGraw Hill. Permission is granted to reproduce for classroom use.

Name _____

thirty	choose	pitcher	snatch	whirl
width	touch	kitchen	stretching	bring
northern	chef	sketched	rush	graph
fifth	chance	ketchup	whine	photo

A. Write the spelling word that means the same as the word below.

1. carry _____   4. pick _____

2. drew _____   5. cook _____

3. complain _____

B. Write the spelling word that best completes each sentence.

6. I took a _____ and raised my hand to answer the question.

7. The runner is _____ her leg muscles before the race.

8. He can bend and _____ his toes without a problem.

9. There is a lot of ice in the _____ parts of the planet.

10. The wind sent the dry leaves into a _____ in the yard.

11. The softball _____ threw a lot of strikes in yesterday's game.

12. My mother is always cooking something new in the _____.

13. You are the _____ person in line, not the fourth.

14. Do you like to put _____ on your hot dog?

15. The teacher helped me draw the _____ in math class.

16. I watch the gull _____ the bread away from the duck.

17. My aunt will be _____ years old next week.

18. Take your time and do not _____ through the test.

19. This is my favorite _____ of our family.

20. The _____ of the room is shorter than its length.

Copyright © McGraw Hill. Permission is granted to reproduce for classroom use.

Name _____

Underline the six misspelled words in the paragraphs below. Write the words correctly on the lines.

Dear Kara,

    Thanks for your letter and the foto. I wish I had a chhance to see the baseball game with you. It sounds like your cousin Mario is quite a pither.

    I went to my fifh baseball game last weekend with my family. It was loud and crowded, but I was in no rushe to leave. My mom says that I was in a wirl of excitement all day!

                                Your friend,
                                Jimmy

1. _____   4. _____

2. _____   5. _____

3. _____   6. _____

Writing Connection

Write about whether you like baseball. Use at least four words from the spelling list to explain your opinion.

_____

_____

_____

_____

_____

_____

_____

Copyright © McGraw Hill. Permission is granted to reproduce for classroom use.

Name _____

Remember

Sometimes single sounds are represented by certain letter combinations, called digraphs or trigraphs. It is important to memorize these sound/spelling combinations.

- /th/ can be spelled *th*
- /sh/ can be spelled *sh, ch, s, ss,* or *sc*
- /ch/ can be spelled *ch* or *tch*
- /hw/ can be spelled *wh*
- /f/ can be spelled *ph* or *gh*
- /ng/ can be spelled *ng*

A. Underline the spelling word in each row that rhymes with the word in bold type. Write the spelling word on the line and read the word aloud.

1. **much** match touch luck _____
2. **sting** bring brag stint _____
3. **fetching** resting guessing stretching _____
4. **pants** stand lamp chance _____
5. **dirty** thirty forty wiry _____
6. **shine** mind whine lane _____
7. **news** loose stew choose _____
8. **catch** clutch snatch snake _____
9. **laugh** graph rough roof _____
10. **flush** crash rush puts _____
11. **clef** chef step leaf _____
12. **etched** skipped punched sketched _____
13. **hurl** hurt whirl while _____
14. **richer** pitcher sister listener _____

B. Write these spelling words in alphabetical order. Alphabetize them to the second letter. *northern, fifth, photo, ketchup, width, kitchen*

15. _____ 17. _____ 19. _____

16. _____ 18. _____ 20. _____

Copyright © McGraw Hill. Permission is granted to reproduce for classroom use.

Name _____

Read each sentence below. Then answer each question about the word in bold.

1. The prefix *un-* means "not." What does **uncommon** mean in the following sentence? "It is not **uncommon** to see birds with pretty feathers."

   _____

2. The prefix *mis-* means "wrong." What does **misprint** mean in the following sentence? "The incorrect spelling of his name in the paper was a **misprint**."

   _____

3. The prefix *sub-* means "below." What does **submarine** mean in the following sentence? "The **submarine** dove below the water."

   _____

4. The prefix *dis-* means "opposite" or "lack of." What does **disadvantage** mean in the following sentence? "Without waterproof feathers, they would be at a **disadvantage**."

   _____

5. The prefix *re-* means "again." What does **reproduce** mean in the following sentence? "The artist will **reproduce** the sculpture in clay."

   _____

Copyright © McGraw Hill. Permission is granted to reproduce for classroom use.

Name _____

> Remember that a **suffix** is a part added to the end of a base word that changes its meaning, and often its part of speech. Knowing the meanings of common suffixes can help you define unfamiliar words.
>
> Take a look at these four suffixes. They all mean "state or quality of" and change root words to nouns.
>
> -ance   -ity/-ty   -ment   -ship

Add the correct suffix from the box above to make each word defined below. Check your answers in a print or digital dictionary. Then use your responses to answer the animal trivia questions.

1. the state of being in awe: amaze _____

2. the quality of being especially mean: cruel _____

3. the state of being good acquaintances: friend _____

4. the state of being irritated: annoy _____

5. the state of being even: equal _____

6. the quality of being satisfied: content _____

7. the state of being an official resident of a country: citizen _____

8. the quality of being firm: solid _____

9. the state of being entertained: amuse _____

10. the quality of being devoted to someone: loyal _____

How many pairs of wings does a bee have? The answer is the number of times you wrote *-ship* above. _____

How many stomachs does a cow have? The answer is the number of times you wrote *-ity* and *-ty* above. _____

How many inches long is a newborn kangaroo? The answer is the number of times you wrote *-ance* above. _____

How many eyelids does a camel have? The answer is the number of times you wrote *-ment* above. _____

Copyright © McGraw Hill. Permission is granted to reproduce for classroom use.

Name _____

- **Irregular plurals** do not follow regular plural rules.
- Many nouns that end in *-f* or *-fe* are made plural by changing the f to a v and adding *-es*, such as *life/lives, loaf/loaves, calf/calves*.
- Some nouns are made plural by changing their vowel sound and spelling, such as *foot/feet, mouse/mice, goose/geese*.
- Some plurals are formed by adding a unique ending to a word that can change the word's pronunciation and number of syllables. For example, *children* has a different vowel sound than *child. Ox* has one syllable, but the plural form has two: *ox/en*.
- Sound out irregular plurals just as you would other words.

Read each sentence aloud. Circle the irregular plural and write it on the line provided.

1. We watched the geese fly into the clouds. _____

2. The men picked up their suitcases and boarded the plane. _____

3. Two halves of the pie equal one whole. _____

4. The patients waited for the dentist to look at their teeth. _____

5. They asked their wives to join them on stage. _____

6. The teams of oxen pulled the plows across the field. _____

7. Are there enough knives for all of the dishes on the table? _____

8. All the women were asked to come onto the dance floor. _____

 **In your writer's notebook, write a short passage about a make-believe animal. Where does it live? What does it look like? Include at least three irregular plurals in your writing. Edit your work for correct spelling of irregular plurals.**

Copyright © McGraw Hill. Permission is granted to reproduce for classroom use.

Name _____

> - Many **irregular plurals** follow their own spelling rules and patterns.
>
> - Plural forms of nouns that end in -*man* are usually spelled -*men:* **woman/women, snowman/snowmen**.
>
> - Plural forms of words that end in *f* or *fe* usually change the *f* to a *v* and add -*es*: **wolf/wolves, leaf/leaves**. Note that the vowel sound stays the same. Read the following example out loud: **book/shelf, book/shelves**.
>
> - In addition, irregular plurals may involve making no change to a word (such as **deer/deer**) or using a new word (**person/people**).
>
> - **Collective nouns** are words that name groups of people, places, or things, such as **class** or **army**.

Read each sentence aloud. Decide whether the underlined noun is *singular* or *plural*. Write your answer on the line.

1. <u>Moose</u> are beautiful but shy creatures. _____

2. How many <u>shrimp</u> come in one bag? _____

3. I watched the <u>sheep</u> shake its head back and forth. _____

4. The <u>mice</u> ran quickly into the hole in the wall. _____

5. Slowly, the lonely <u>buffalo</u> moved across the grassy plains. _____

 **Think about the groups of animals you see at the zoo or on television. What do you think they like to do in their habitats? Write at least three sentences with irregular plural nouns. Then check your work for correct spelling.**

Copyright © McGraw Hill. Permission is granted to reproduce for classroom use.

Name _____

- Some irregular plurals are not based on rules and must be memorized.
- There is a rule for forming plural nouns that end in *-f* or *-fe*, but not all nouns follow this rule, such as *roof/roofs*.
- Some nouns have the same singular and plural forms, such as *deer/deer*.
- Some nouns use a different ending to form the plural, such as **man/men**.
- Some nouns change completely from singular to plural, such as **mouse/mice**.

Read each sentence. Circle the word that is the correct plural form. Then write the sentence on the line provided.

1. The (loafs, loaves) of bread smelled delicious!

_____

2. I watched as the (fish, fishs) jumped in and out of the water.

_____

3. How many (persons, people) can fit in this little car?

_____

4. There were ten (childes, children) on the playground.

_____

 **Read these sentences from "The Ant and the Grasshopper." Underline the irregular plural nouns. In your writer's notebook, explain why you think Termite introduced Ant and Grasshopper as his buddies.**

> **Maybe you have heard of them from other familiar stories. Let's see what my buddies are up to!**

Copyright © McGraw Hill. Permission is granted to reproduce for classroom use.

Name _____

> - Some nouns have **irregular plurals** that do not follow regular plural rules. They are either based on their own rules or do not follow a rule at all and must be memorized.
> - Irregular plurals may involve changing the *f* to a *v* and adding *-es* in words that end in *-f* or *-fe*, changing a middle vowel sound and spelling, or using different endings.
> - In addition, irregular plurals may involve making no change to a word (such as *deer/deer*) or using a completely new word (*person/people*).
> - **Collective nouns** are words that name groups of people, places, or things, such as *class* or *army*.

Rewrite the sentences below correcting mistakes in plurals.

1. The pack of wolfes included males, femals, and cubs.

   _____

2. My foots and calfs are sore from walking on the trails yesterday.

   _____

3. The womans entered the room even though they were afraid of the mouses.

   _____

4. How many chevs are needed for the feast this weekend?

   _____

5. The trouts are passing through these riveres at this time of year.

   _____

Copyright © McGraw Hill. Permission is granted to reproduce for classroom use.

Name _____

A. Read the paragraph. Choose the best answer to correct each question.

(1) The person were determined to catch them. (2) The thief who stole fifty-nine pairs of shoes were running away. (3) They had grabbed the boxes off the shelf. (4) How many foot do these guys have, anyway?

1. How would you write the plural of *person* in sentence 1?

   A person

   B persons

   C people

   D peoples

2. How would you write the plural of *thief* in sentence 2?

   F thieves

   G thiefs

   H thieve

   J thief

3. How would you write the plural of *shelf* in sentence 3?

   A shelf

   B shelves

   C shelfs

   D shelve

4. How would you write the plural of *foot* in sentence 4?

   F feet

   G feets

   H foot

   J foots

B. Read the student draft and choose the best answer to each question.

(1) There are so many species at this zoo! (2) I see oxen grazing in a field. (3) A bunch of childs are looking at some penguins swimming in a large pond. (4) Some moose are yawning, and I can see their teeth! (5) Next time, I am visiting the elk first.

5. What change, if any, should be made to *childs* in sentence 3?

   A childrens

   B children

   C child

   D Make no change

6. What change, if any, should be made to *moose* in sentence 4?

   F mooses

   G mises

   H mouses

   J Make no change

Copyright © McGraw Hill. Permission is granted to reproduce for classroom use.

Name _____

Fold back the paper along the dotted line. Use the blanks to write each word as it is read aloud. When you finish the test, unfold the paper. Use the list at the right to correct any spelling mistakes.

1. _____
2. _____
3. _____
4. _____
5. _____
6. _____
7. _____
8. _____
9. _____
10. _____
11. _____
12. _____
13. _____
14. _____
15. _____
16. _____
17. _____
18. _____
19. _____
20. _____

Review Words
21. _____
22. _____
23. _____

Challenge Words
24. _____
25. _____

1. shred
2. shriek
3. shrimp
4. shrink
5. script
6. screw
7. screech
8. straighten
9. straps
10. strand
11. sprout
12. sprawl
13. sprang
14. splashing
15. splotch
16. thrill
17. throb
18. throat
19. thrift
20. through
21. choose
22. photo
23. whine
24. threaten
25. strictly

Copyright © McGraw Hill. Permission is granted to reproduce for classroom use.

Name _____

> A **three-letter blend** is a combination of three consonants found at the beginning of a word. These blends include:
>
> - *scr* as in *scribe*   - *spl* as in *splash*
> - *str* as in *strangle*   - *thr* as *in throw*
> - *spr* as in *spritely*

DECODING WORDS

The first syllable of *threading* contains the three-letter blend *thr* and the vowel team *ea*. The second syllable contains the ending *-ing*. Blend the sounds and read the word aloud.

Write the spelling words that contain each three-letter blend. Then read the words aloud.

thrill	script	straps	sprang	sprout
sprawl	thrift	shrink	screech	throat
shred	splashing	throb	splotch	screw
strand	shrimp	shriek	straighten	through

thr

1. _____

2. _____

3. _____

4. _____

5. _____

scr

6. _____

7. _____

8. _____

spl

9. _____

10. _____

shr

11. _____

12. _____

13. _____

14. _____

str

15. _____

16. _____

17. _____

spr

18. _____

19. _____

20. _____

Look through this week's selection for more words to sort. Create a word sort for a partner in your writer's notebook.

Copyright © McGraw Hill. Permission is granted to reproduce for classroom use.

Name _____

A three-letter blend is a combination of three consonants found at the beginning of a word. These blends include:

- *scr* as in *scribe*
- *spl* as in *splash*
- *str* as in *strangle*
- *thr* as in *throw*
- *spr* as in *spritely*

DECODING WORDS

The first syllable of *threading* contains the three-letter blend *thr* and the vowel team *ea*. The second syllable contains the ending *-ing*. Blend the sounds and read the word aloud.

Write the spelling words that contain each three-letter blend. Then read the words aloud.

thrill	script	spring	sprang	sprout
split	thrift	shrink	screech	throat
shred	splash	throb	throne	screw
strand	shrimp	shrunk	straight	through

thr

1. _____
2. _____
3. _____
4. _____
5. _____
6. _____

scr

7. _____
8. _____
9. _____

spl

10. _____
11. _____

shr

12. _____
13. _____
14. _____
15. _____

str

16. _____
17. _____

spr

18. _____
19. _____
20. _____

 **Look through this week's selection for more words to sort. Create a word sort for a partner in your writer's notebook.**

Copyright © McGraw Hill. Permission is granted to reproduce for classroom use.

Name _____

A. Write the spelling words that contain each three-letter blend.

thrillingly	script	stringy	sprang	sprout
sprawl	throttle	shrink	screech	throat
shredding	splashing	throb	splotch	scrawny
strand	shrugged	shriek	straighten	throughout

thr

1. _____

2. _____

3. _____

4. _____

5. _____

scr

6. _____

7. _____

8. _____

spl

9. _____

10. _____

shr

11. _____

12. _____

13. _____

14. _____

str

15. _____

16. _____

17. _____

spr

18. _____

19. _____

20. _____

B. Compare the words *strand* and *sprang.* How are they alike? How are they different?

_____

_____

_____

 **Look through this week's selection for more words to sort.
Create a word sort for a partner in your writer's notebook.**

Copyright © McGraw Hill. Permission is granted to reproduce for classroom use.

Name _____

shred	script	straps	sprang	throb
shriek	screw	strand	splashing	throat
shrimp	screech	sprout	splotch	thrift
shrink	straighten	sprawl	thrill	through

A. Write the spelling word that best completes each sentence.

1. A _____ of the old rope fell on the floor.

2. Shopping for sales is a sure sign of _____.

3. Please _____ your room before your friend arrives.

4. She will _____ with laughter at that funny joke.

5. We must go _____ the tunnel to get into the city.

6. Is that a messy _____ on your white sweater?

7. I do not want my favorite jeans to _____ in the wash.

8. The kids are _____ happily in the little tub.

9. We watched the cat _____ lazily in the sun.

10. If you hit the brakes too hard, the tires will _____.

11. My _____ was scratchy after singing at the concert.

12. The play was a big hit because the _____ was so funny.

13. The leather _____ hung down from the saddle.

B. Write the spelling word that belongs with the other words in the group.

14. jumped, leaped, _____

15. clam, lobster, _____

16. pleasure, excitement, _____

17. tear, rip, _____

18. push, grow, _____

19. pulse, beat, _____

20. nail, bolt, _____

Copyright © McGraw Hill. Permission is granted to reproduce for classroom use.

Name _____

Underline the six misspelled words in the paragraphs below. Write the words correctly on the lines.

Many people like to wear jewelry. You will often see a woman with a necklace around her thuroat. Some jewelry pieces are worth a lot of money because they are very old. This jewelry can be a real trill to wear. A shrand of aged pearls can be worth more than a house!

Some people sell jewelry at yard sales. They sparwl necklaces and bracelets out on tables. If you see a piece of jewelry that you like, do not shiek or shout. Calmly ask how much it costs. You might be able to show some thhrift by talking the person into selling it for less.

1. _____ 4. _____

2. _____ 5. _____

3. _____ 6. _____

Writing Connection

Write about something else that is worth a lot of money. Use at least four words from the spelling list.

_____
_____
_____
_____
_____
_____
_____
_____

Copyright © McGraw Hill. Permission is granted to reproduce for classroom use.

Name _____

Copyright © McGraw Hill. Permission is granted to reproduce for classroom use.

Remember

A **three-letter blend** is a combination of three consonants found at the beginning of a word. These blends include:

- *scr* as in *scribble*
- *str* as in *strangely*
- *spr* as in *springy*
- *spl* as in *splat*
- *thr* as in *threaten*

shred	script	straps	sprang	throb
shriek	screw	strand	splashing	throat
shrimp	screech	sprout	splotch	thrift
shrink	straighten	sprawl	thrill	through

A. Fill in the missing letters of each word to form a spelling word. Then read the word aloud.

1. ___ ___ ___ out
2. ___ ___ ___ ob
3. ___ ___ ___ iek
4. ___ ___ ___ eech
5. ___ ___ ___ ill
6. ___ ___ ___ aps
7. ___ ___ ___ ink
8. ___ ___ ___ ashing
9. ___ ___ ___ ough
10. ___ ___ ___ ipt

11. ___ ___ ___ oat
12. ___ ___ ___ ew
13. ___ ___ ___ ang
14. ___ ___ ___ aighten
15. ___ ___ ___ imp
16. ___ ___ ___ otch
17. ___ ___ ___ ift
18. ___ ___ ___ and
19. ___ ___ ___ ed
20. ___ ___ ___ awl

B. Write these spelling words in alphabetical order. Alphabetize them to the fourth letter. *shrimp, throb, straighten, shred, thrift*

21. _____
22. _____
23. _____

24. _____
25. _____

Name _____

> When you add different prefixes, suffixes, and inflectional endings to a base word, you create a group of **related words** with similar meanings. Recognizing and defining related words will help you expand your vocabulary.

Read each base word below. Add prefixes, suffixes, and inflectional endings (-ed, -ing, -s, -er, -est) to form related words and write them in the blanks. Use a print or online dictionary to help.

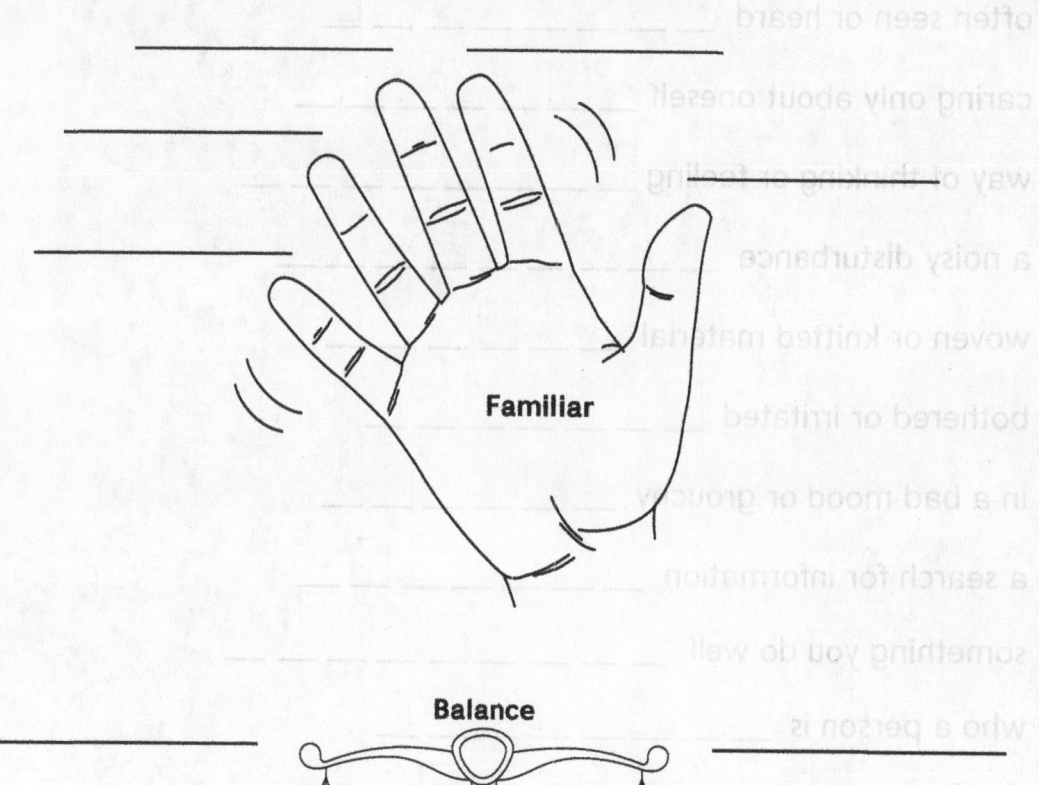

Familiar

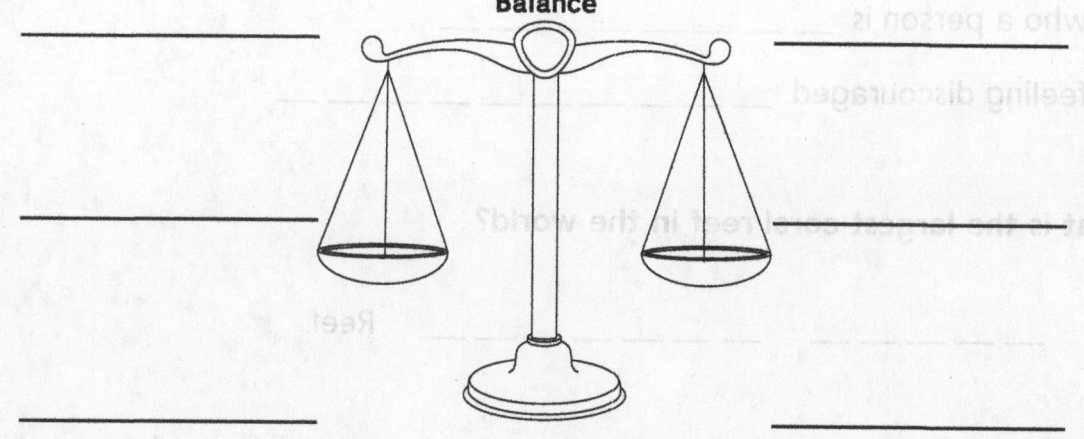

Balance

Copyright © McGraw Hill. Permission is granted to reproduce for classroom use.

Name _____

Write each vocabulary word from the box next to its meaning. Then write the letters from the boxes to answer the trivia question at the bottom of the page.

fabric	cranky	annoyed	familiar
selfish	trudged	attitude	inquiry
specialty	identity	commotion	frustrated

1. walked slowly and steadily __ __ __ ☐ __ __ __
2. often seen or heard __ __ __ __ __ __ __ ☐
3. caring only about oneself __ ☐ __ __ __ __ __
4. way of thinking or feeling ☐ __ __ __ __ __ __ __
5. a noisy disturbance __ __ __ __ __ ☐ __ __ __
6. woven or knitted material __ __ ☐ __ __ __
7. bothered or irritated ☐ __ __ __ __ __ __
8. in a bad mood or grouchy __ ☐ __ __ __ __
9. a search for information __ __ __ __ __ ☐ __
10. something you do well __ __ __ __ ☐ __ __ __ __
11. who a person is __ __ ☐ __ __ __ __ __
12. feeling discouraged __ __ __ __ __ ☐ __ __ __ __

What is the largest coral reef in the world?

The __ __ __ __ __ __ __ __ __ __ __ Reef.

Copyright © McGraw Hill. Permission is granted to reproduce for classroom use.

Name _____

> • A **possessive noun** shows ownership.
>
> • When a possessive noun is used before another noun, it shows to what or whom that noun belongs: *Anthony's shoes*.
>
> • To form the possessive of a singular noun, add an **apostrophe** and an *-s* to the end of the noun: *bear/bear's*.

Read each sentence. Write the possessive form of the underlined singular noun.

1. The <u>family</u> trip was cancelled because of the rain. _____

2. My mother went to the <u>school</u> fundraiser event. _____

3. The <u>kite</u> tail was missing, so we attached some ribbon. _____

4. <u>Annie</u> class is going on a field trip next week. _____

5. The <u>television</u> screen is old and not working well. _____

6. <u>Grandma</u> car needs to be taken to the auto repair shop. _____

7. The <u>snake</u> skin sheds from its body every few months. _____

8. I could not wait to watch <u>America</u> favorite pastime—baseball! _____

 **In your writer's notebook, describe the different kinds of hair your friends, family, and pets have. Be sure to add an apostrophe and *-s* for all possessive nouns. Check your work to make sure you have formed the possessives correctly.**

Copyright © McGraw Hill. Permission is granted to reproduce for classroom use.

Name _____

- When a **possessive noun** is used before another noun, it shows to what or whom that noun belongs.
- To form the possessive of a singular noun, add an **apostrophe** and an **-s** to the end of the noun: *cat/cat's*.
- To form the possessive of a plural noun that ends in *s*, add only an apostrophe to the end of the noun: *cats/cats'*.
- To form the possessive of a plural noun that does not end in *s*, add an apostrophe and an **-s** to the end of the noun: *children/children's*.

Read each sentence. Write the possessive form of the underlined plural noun.

1. The mayor honored the two <u>firefighters</u> heroic act. _____

2. The <u>people</u> opinion is that none of the candidates are good. _____

3. The <u>women</u> purses were all black and quite large. _____

4. The <u>workers</u> lunch was waiting for them in the cafeteria. _____

5. Several <u>countries</u> athletes ran in the race. _____

6. My <u>sheep</u> wool will keep them warm. _____

Reading/Writing Connection

Reread this excerpt from "Pecos Bill and the Bear Lake Monster." Circle the possessive nouns. In your writer's notebook, write about what you would do if you were king or queen of a country. Use three possessive nouns in your writing.

All of a sudden the water churned and foamed and ten-foot waves started crashing over Bill's head. A monster reared out of the water with its mouth open and roared. Bill had seen caverns smaller than that snake's mouth, and its roar shook the surrounding mountains. Without missing a beat, Pecos Bill jumped onto the monster's neck and slipped a loop of rope into its mouth. Then he held the ends like reins.

Copyright © McGraw Hill Permission is granted to reproduce for classroom use.

Name _____

- Use an apostrophe and an *-s* to form the possessive of a singular noun: *person's*.
- Use an apostrophe and an *-s* to form the possessive of a plural noun that does not end in *s*: *people's*.
- Use an apostrophe alone to form the possessive of a plural that ends in *s*: *fishes'*.

Read each sentence. Rewrite the possessive nouns with correct punctuation.

1. This movies title is so bad that it is funny!

_____

2. Benjis hometown is miles away from where he lives now.

_____

3. Turtles shells are all different in some ways and similar in other ways.

_____

4. The gentlemens names were all noted at the front desk.

_____

Writing Connection **Write three sentences about a family member. Include two possessive nouns.**

_____
_____
_____
_____
_____
_____

Copyright © McGraw Hill. Permission is granted to reproduce for classroom use.

Name _____

> • A **possessive noun** shows ownership.
>
> • To form the possessive of a singular noun, add an **apostrophe** and an **-s** to the end of the noun.
>
> • To form the possessive of a plural noun that ends in **s**, add only an apostrophe to the end of the noun.
>
> • To form the possessive of a plural noun that does not end in **s**, add an apostrophe and an **-s** to the end of the noun.

Rewrite the paragraphs below, correcting mistakes in possessive nouns.

1. Madisons school was having a food drive. Her sisters school was having a fundraiser. Both schools goals were to help victims of last months hurricane. The childrens parents helped them collect food and money to meet their goals.

_____

_____

_____

_____

2. Polar bears live difficult lives. A polar bears days are usually spent alone, unless a mother has cubs. Polar bears coats are very thick to help keep them warm when the areas temperature is below zero. It is not easy to be a polar bear!

_____

_____

_____

_____

Copyright © McGraw Hill. Permission is granted to reproduce for classroom use.

Name _____

Read the paragraph and choose the best answer to each question.

(1) The ten judges decisions were final. (2) Cassandras floor routine was the best anyone had ever seen. (3) The other countries judges were in agreement. (4) The winner of the gold medal for the womens gymnastics finals had been chosen.

(5) She saw her mothers tears all the way from the podium. (6) She could see the looks of pride on her familys faces. (7) Just wait until they saw the routine she was planning for next time!

1. How should you write the word *judges* in sentence 1?

   A judges's

   B judges'

   C judge's

   D Make no change

2. How should you write the word *Cassandras* in sentence 2?

   F Cassandras'

   G Cassandras's

   H Cassandra's

   J Make no change

3. How should you write the word *countries* in sentence 3?

   A countries'

   B countrie's

   C countries's

   D countrys

4. How should you write the word *womens* in sentence 4?

   F women's

   G womens'

   H womens's

   J woman's

5. How should you write the word *mothers* in sentence 5?

   A mothers'

   B mother's

   C mothers's

   D Make no change

6. How should you write the word *familys* in sentence 6?

   F familie's

   G familys'

   H families'

   J family's

Copyright © McGraw Hill. Permission is granted to reproduce for classroom use.

Name _____

Fold back the paper along the dotted line. Use the blanks to write each word as it is read aloud. When you finish the test, unfold the paper. Use the list at the right to correct any spelling mistakes.

1. _____
2. _____
3. _____
4. _____
5. _____
6. _____
7. _____
8. _____
9. _____
10. _____
11. _____
12. _____
13. _____
14. _____
15. _____
16. _____
17. _____
18. _____
19. _____
20. _____

Review Words
21. _____
22. _____
23. _____

Challenge Words
24. _____
25. _____

1. dart
2. guard
3. award
4. backyard
5. argue
6. spark
7. target
8. smart
9. charge
10. carpet
11. warp
12. door
13. fort
14. morning
15. stork
16. cord
17. worn
18. stormy
19. core
20. bore
21. screech
22. shrimp
23. throat
24. charcoal
25. forecast

Copyright © McGraw Hill. Permission is granted to reproduce for classroom use.

Name _____

An *r-controlled* vowel is a vowel followed by the letter *r*. The sound /är/ is usually spelled *ar*, as in <u>car</u>d. The sound /ôr/ is usually spelled *or*, *oor*, *oar*, and *ore*, as in the words *bore*, *floor*, *boar*, and *store*.

DECODING WORDS

The first syllable in *forcing* contains the *r-controlled* vowel sound /ôr/. The second syllable has the ending *-ing*. Blend the sounds and read the word aloud: /fôrs/ /ing/.

Write the spelling words with the matching spelling patterns.

stork	bore	guard	fort	warp
charge	spark	carpet	backyard	smart
award	cord	worn	dart	core
morning	door	stormy	target	argue

ore

1. _____

2. _____

or

3. _____

4. _____

5. _____

6. _____

7. _____

8. _____

oor

9. _____

ar

10. _____

11. _____

12. _____

13. _____

14. _____

15. _____

16. _____

17. _____

18. _____

19. _____

20. _____

 **Use the spelling rules above to write a short fable. Include four words from the spelling list. Check your work for errors.**

Copyright © McGraw Hill. Permission is granted to reproduce for classroom use.

Name _____

> An *r-controlled vowel* is a vowel followed by the letter *r*. The sound /är/ is usually spelled *ar*, as in *card*. The sound /ôr/ is usually spelled *or*, *oor*, *oar*, and *ore*, as in the words *bore*, *floor*, *boar*, and *store*.

DECODING WORDS

The first syllable in *forcing* contains the r-controlled vowel sound /ôr/. The second syllable has the ending *-ing*. Blend the sounds and read the word aloud: /fôrs/ /ing/.

Write the spelling words with the matching spelling patterns.

stork	bore	card	fort	warp
bark	spark	carpet	backyard	smart
yard	cord	worn	dart	core
floor	door	stormy	far	large

ore

1. _____

2. _____

or

3. _____

4. _____

5. _____

6. _____

7. _____

oor

8. _____

9. _____

ar

10. _____

11. _____

12. _____

13. _____

14. _____

15. _____

16. _____

17. _____

18. _____

19. _____

20. _____

 **Use the spelling rules above to write a short fable. Include four words from the spelling list. Check your work for errors.**

Copyright © McGraw Hill. Permission is granted to reproduce for classroom use.

Name_____

Write the spelling words with the matching spelling patterns. If a word has more than one spelling pattern, write it under both headings.

predator	forecast	guard	force	forward
charge	spark	carpet	barnyard	guitar
charcoal	afford	uproar	seminar	Oregon
morning	scorch	aboard	enlarge	argue

ore

1. _____

2. _____

or

3. _____

4. _____

5. _____

6. _____

7. _____

8. _____

oar

9. _____

10. _____

ar

11. _____

12. _____

13. _____

14. _____

15. _____

16. _____

17. _____

18. _____

19. _____

20. _____

21. _____

Compare the words *award* and *warp*. How are they alike? How are they different?

_____

_____

 Use the spelling rules above to write a short fable. Include four words from the spelling list. Check your work for errors.

Copyright © McGraw Hill. Permission is granted to reproduce for classroom use.

Name _____

dart	argue	charge	fort	worn
guard	spark	carpet	morning	stormy
award	target	warp	stork	core
backyard	smart	door	cord	bore

A. An *analogy* is a statement that compares sets of words. Write the spelling word to complete each analogy below.

1. *Dollar* is to *bill* as *prize* is to _____.

2. *Laugh* is to *cry* as *agree* is to _____.

3. *Eat* is to *dine* as *curve* is to _____.

4. *Begin* is to *end* as *excite* is to _____.

5. *Powerful* is to *strong* as *bright* is to _____.

6. *White* is to *black* as *new* is to _____.

7. *Jet* is to *plane* as *bull's-eye* is to _____.

B. Write the spelling word that matches each definition below.

8. rug _____

9. rope _____

10. area behind a house _____

11. place for soldiers _____

12. one who watches _____

13. rainy _____

14. dawn _____

15. tiny fire _____

16. in an entrance _____

17. thrown in a game _____

18. large bird _____

19. center _____

20. electricity _____

Copyright © McGraw Hill. Permission is granted to reproduce for classroom use.

Name _____

Underline the six misspelled words in the paragraphs below. Write the words correctly on the lines.

It was a stourmy night when Benjamin Franklin discovered electricity. Lightning hit the torget of his experiment and traveled down a kite string. Ben felt an incredible spairk when he touched the metal key tied there. Electricity!

No one could arrgue that electricity is not now an important part of our lives. Today, we use electricity to light our street, home, and even the backyad. It is necessary for many of the things we do from marning to night.

1. _____   4. _____

2. _____   5. _____

3. _____   6. _____

Writing Connection

Write about how electricity has improved your life in some way. Use at least four words from the spelling list.

_____

_____

_____

_____

_____

_____

_____

_____

Copyright © McGraw Hill. Permission is granted to reproduce for classroom use.

Name _____

Copyright © McGraw Hill. Permission is granted to reproduce for classroom use.

Remember

An *r-controlled vowel* is a vowel followed by the letter *r*. The sound /är/ is usually spelled *ar*, as in <u>car</u>d. The sound /ôr/ is usually spelled *or*, *oor*, *oar*, and *ore*, as in the words *bore*, *floor*, *boar*, and *store*.

A. Circle the spelling word in each row that rhymes with the word in bold type. Read the spelling word aloud and write it on the line.

1. **chore**   door   dare   sort   _____
2. **scarred** snared   carted   guard   _____
3. **large**   charge   charm   flag   _____
4. **horn**   word   worn   war   _____
5. **fork**   spook   stork   lark   _____
6. **star**t   hard   note   dart   _____
7. **aboard**   award   colored   apart   _____
8. **four**   first   pair   bore   _____
9. **short**   pour   fort   fit   _____
10. **cart**   smart   smelled   port   _____
11. **board**   cord   card   crowed   _____
12. **shark**   stork   clock   spark   _____
13. **pour**   pair   core   cope   _____
14. **warning** morning   forty   started   _____

B. Write these spelling words in alphabetical order: *carpet, argue, backyard, warp, stormy, target.*

15. _____   17. _____   19. _____

16. _____   18. _____   20. _____

Name _____

Read each passage. Underline the antonyms that help you figure out the meaning of each word in bold. Then write the word's meaning on the line.

1. Father: Stop wasting your time. Your dragon looks like the horrible mountain dragon, who has swooped down on the village and eaten water buffalo, pigs, and even people!
   Liang: That dragon is dangerous, but some dragons are **harmless**.

   _____

   _____

2. Father: Good luck to anyone who tries! It's **impossible**!
   Liang: I think it's possible. As a matter of fact, I think I can do it.

   _____

   _____

3. Mother: I believe in him. For once, please, believe in your son, too. . . .
   Father: (*patting Liang on the back*) I will never **doubt** you again.

   _____

   _____

Copyright © McGraw Hill. Permission is granted to reproduce for classroom use.

Name _____

Knowing **Greek roots** and their meanings can help you figure out the meaning of unfamiliar words. Here are a few Greek roots and their meanings:

auto – *self*   **graph** – *write*   **meter** – *measure*   **scop** – *see*

How many words can you think of with the Greek roots *auto, graph, meter,* and *scop*? Consult a print or digital dictionary to read the word aloud. Then write the words under the correct Greek root.

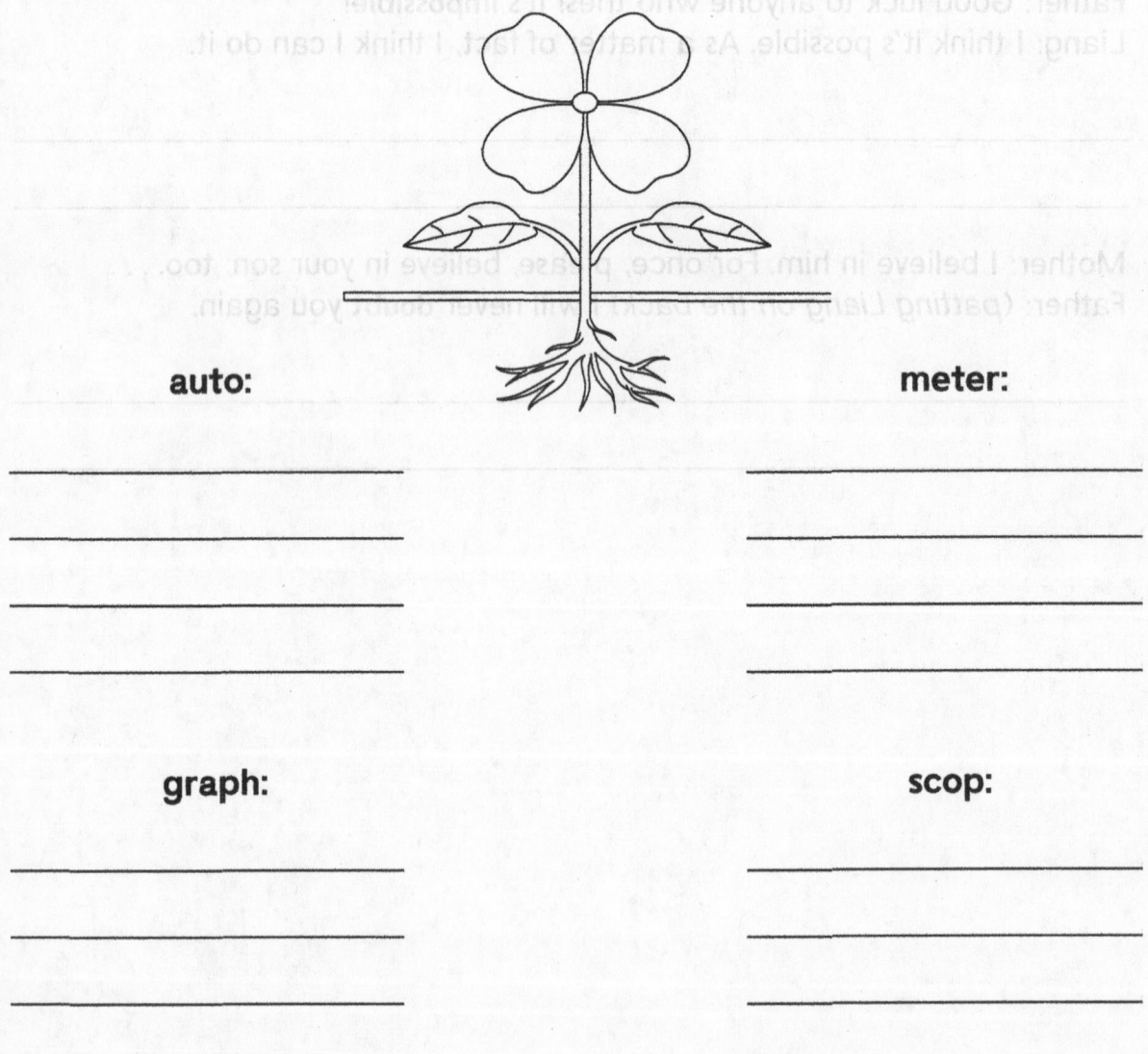

auto:

_____

_____

_____

_____

meter:

_____

_____

_____

_____

graph:

_____

_____

_____

scop:

_____

_____

_____

Copyright © McGraw Hill. Permission is granted to reproduce for classroom use.

Name _____

> • Sentences can be combined by using the word *and* to join two nouns in the subject. Leave out any words that repeat and make sure that subjects and verbs agree.
>
>   *Jamal washes the dishes. Teri washes the dishes. Jamal and Teri wash the dishes.*
>
> • A combined sentence has a complete subject and a complete predicate.

Read each pair of sentences. Circle the subject in each sentence. Then combine the sentences by using the word *and* to join the two nouns in the subject.

1. Kelsey goes to summer camp. Alvin goes to summer camp.

   _____

2. The rabbit hides under a bush. The squirrel hides under a bush.

   _____

3. My sister likes to watch football. I like to watch football.

   _____

4. The teacher knows the correct answer. The student knows the correct answer.

   _____

5. Mom eats dinner with me at the table. Aunt Macy eats dinner with me at the table.

   _____

 **Imagine you could take all of your friends on vacation. In your writer's notebook, write a short passage about whom you would bring and what you would do. Use the sentences as a model. Then check your work.**

Copyright © McGraw Hill. Permission is granted to reproduce for classroom use.

Name _____

> • Sentences can be combined by using the word *and* to join two nouns in the subject.
>
> • A **predicate noun** follows a linking verb and renames the subject.
>
> • Sentences can be combined by using the word *and* to join two nouns in the predicate. Leave out any words that repeat and make sure that subjects and verbs agree.
>
> *Tana is a student. Tana is a ballerina. Tana is a student and a ballerina.*

Read each pair of sentences. Circle the predicate noun in each sentence. Then combine the sentences by using the word *and* to join the two predicate nouns.

1. The woman is an actress. The woman is a waitress.

   _____

2. My dog seemed like a statue. He seemed like a rock.

   _____

3. I am a student. I am a volunteer.

   _____

4. My parents are citizens. My parents are community leaders.

   _____

 **Read this sentence from "Fog." Underline the nouns that have been combined. In your writer's notebook, rewrite the sentence into two sentences with the nouns separated. Then explain why you think the poet combined these nouns to make one sentence instead of two.**

It sits looking over harbor and city on silent haunches and then moves on.

Copyright © McGraw Hill. Permission is granted to reproduce for classroom use.

Name _____

- Use a comma after an **introductory phrase** at the beginning of a sentence. *In the beginning, singing so loudly was fun.*

- An **appositive** is a noun that describes the noun that comes right before it. Appositives are separated from the rest of the sentence with a comma before and after them. *Shawna, my cousin, is very tall.*

- **Interjections** express emotion and are often followed by an exclamation point. *Oh, no! Our basement is flooding.*

Read each sentence. On the line, write whether the underlined word or words are a *phrase,* **an** *appositive,* **or an** *interjection.* **Then rewrite the sentence using correct punctuation.**

1. Eli <u>a strong soccer player</u> scored the most goals. _____

_____

2. <u>Once upon a time</u> there was a beautiful princess. _____

_____

3. <u>Ouch</u> I stepped on something sharp. _____

_____

Writing Connection | **Use the sentences as a model. Write a short story about discovering a mouse in your kitchen. Include one introductory phrase, one appositive, and one interjection.**

_____

_____

_____

_____

_____

Copyright © McGraw Hill. Permission is granted to reproduce for classroom use.

Name _____

- Sentences can be combined by using the word **and** to join two nouns in the subject or two nouns in the predicate. Leave out any words that repeat and make sure that subjects and verbs agree.
- **Introductory phrases** and **appositives** are punctuated with commas.
- **Interjections** express emotion and are often followed by an exclamation point.

Rewrite the paragraphs below, correcting mistakes in punctuation.

1. Long ago there was a woodcutter with three sons. The woodcutter a strong man would spend his day chopping trees. Meanwhile, his sons would argue the entire time he was gone. Then one day the woodcutter used a batch of twigs to show they were stronger when they were together as one. Ah the woodcutter's sons never fought again.

_____

_____

_____

_____

2. Kids also called growing machines get taller and taller every year. This is because their bones are still growing. Like most people you probably think that we stop growing when we become adults. This is not true. Your nose and ears never stop growing. Wow although this is odd, it does explain why many older people have large noses and ears.

_____

_____

_____

_____

Copyright © McGraw Hill. Permission is granted to reproduce for classroom use.

Name _____

Read the selection that follows. Then answer the questions.

(1) My mother is an excellent mathematician. (2) My mother is an excellent woodworker. (3) My father is a great musician. (4) My sister is a great musician.

1. Which predicate nouns should be joined in sentences 1 and 2?
   A *my* and *mother*
   B *excellent* and *woodworker*
   C *excellent* and *mathematician*
   D *woodworker* and *mathematician*

2. Which subject nouns should be joined in sentences 3 and 4?
   F *my* and *great*
   G *father* and *sister*
   H *great* and *musician*
   J *father* and *musician*

Read the student draft that follows. Then answer the questions.

(1) We will be good listeners at the art show. (2) We will be good learners at the art show. (3) Jessica painted a picture. (4) Brandon painted a picture.

3. How would you best combine sentences 1 and 2?
   A We will be good listeners and learners at the art show.
   B We and we will be good listeners at the art show.
   C We will be good and good listeners at the art show.
   D We will be good listeners at the art show; we will be good learners at the art show.

4. How would you best combine sentences 3 and 4?
   F Jessica painted a picture. Brandon painted a picture.
   G Jessica painted a picture, and Brandon painted a picture.
   H Jessica and Brandon painted a picture.
   J Jessica painted a picture, Brandon painted a picture.

Copyright © McGraw Hill. Permission is granted to reproduce for classroom use.

Name _____

Fold back the paper along the dotted line. Use the blanks to write each word as it is read aloud. When you finish the test, unfold the paper. Use the list at the right to correct any spelling mistakes.

1. _____
2. _____
3. _____
4. _____
5. _____
6. _____
7. _____
8. _____
9. _____
10. _____
11. _____
12. _____
13. _____
14. _____
15. _____
16. _____
17. _____
18. _____
19. _____
20. _____

Review Words 21. _____
22. _____
23. _____

Challenge Words 24. _____
25. _____

1. sickly
2. hardly
3. quickly
4. slowly
5. carefully
6. wonderful
7. beautiful
8. graceful
9. spoonful
10. darkness
11. shapeless
12. ageless
13. illness
14. goodness
15. spotless
16. painless
17. weakness
18. darkest
19. clearest
20. thoughtful
21. door
22. smart
23. argue
24. brilliantly
25. straightest

Copyright © McGraw Hill. Permission is granted to reproduce for classroom use.

Name _____

A suffix is added to the end of a word to change the word's meaning.

- *-ness* means *the state of*
- *-ly* means *in a certain way*
- *-est* means *most*

- *-ful* means *full of*
- *-fully* means *in a certain way full of*

DECODING WORDS

When a word ends in a consonant and *y*, change the *y* to an *i* before adding *-ful, -less,* or *-ly*. This usually changes the vowel sound. When you add *-ful* to *pity*, the long *e* becomes a short *i: pi/ti/ful.*

Write the spelling words that contain each suffix. Then read the words aloud.

spotless	carefully	spoonful	illness	graceful
wonderful	hardly	darkness	darkest	goodness
shapeless	ageless	quickly	slowly	sickly
thoughtful	beautiful	weakness	clearest	painless

-ness

1. _____
2. _____
3. _____
4. _____

-ly

5. _____
6. _____
7. _____
8. _____

-est

9. _____
10. _____

-ful

11. _____
12. _____
13. _____
14. _____
15. _____

-less

16. _____
17. _____
18. _____
19. _____

-fully

20. _____

Look through this week's selection for more words to sort. Create a word sort for a partner in your writer's notebook.

Copyright © McGraw Hill. Permission is granted to reproduce for classroom use.

Name _____

Suffixes are added to the end of a word to slightly change a word's meaning. Here is a list of some suffixes and their meanings:

- *-ness* means *the state of*
- *-ly* means *in a certain way*
- *-est* means *most*
- *-ful* means *full of*
- *-fully* means *in a certain way full of*

SPELLING TIP

When adding a suffix to a word that ends in a *y*, like *beauty*, remember to change the *y* to *i*. Then add the suffix.

Write the spelling words that contain each suffix. Then read the words aloud.

spotless	carefully	spoonful	illness	graceful
wonderful	hardly	darkness	darkest	goodness
shapeless	ageless	quickly	slowly	sickly
oldest	thankful	weakness	clearest	painless

-ness

1. _____
2. _____
3. _____
4. _____

-ly

5. _____
6. _____
7. _____
8. _____

-est

9. _____
10. _____
11. _____

-ful

12. _____
13. _____
14. _____
15. _____

-less

16. _____
17. _____
18. _____
19. _____

-fully

20. _____

 **Look through this week's selection for more words to sort. Create a word sort for a partner in your writer's notebook.**

Copyright © McGraw Hill. Permission is granted to reproduce for classroom use.

Name _____

A. Write the spelling words that contain each suffix.

acrobatic	carefully	spoonful	illness	weakness
darkness	shapeless	gymnastic	darkest	clearest
fantastic	allergic	spotless	wonderful	thoughtful
ageless	graceful	beautifully	painless	goodness

-ness

1. _____

2. _____

3. _____

4. _____

-ic

5. _____

6. _____

7. _____

8. _____

-est

9. _____

10. _____

-ful

11. _____

12. _____

13. _____

14. _____

-less

15. _____

16. _____

17. _____

18. _____

-fully

19. _____

20. _____

B. Compare the words *darkness* and *darkest*. How are they alike? How are they different?

_____

_____

_____

 **Look through this week's selection for more words to sort. Create a word sort for a partner in your writer's notebook.**

Copyright © McGraw Hill. Permission is granted to reproduce for classroom use.

Name _____

A. Write the spelling word that best completes each sentence.

sickly	carefully	spoonful	illness	weakness
hardly	wonderful	darkness	goodness	darkest
quickly	beautiful	shapeless	spotless	clearest
slowly	graceful	ageless	painless	thoughtful

1. The road was _____ where there were no street lights.

2. The student _____ checked her test answers.

3. I had a _____ time at the lake and would like to go back!

4. My grandmother looks so young that people say she is

   _____.

5. I took a _____ of medicine and felt better.

6. The car moved so _____ that I thought we'd never get there.

7. The scrape on my knee was _____ and healed quickly.

8. The _____ model was known for her pretty face.

9. She gave me this for free out of the _____ of her heart.

10. The sky had no clouds and was the _____ I had ever seen it.

B. Write the spelling word that matches each definition below.

11. lack of light _____   16. not healthy _____

12. perfectly clean   17. elegant in form _____

   _____   18. kind and considerate

13. lack of strength

   _____   19. without form _____

14. sickness _____   20. in a fast way _____

15. barely _____

Copyright © McGraw Hill. Permission is granted to reproduce for classroom use.

Name _____

Underline the three misspelled words in each paragraph below. Write the words correctly on the lines.

Red's grandmother had an illniss. Red didn't like the darknes of the woods around Grandmother's house, but she wanted to help Grandmother feel better. She quicklie ran through the woods to bring Grandmother a basket of food.

She was almost there when she saw a dark, shapelass figure ahead. She turned to run, but then she heard Grandmother calling her. Grandmother told Red that her weaknis had gone away and she had come to meet her. Then Grandmother thanked Red for the wonderfull basket of food.

1. _____ 4. _____

2. _____ 5. _____

3. _____ 6. _____

Writing Connection

Tell your own tale about a favorite fairy tale character. Use at least four words from the spelling list.

_____
_____
_____
_____
_____
_____
_____
_____
_____

Copyright © McGraw Hill. Permission is granted to reproduce for classroom use.

Name _____

Remember

Suffixes are added to the end of a word to slightly change a word's meaning. Here is a list of some common suffixes and their meanings:

- *-ness* means "the state of"
- *-ful* means "full of"
- *-ly* means "in a certain way"
- *-fully* means "in a certain way full of"
- *-est* means "most"

Suffixes form the final syllable or syllables in a word. A suffix can change the spelling and pronunciation of the base word to which it is added. For example, when the suffix *-fully* is added to *beauty,* the long *e* spelled *y* becomes a short *i* spelled *i: beau/ti/ful/ly.*

sickly	carefully	spoonful	illness	weakness
hardly	wonderful	darkness	goodness	darkest
quickly	beautiful	shapeless	spotless	clearest
slowly	graceful	ageless	painless	thoughtful

Write the missing letters of a suffix to make a spelling word. Read the words aloud, then write the complete word in your writer's notebook.

1. shape ____ ____ ____ ____
2. sick ____ ____
3. weak ____ ____ ____ ____
4. spoon ____ ____ ____
5. clear ____ ____ ____
6. beauti ____ ____ ____
7. quick ____ ____
8. age ____ ____ ____ ____
9. thought ____ ____ ____
10. dark ____ ____ ____

11. care ____ ____ ____ ____ ____
12. pain ____ ____ ____ ____
13. slow ____ ____
14. ill ____ ____ ____ ____
15. grace ____ ____ ____
16. dark ____ ____ ____ ____
17. hard ____ ____
18. spot ____ ____ ____ ____
19. good ____ ____ ____ ____
20. wonder ____ ____ ____

Copyright © McGraw Hill. Permission is granted to reproduce for classroom use.

Name _____

Remember that **related words** have the same base word. The meaning of the word is changed slightly with the addition of prefixes, suffixes, and inflectional endings. Examine the following related words with the base word *act* and think about their meanings.

react   action   reaction   acted   acting   activate

These groups of related words need some help! Read the words aloud and cross out the words that do not belong. When you are finished, the remaining words should all have the same base.

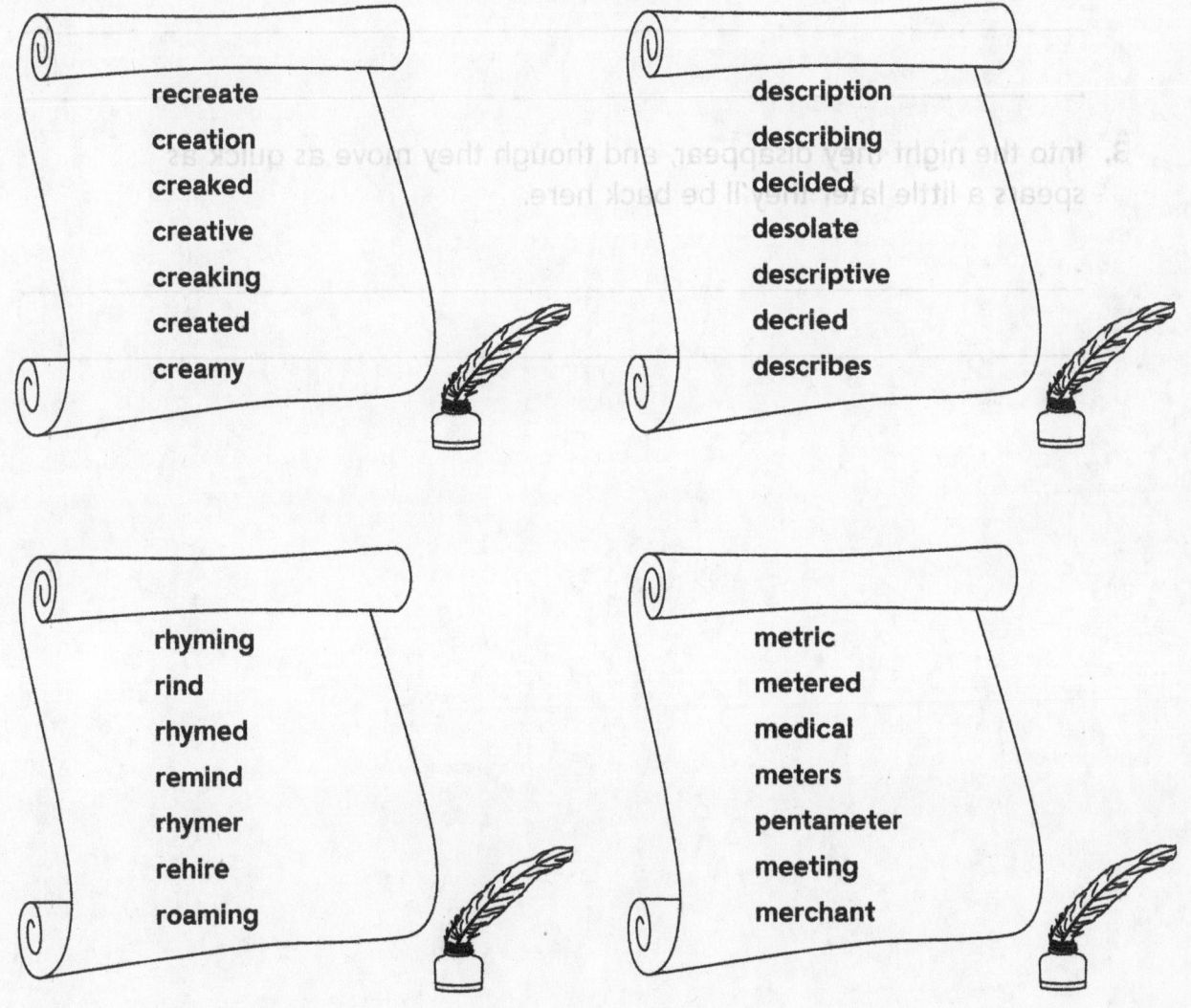

recreate
creation
creaked
creative
creaking
created
creamy

description
describing
decided
desolate
descriptive
decried
describes

rhyming
rind
rhymed
remind
rhymer
rehire
roaming

metric
metered
medical
meters
pentameter
meeting
merchant

Copyright © McGraw Hill. Permission is granted to reproduce for classroom use.

Name _____

Read each passage from "Deer." Underline the simile or metaphor in the sentence. Then write the two things that are being compared on the lines.

1. We see them sitting under trees at night, in my yard, like a photo of a family.

   _____

   _____

2. Then they dart away, their tails held high, six white arrows point at the sky.

   _____

   _____

3. Into the night they disappear, and though they move as quick as spears a little later they'll be back here.

   _____

   _____

Copyright © McGraw Hill. Permission is granted to reproduce for classroom use.

Name _____

- A **verb** tells what the subject does: *run, take, smelled*.

- A verb can include more than one word. There may be a **main verb** and a **helping verb**: *can come, has baked, am walking*.

Read each sentence and find the verb. Write it on the line provided.

1. The white cat sleeps on the sofa. _____

2. She was counting the fluffy clouds. _____

3. The lights blinked on and off quickly. _____

4. He sang that song perfectly! _____

5. We will visit my grandparents next week. _____

Connect to Community | **Talk to a parent or another trusted adult about fire departments. Who pays the firefighters? What kind of training do they get? Then write a paragraph about why you think fire departments are important. Edit your paragraph to make sure each sentence has a subject and a verb.**

_____

_____

_____

_____

_____

_____

Copyright © McGraw Hill. Permission is granted to reproduce for classroom use.

Name _____

> • A **verb** tells what the subject does.
>
> • An **action verb** tells what the subject does, did, or will do.
>
> • Action verbs can have different **tenses**. They can show action in the **past, present,** or **future**. *Tameka ran. Ali gives. Sarah will drink.*

Read each sentence and circle the action verb. On the line, write *past,* **present,** or *future* **to name the tense of each circled verb.**

1. The angry baby cries loudly for her bottle. _____

2. The weatherman will predict the weather after this commercial break.

   _____

3. She played the piano beautifully at the concert. _____

4. Scientists will search for the tomb inside the pyramid. _____

5. The audience laughed at the comedian's jokes. _____

6. Birds protect their babies from predators. _____

7. My friend and I will walk home from school together. _____

8. The computer made a loud and unusual noise. _____

Reading/Writing Connection

Read the paragraph below. Circle all the action verbs. What tense are all the verbs in? In your writer's notebook, explain how the article would be different if a different tense had been used.

Over my steering wheel, I watched the heavy, dark gray clouds roll in. The sky became a darker shade of gray, and raindrops soon scattered across my windshield. A big storm was almost here. I glanced at the boxes of clothes in the large back seat. I smiled to myself.

Copyright © McGraw Hill. Permission is granted to reproduce for classroom use.

> - Underline or italicize titles of television shows, movies, books, and albums of songs; and names of newspapers and magazines: *The Wizard of Oz* and <u>The Global Weekly</u>.
> - Use quotation marks around titles of stories, articles, essays, songs, and poems: "How the West Was Won."
> - Capitalize every word in a title except articles, conjunctions, and prepositions that are not at the beginning or end of the title: "How to Change the Car's Oil."

Write each sentence correctly using capital letters and correct punctuation for titles.

1. Have you ever read the book Peter Pan by J. M. Barrie?

   _____

2. I like the article Real school Kids in the magazine School Times.

   _____

3. My sister went to see the new movie life on mars last Saturday.

   _____

4. I miss you is my favorite song on the album "Songs from the heart."

   _____

5. I read aloud the poem <u>My Shadow</u> by Robert Louis Stevenson.

   _____

 **In your writer's notebook, write a list of your favorite books, movies, or TV shows. Check that you have capitalized the correct words in each title. Check for any spelling mistakes. You can use a dictionary to help you.**

Copyright © McGraw Hill. Permission is granted to reproduce for classroom use.

Name _____

- A **verb** tells what the subject does. An **action verb** can show action in the **past, present,** or **future**.
- Most titles are either underlined or italicized. Quotation marks are used for titles of stories, articles, essays, songs, and poems.
- Every word in a title should be capitalized except articles, conjunctions, and prepositions that are not at the beginning or end of the title.

Rewrite the paragraphs below, correcting mistakes in verb tenses and titles.

COMMON ERRORS

It is important to make sure that your writing stays in a single tense. The verbs do not jump back and forth between past, present, and future.

1. Deven likes the action movie "the cowboy." It has great music and an exciting plot. His sister Anya likes the comedy "strawberry hill" because it is so funny. It also will include her favorite song, "don't look back."

_____
_____
_____
_____

2. I will read an article in the newspaper "The Sun Times" yesterday. It was called How to Choose a vacation spot. It reminded me of a book I will read called My Summer Vacation. I run to tell my mom about it.

_____
_____
_____
_____

Copyright © McGraw Hill. Permission is granted to reproduce for classroom use.

Name _____

A. Answer the questions below.

1. Which sentence has a present-tense action verb?

   A People walked past the lake.

   B The leaves flutter in the breeze.

   C Sunshine warmed the ground.

   D Summer will arrive soon.

2. Which sentence has a present-tense action verb?

   F The horse ran the fastest.

   G It will rain this evening.

   H I hide quietly behind a tree.

   J You will win the contest.

B. Read the student draft. Then choose the best answer to each question for the underlined verb.

    (1) Ella's band <u>play</u> three songs and then left the stage. (2) "That was awesome!" I <u>tell</u> her later in the green room. (3) "When do you think you <u>play</u> again?" I asked. (4) "I definitely <u>want</u> to be there for your next show!"

3. What is the correct verb tense for sentence 1?

   A play

   B played

   C will play

   D playing

4. What is the correct verb tense for sentence 2?

   F tell

   G told

   H will tell

   J telling

5. What is the correct verb tense for sentence 3?

   A play

   B played

   C will play

   D playing

6. What is the correct verb tense for sentence 4?

   F want

   G wanted

   H will want

   J wanting

Copyright © McGraw Hill. Permission is granted to reproduce for classroom use.

Name _____

Fold back the
paper along the
dotted line. Use
the blanks to
write each word
as it is read aloud.
When you finish
the test, unfold
the paper. Use the
list at the right
to correct any
spelling mistakes.

1. _____   1. herb
2. _____   2. person
3. _____   3. sternly
4. _____   4. serpent
5. _____   5. worse
6. _____   6. pearl
7. _____   7. dirty
8. _____   8. birth
9. _____   9. shirt
10. _____ 10. twirl
11. _____ 11. swirl
12. _____ 12. purse
13. _____ 13. curl
14. _____ 14. curve
15. _____ 15. curb
16. _____ 16. hurl
17. _____ 17. turkey
18. _____ 18. turnip
19. _____ 19. purpose
20. _____ 20. blurred

Review Words   21. _____ 21. slowly
22. _____ 22. quickly
23. _____ 23. beautiful

Challenge Words   24. _____ 24. spurt
25. _____ 25. further

Copyright © McGraw Hill. Permission is granted to reproduce for classroom use.

Name _____

When a vowel sound is followed by the letter *r*, the *r* changes the vowel sound to /ûr/. These vowels are called **r-controlled vowels**. The /ûr/ sound is spelled

- *er*, as in *herd*
- *or*, as in *worse*
- *ir*, as in *bird*
- *ear*, as in *heard*
- *ur*, as in *hurt*

SPELLING TIP

Though *er, ir, ur, or,* and *ear* are spelled with two or three letters, they blend into one sound. Remember to use the correct spelling pattern when you hear the /ûr/ sound.

Write the spelling words with the matching *r*-controlled spellings.

hurl	curl	shirt	worse	turkey
person	pearl	turnip	birth	twirl
purse	dirty	swirl	curb	purpose
blurred	curve	sternly	herb	serpent

ur
1. _____
2. _____
3. _____
4. _____
5. _____
6. _____
7. _____
8. _____
9. _____

or
10. _____

er
11. _____
12. _____
13. _____
14. _____

ir
15. _____
16. _____
17. _____
18. _____
19. _____

ear
20. _____

Look through this week's selection for more words to sort. Read the words aloud and create a word sort for a partner in your writer's notebook.

Copyright © McGraw Hill. Permission is granted to reproduce for classroom use.

Name _____

> When a vowel sound is followed by the letter *r*, the *r* changes the vowel sound to /ûr/. These vowels are called *r*-controlled **vowels**. The /ûr/ sound is spelled
>
> - *er*, as in *herd*   - *or*, as in *worse*
> - *ir*, as in *bird*   - *ear*, as in *heard*
> - *ur*, as in *hurt*

SPELLING TIP

Though *er, ir, ur, or,* and *ear* are spelled with two or three letters, they blend into one sound. Remember to use the correct spelling pattern when you hear the /ûr/ sound.

Write the spelling words with the matching *r*-controlled spellings.

hurl	curl	shirt	worse	turkey
person	pearl	turns	birth	twirl
purse	dirty	third	purr	learn
surf	nurse	perfect	herb	serve

ur

1. _____
2. _____
3. _____
4. _____
5. _____
6. _____
7. _____
8. _____

or

9. _____

er

10. _____
11. _____
12. _____
13. _____

ir

14. _____
15. _____
16. _____
17. _____
18. _____

ear

19. _____
20. _____

 **Look through this week's selection for more words to sort. Read the words aloud and create a word sort for a partner in your writer's notebook.**

Copyright © McGraw Hill. Permission is granted to reproduce for classroom use.

Name _____

Write the spelling words with the matching *r*-controlled spellings.

hurl	further	squirming	emergency	turkey
permit	pearl	turnip	birthmark	superbly
purse	whirlwind	swirl	curbed	purpose
blurred	curved	sternly	herbs	serpent

ur   **er**   **ir**

1. _____   10. _____   16. _____

2. _____   11. _____   17. _____

3. _____   12. _____   18. _____

4. _____   13. _____   19. _____

5. _____   14. _____   20. _____

6. _____   15. _____   **ear**

7. _____   20. _____

8. _____

9. _____

Compare the words *twirl* and *swirl*. How are they alike? How are they different?

_____

_____

_____

 **Look through this week's selection for more words to sort. Read the words aloud and create a word sort for a partner in your writer's notebook.**

Copyright © McGraw Hill. Permission is granted to reproduce for classroom use.

Name _____

herb	worse	shirt	curl	turkey
person	pearl	twirl	curve	turnip
sternly	dirty	swirl	curb	purpose
serpent	birth	purse	hurl	blurred

A. Write the spelling word that belongs with the other words in the group.

1. life, death, _____

2. spice, seasoning, _____

3. child, woman, _____

4. reason, goal, _____

5. street, sidewalk, _____

6. monster, snake, _____

7. bag, pocketbook, _____

8. messy, muddy, _____

9. firmly, sharply, _____

10. bend, turn, _____

B. Write the spelling word that best completes each sentence.

11. Are you feeling better or _____ than yesterday?

12. Her tight _____ would not straighten.

13. The leaves _____ around on a windy day.

14. A _____ is a root vegetable, just as a carrot is.

15. My sight _____ as I fought back tears.

16. Did you see the drum major _____ her baton?

17. You might find a _____ inside an oyster.

18. Do you eat _____ for Thanksgiving dinner?

19. The tag inside my _____ made my neck itch.

20. I wanted to _____ the ball as far as I could throw it.

Copyright © McGraw Hill. Permission is granted to reproduce for classroom use.

Name _____

**Underline the three misspelled words in each paragraph below.
Write the words correctly on the lines.**

I woke up late yesterday. I grabbed some clothes, put them on, and got to the cerb just as the bus came. Whew! When I got to school, though, I saw that I had put on derty clothing. I was so embarrassed. But now I have a plan. I will lay out clean pants and a clean shurt at night. That way, if I oversleep, I'll have clean clothes to grab!

My eyes blirred as I looked down at my desk. Could things get any wurse? I just couldn't see the board. I knew I needed glasses. What was the perpose of pretending? I knew I needed to talk to my parents. After I did, I felt so much better. They made a date with the eye doctor right away!

1. _____   4. _____

2. _____   5. _____

3. _____   6. _____

Writing Connection

Write about a person who has helped you solve a problem. Use at least four words from the spelling list.

_____

_____

_____

_____

_____

_____

_____

_____

_____

Copyright © McGraw Hill. Permission is granted to reproduce for classroom use.

Name _____

Remember

When a vowel sound is followed by the letter *r*, the *r* changes the vowel sound to /ûr/. These vowels are called ***r*-controlled vowels**. The /ûr/ sound is spelled:

- *er*, as in *her*
- *ir*, as in *squirt*
- *ur*, as in *curd*
- *or*, as in *worse*
- *ear*, as in *heard*

A. Underline the spelling word in each row that rhymes with the word in bold type. Read the word aloud and write the spelling word on the line.

1.	**whirl**	swirl	wind	fur	_____
2.	**heard**	steer	fed	blurred	_____
3.	**worsen**	lesson	winded	person	_____
4.	**perky**	turkey	corny	funny	_____
5.	**spurt**	spent	shirt	blur	_____
6.	**verb**	curb	nerve	fern	_____
7.	**nurse**	must	bees	worse	_____
8.	**girl**	grunt	hurl	ball	_____
9.	**worth**	wart	birth	teeth	_____
10.	**verse**	purse	belts	serve	_____
11.	**serve**	knee	love	curve	_____
12.	**blurb**	bulb	glad	herb	_____
13.	**earl**	twirl	tell	end	_____

B. Write these spelling words in alphabetical order. Alphabetize them to the second letter: *pearl, serpent, turnip, curl, sternly, purpose, dirty.*

14._____ 17._____ 20._____

15._____ 18._____

16._____ 19._____

Copyright © McGraw Hill. Permission is granted to reproduce for classroom use.

Name _____

Remember that **related words** have the same base word, or root, and different prefixes, suffixes, and inflectional endings. Examine this group of related words:

preassign   reassign   assigned   assigning   assignable   assignment

How are their meanings similar? How are they different?

Add the suggested prefixes, suffixes, and inflectional endings to each base below to create a group of related words.

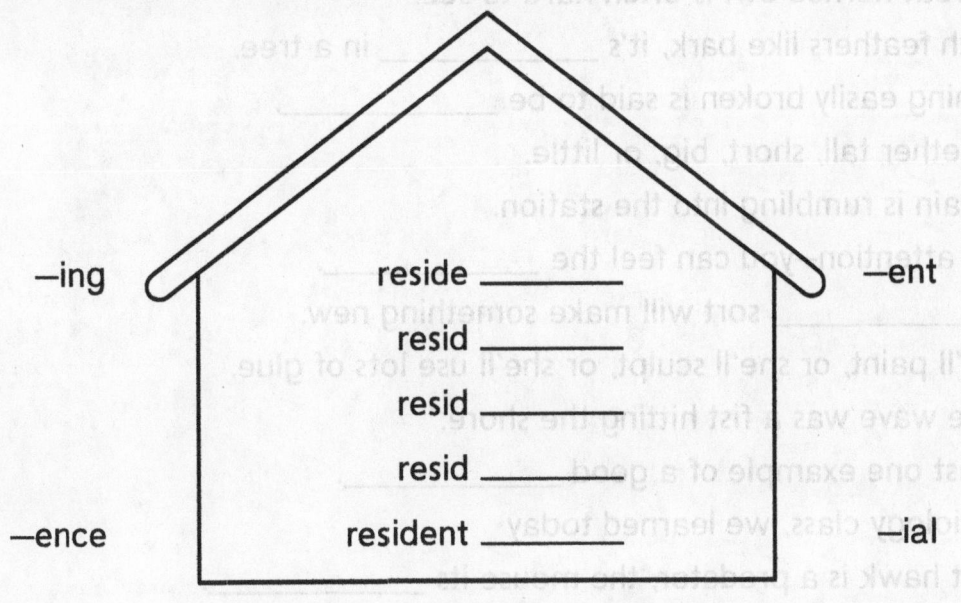

−ing

reside _____

resid _____

resid _____

resid _____

resident _____

−ent

−ence

−ial

im-   -ed

mature _____

matur _____

-ly   -ity

_____mature

matur _____

-ing

matur _____

Copyright © McGraw Hill. Permission is granted to reproduce for classroom use.

Name _____

Be a poet! Write a vocabulary word from the box to complete each rhyming couplet.

vibrations	metaphor	simile	outstretched
creative	descriptive	pounce	prey
brittle	rhyme	camouflaged	meter

1. If it has *like* or *as* and compares two things swimmingly,
   Your teacher will tell you to call it a _____.

2. A great horned owl is often hard to see.
   With feathers like bark, it's _____ in a tree.

3. A thing easily broken is said to be _____,
   Whether tall, short, big, or little.

4. A train is rumbling into the station.
   Pay attention—you can feel the _____.

5. A _____ sort will make something new.
   She'll paint, or she'll sculpt, or she'll use lots of glue.

6. "The wave was a fist hitting the shore."
   Is just one example of a good _____.

7. In biology class, we learned today
   That hawk is a predator; the mouse its _____.

8. Though poets may try it most of the time,
   It is never a given that their poems will _____.

9. My bright little kitten is about to _____,
   But away, away, the ball will bounce.

10. I hope this doesn't seem too far-fetched,
    But I'm seven feet tall with my arms _____.

11. The pattern you hear, of words stressed and unstressed,
    In poems is _____. Now, aren't you impressed?

12. Writers of _____ texts will prefer
    To use specific adjectives, nouns, and verbs.

Copyright © McGraw Hill. Permission is granted to reproduce for classroom use.

Name _____

> • The **verb tense** tells when in time an action is happening. A verb in the **present tense** shows that the action is happening now or over and over.
>
> *My parents walk the dog every morning before work.*
>
> • A present-tense verb must **agree** with the subject of the sentence. For singular subjects, add -*s* to most verbs. *Teri takes piano lessons on Wednesday.*
>
> • Use *am, is,* or *are* with the -*ing* form of a main verb to create the **progressive form** of a present-tense verb: *is walking, are talking.*

Circle the present-tense verb in each sentence. Rewrite the sentence with the progressive form of the verb.

1. She turns the light on.

_____

2. We ride the bus to school.

_____

3. He eats a turkey sandwich.

_____

4. I paint a picture of my backyard.

_____

5. Mom and Dad try to build the bookcase.

_____

 **Use the sentences as a model. In your writer's notebook, write a paragraph about a pet or a wild animal. Use the present tense and the progressive form. Draw one line under each progressive verb that you use. Use at least three progressive verbs.**

Copyright © McGraw Hill. Permission is granted to reproduce for classroom use.

Name _____

> • A verb in the **present tense** shows that the action is happening now or over and over.
>
> • A verb in the **past tense** shows that the action has already happened: *hurried*. Use *was* or *were* with the *-ing* form of a main verb to create the **progressive form** of a past-tense verb: *was hurrying*.
>
> • A verb in the **future tense** shows action that will happen: *will hurry*. Use *will be* with the *-ing* form of a main verb to create the **progressive form** of a future-tense verb: *will be hurrying*.

Read each sentence and underline the verb. On the line provided, identify the verb as *past, past progressive, future,* **or** *future progressive.*

1. The telephone was ringing all day. _____

2. I watched the deer in the woods. _____

3. My grandmother will call soon. _____

4. Dr. Lewis will be teaching a course next year. _____

5. The television broke a long time ago. _____

Read this excerpt from "Partaking in Public Service." Write the future progressive verb form for each underlined verb.

Kids <u>join</u> local volunteer groups to help their communities. They <u>work</u> together to improve their schools and neighborhoods. Community projects may include planting gardens or collecting food and clothing. Some <u>raise</u> money for local charities.

_____

_____

Copyright © McGraw Hill. Permission is granted to reproduce for classroom use.

Name _____

- A singular subject must have a singular verb.

- With a singular third-person subject, add -s or -es to most present-tense verbs. *Amir starts a business.*

- If the subject is *I, you,* a plural noun, or a plural pronoun, do not add -s or -es to a present-tense verb. *We start a business.*

- If a clause or phrase intervenes, or comes between, a subject and verb, the subject and verb must still agree. *The marbles, including the red one, belong to Fred.*

Read each sentence. On the line provided, write the correct present-tense form of the verb in parentheses.

1. Miguel, who is our friend, _____ the doorbell at his neighbor's house. (ring)

2. Shamese and Kim _____ twice around the track. (run)

3. I _____ a salad and an apple for lunch. (choose)

4. She _____ at the silly costume. (chuckle)

5. We _____ our lines for the play. (practice)

6. Renee _____ her chores early on the weekend. (do)

 **Imagine that you take a trip to another country. Write three sentences in your writer's notebook about what you see there. Include at least three verbs and underline them.**

Copyright © McGraw Hill. Permission is granted to reproduce for classroom use.

Name _____

> • The **tense** of a verb tells if the action is happening in the **past, present,** or **future.**
>
> • To create **progressive forms** of verbs, include a form of *to be* before the *-ing* form of the main verb.
>
> • A singular subject must have a singular verb. With a singular third-person subject, add *-s* or *-es* to a present-tense verb. If the subject is *I, you,* a plural noun, or a plural pronoun, do not add *-s* or *-es* to a present-tense verb.

Rewrite the sentences below based on the information in the parentheses. Correct mistakes in verb tenses and in subject-verb agreement.

1. We was cheering for our team at the football game. (past progressive)

   _____

2. You is go to the science fair next weekend. (future)

   _____

3. Cammy is reach for the sugar on the top shelf. (present)

   _____

4. I was gets another balloon for her. (past progressive)

   _____

5. The train will be zoom past my stop! (future progressive)

   _____

Copyright © McGraw Hill. Permission is granted to reproduce for classroom use.

Name _____

A. Answer the questions below.

1. Which sentence has the correct subject-verb agreement?

    A You brings your flute, which your sisters also play, to school.

    B He know all the questions and the answer.

    C Ms. Katz, one of our teachers, give a test today.

    D Trisha, who is an excellent student, asks for a pencil.

2. Which sentence has the correct subject-verb agreement?

    F We eats breakfast early.

    G They drives down the road.

    H The neighbor water his lawn.

    J I watched an hour of television.

B. Read the student draft. Then choose the best answer to each question.

   (1) So many things happen on my street in the summer. (2) Uncle Bill tells stories on the stoop. (3) We climb the jungle gym in the neighbor's backyard. (4) Jennifer skips on the sidewalk. (5) The ball rolls down the street.

3. What is the past-tense form of the verb in sentence 1?

    A happened

    B was happening

    C will be happening

    D Make no change

4. What is the past progressive form of the verb in sentence 2?

    F told

    G was telling

    H were telling

    J Make no change

5. What is the future-tense form of the verb in sentence 3?

    A climbed

    B will climb

    C will be climbing

    D Make no change

6. What is the future progressive form of the verb in sentence 5?

    F will be rolling

    G will roll

    H was rolling

    J Make no change

Copyright © McGraw Hill. Permission is granted to reproduce for classroom use.

Name _____

Fold back the paper along the dotted line. Use the blanks to write each word as it is read aloud. When you finish the test, unfold the paper. Use the list at the right to correct any spelling mistakes.

1. _____
2. _____
3. _____
4. _____
5. _____
6. _____
7. _____
8. _____
9. _____
10. _____
11. _____
12. _____
13. _____
14. _____
15. _____
16. _____
17. _____
18. _____
19. _____
20. _____

Review Words   21. _____
22. _____
23. _____

Challenge Words   24. _____
25. _____

1. wrinkle
2. wriggle
3. wrapper
4. wrench
5. answer
6. knead
7. knives
8. known
9. kneel
10. knew
11. plumber
12. combs
13. thumbs
14. lambs
15. condemn
16. resign
17. doubtful
18. hour
19. honest
20. honor
21. person
22. curl
23. shirt
24. knuckles
25. wrestle

Copyright © McGraw Hill. Permission is granted to reproduce for classroom use.

Name _____

> The spellings for /m/, /n/, and /r/ often contain silent letters.
>
> - The letter *b* is often silent when an *m* comes before it: *dumb*.
> - The letters *g* and *k* are often silent when they come before the letter *n*: *gnome* and *known*.
> - The letter *w* is silent when it comes before the letter *r*: *written*.

Decoding Words

Words like c**a**ke, comp**e**te, and inv**i**te have **vowel-consonant-e (VCe) syllables**. The vowel before the consonant is long, and the final *e* is silent. Read the words aloud.

Read aloud and write the spelling words that contain the silent letter.

wrinkle	answer	wrapper	wriggle	known
thumbs	honesty	knew	lambs	hour
kneel	knives	plumber	condemn	knead
resign	doubtful	combs	wrench	honor

silent b

1. _____
2. _____
3. _____
4. _____
5. _____

silent h

6. _____
7. _____
8. _____

silent k

9. _____
10. _____
11. _____
12. _____
13. _____

silent n

14. _____

silent w

15. _____
16. _____
17. _____
18. _____
19. _____

silent g

20. _____

Look for multisyllabic words with VCe syllables. Read the words aloud. Create a word sort for a partner in your writer's notebook.

Copyright © McGraw Hill. Permission is granted to reproduce for classroom use.

Name _____

The spellings for /m/, /n/, and /r/ often contain silent letters.

- The letter *b* is often silent when an *m* comes before it: *dumb*.
- The letters *g* and *k* are often silent when they come before the letter *n*: *gnome* and *known*.
- The letter *w* is silent when it comes before the letter *r*: *written*.

Decoding Words

Words like c<u>a</u>ke, comp<u>e</u>te, and inv<u>i</u>te have **vowel-consonant-*e* (VC*e*) syllables**. The vowel before the consonant is long, and the final *e* is silent. Read the words aloud.

Write the spelling words that contain the silent letter.

write	knot	wrap	wrist	known
thumbs	honest	knew	lambs	hour
crumb	knives	plumber	climb	knob
sign	doubt	combs	knee	honor

silent *b*

1. _____

2. _____

3. _____

4. _____

5. _____

6. _____

7. _____

silent *k*

8. _____

9. _____

10. _____

11. _____

12. _____

13. _____

silent *h*

14. _____

15. _____

16. _____

silent *w*

17. _____

18. _____

19. _____

silent *g*

20. _____

 **Look for multisyllabic words with VC*e* syllables to sort. Read the words aloud and create a word sort for a partner in your writer's notebook.**

Copyright © McGraw Hill. Permission is granted to reproduce for classroom use.

Name _____

Write the spelling words that contain the silent letter.

wrinkle	wreckage	wrapper	wriggle	knowledge
thumbs	honesty	assignment	lambs	knapsack
kneel	knives	plumber	autumn	knead
resign	doubtless	combs	wrench	honorable

silent b   **silent n**   **silent g**

1. _____   11. _____   19. _____

2. _____   **silent h**   20. _____

3. _____   12. _____

4. _____   13. _____

5. _____   **silent w**

silent k   14. _____

6. _____   15. _____

7. _____   16. _____

8. _____   17. _____

9. _____   18. _____

10. _____

Look through this week's selection for more words to sort. Read the words aloud and create a word sort for a partner in your writer's notebook.

Copyright © McGraw Hill. Permission is granted to reproduce for classroom use.

Name _____

wrinkle	answer	kneel	thumbs	doubtful
wriggle	knead	knew	lambs	hour
wrapper	knives	plumber	condemn	honesty
wrench	known	combs	resign	honor

A. Write the spelling word that best completes each sentence.

1. I have the _____ to your question.

2. The soldier's actions showed courage and _____.

3. Call the _____ to fix the kitchen faucet.

4. The brushes and _____ were lined up on the dresser.

5. I am able to bend my _____ back to my wrist.

6. I need a _____ to help me fix this.

7. Don't your knees hurt when you _____ for a long time?

8. I will iron the shirt until the last _____ is gone!

9. He will have to go to bed in one _____.

10. It is a _____ fact that Earth both rotates and revolves.

B. Write the spelling word that means the same as each word listed below.

11. realized _____

12. truthfulness _____

13. press _____

14. disapprove _____

15. unlikely _____

16. leave _____

17. jiggle _____

18. sheep _____

19. utensils _____

20. covering _____

Copyright © McGraw Hill. Permission is granted to reproduce for classroom use.

Name _____

Underline the six misspelled words in the paragraphs below. Write the words correctly on the lines.

    My brother Sam could never make up his mind about what he wanted to be when he grew up. He just new that he wanted to do something interesting. At one time, he wanted to be a farmer. He thought about raising sheep and lams. But he also liked tools. He would make a great plumer, too. It was a tough choice!

    Then one day he decided to be a judge. It was the perfect job for him! He was known for his onesty and was good at finding the ansers to problems. But then Sam changed his mind again, so I am doutful that he is ready to make a choice. Whatever he decides, I know my brother will be great at it!

1. _____   4. _____

2. _____   5. _____

3. _____   6. _____

Writing Connection | **Write about an interesting job of someone you know. Use at least four words from the spelling list. Review the spelling rules for silent letters before you write.**

_____

_____

_____

_____

_____

_____

_____

Copyright © McGraw Hill. Permission is granted to reproduce for classroom use.

Name _____

Copyright © McGraw Hill. Permission is granted to reproduce for classroom use.

Remember

The spellings for /m/, /n/, and /r/ often contain silent letters.

- The letter *b* is often silent when an *m* comes before it, as in *plumbing*.
- The letters *g* and *k* are often silent when they come before the letter *n*, as in *gnats* and *knowing*.
- The letter *w* is silent when it comes before the letter *r*, as in *writing*.

wrinkle	answer	kneel	thumbs	doubtful
wriggle	knead	knew	lambs	hour
wrapper	knives	plumber	condemn	honesty
wrench	known	combs	resign	honor

A. Fill in the missing letter of each word to form a spelling word. Then read the word aloud.

1. _____ riggle
2. dou _____ tful
3. _____ nown
4. plum _____ er
5. thum _____ s
6. condem _____
7. _____ nead

8. _____ onor
9. _____ rench
10. com _____ s
11. _____ neel
12. resi _____ n
13. _____ nives
14. lam _____ s

15. _____ onesty
16. _____ rinkle
17. ans _____ er
18. _____ new
19. _____ our
20. _____ rapper

B. Write these spelling words in alphabetical order. Alphabetize them to the third letter: *wrinkle, honor, wrench, hour, resign*.

21. _____
22. _____
23. _____
24. _____
25. _____

Name _____

Read the following sentences from "How Vera Helped." Underline the context clues that help you figure out the meaning of each word in bold. Use the clues and your background knowledge to write a short definition of the word on the line. Then use the word correctly in a sentence.

1. Vera had been collecting food since the beginning of the school year. . . . It was November now, and Brad was **questioning** what happened to all those juice boxes and food he gave away.

_____

_____

2. Her shopping bag was **bulging**, with boxes pushing out against the bag.

_____

3. When Vera walked into her house, Brad said out loud, "Wow, maybe she does eat it all. Maybe her family needs the food." He felt unsure as he said it, since her family had a lovely house with a tidy yard. But he was truly **perplexed**. He didn't know what to think.

_____

_____

4. She knocked on the front door. A moment later, an **elderly** man opened the door. Brad couldn't hear what the older man said to Vera, but they both smiled.

_____

_____

_____

Copyright © McGraw Hill. Permission is granted to reproduce for classroom use.

Name _____

> Often when you add certain **inflectional endings (-es, -ed)** or **suffixes (-er, -est, -ful, -ly, -ness)** to a base word, you must change the spelling of that base word.
>
> When a base word ends with a consonant and *y*, change the *y* to *i* before adding some endings: *marry/marries; cry/cried; lazy/laziest; happy/happiness.*
>
> When a base word ends with a short vowel and a consonant, double the consonant before adding some endings: *knit/knitted; slim/slimmer; hot/hottest.*
>
> When a base word ends with a silent *e*, drop the *e* before adding an ending that begins with a vowel: *bake/baked; hike/hiker; close/closest.*

Read each word in the box aloud. Decide which rule has been followed to add the inflectional ending or suffix. Write the word under the correct rule. Some of the words do not demonstrate any rule. Write them under *No Rule*.

batter	sillier	taped	rarest
busiest	patted	sheer	cities
carries	letter	species	wetter
invest	trader	thinnest	tamest

Change *y* to *i*

_____
_____
_____
_____

Drop Final *e*

_____
_____
_____
_____

Double Final Consonant

_____
_____
_____
_____

No Rule

_____
_____
_____
_____

Copyright © McGraw Hill. Permission is granted to reproduce for classroom use.

Name _____

> • The **main verb** in a sentence tells what the subject does or is.
>
>   *She <u>washes</u> the dog.*
>
> • A **helping verb** helps the main verb tell about an action or make a statement.
>
>   *She <u>is</u> washing the dog.*

Read each sentence. Circle the main verb. Underline the helping verb.

1. We are going to the store for milk.

2. I will help you in the kitchen.

3. He has taken this test once before.

4. The shoe is missing from the closet.

5. My mother is waiting in the parking lot.

6. You will want dessert soon.

Write a short paragraph about a time you were really looking forward to something, but it didn't turn out as you had planned. Use helping verbs in your sentences.

_____

_____

_____

_____

_____

Copyright © McGraw Hill. Permission is granted to reproduce for classroom use.

Name _____

> - A **helping verb** helps the main verb tell about an action or make a statement.
> - Helping verbs such as *have, has, had, is, am, are, was, were,* and *will* are used to show present, past, and future tense.
> - Some helping verbs, called modals, do not show tense. The principal modals are *can, could, may, might, must, ought, shall, should, will,* and *would.* They show possibility or obligation.

Read each sentence. Circle the helping verb. On the line provided, write whether the verb is in the *past, present,* or *future* tense. If there is no tense, write *none*.

1. She had prepared well for the test. _____

2. I will rest before the big game. _____

3. We have completed the puzzle! _____

4. The alligator may choose a resting spot soon. _____

5. The river can rise very quickly. _____

6. Our friends might have a party. _____

7. Jules had forgotten the answer. _____

Writing Connection Write a story in your writer's notebook about a real or imaginary trip. Use at least three past tense helping verbs in your writing. Then check your writing for correct use of helping verbs.

Copyright © McGraw Hill. Permission is granted to reproduce for classroom use.

Name _____

> - A **contraction** is a word that combines two words and leaves out one or more letters from one or both words: *do not/don't.*
> - Use an **apostrophe** in a contraction for the letters that have been left out: *cannot/can't.*
> - Use parentheses around material that is added to a sentence but not important to the meaning. Include an opening and closing parenthesis.
>
>   *My cat (whose name is Cookie) sometimes digs in the garbage.*

A. Read each sentence. Write the contraction for each set of underlined words.

1. The dentist <u>should not</u> have to pull the patient's tooth. _____

2. We <u>have not</u> gone swimming in the pool yet. _____

3. <u>They will</u> want to come along with us. _____

4. I think <u>she is</u> two years older than I am. _____

B. Add parentheses where they are needed in each sentence.

5. My dog's collar which is old needs to be replaced.

   _____

6. The restaurant offered chocolate chip pancakes my favorite.

   _____

 Write a short passage in your writer's notebook about an invention you would like to see in the future. Use contractions for the following word pairs: *will not, we will, I am.* Underline these contractions and any others that you include. Then edit your work for correct use of contractions.

Copyright © McGraw Hill. Permission is granted to reproduce for classroom use.

Name _____

- A sentence's **main verb** tells what the subject does or is. A **helping verb** helps the main verb tell about an action or make a statement.
- Helping verbs can show present, past, and future tenses, or they may not show any tense.
- A **contraction** is a word that combines two words and replaces one or more letters from one or both words with an **apostrophe**.
- Use opening and closing **parentheses** around material that is not important.

Rewrite the sentences below, correcting mistakes in helping and main verbs, contractions, and parentheses.

COMMON ERRORS

Some contractions form homophones with other words, such as *they're* with *their* and *there*. Try saying *they are* with the sentence in your head to make sure *they're* is the correct choice.

1. Mrs. Ryan my math teacher) have formed a club after school.

   _____

   _____

2. We will hiked the trail if it does'nt rain.

   _____

3. I have get my permission slip signed already.

   _____

4. Dont you want to get some ice cream (your favorite dessert?

   _____

5. I is streaming this song because i'ts my favorite one of all time!

   _____

Copyright © McGraw Hill. Permission is granted to reproduce for classroom use.

Name _____

A. Read the paragraphs. Then answer the questions.

(1) My mother prepared to cut the cake. (2) First, I wanted to open some of my presents. (3) My friends had paid attention to all my hints! (4) I opened many things that were on my wish list.

(5) My mom said it was time to cut the cake. (6) It was a chocolate cake with chocolate frosting. (7) I breathed in the smell of candle smoke as I held out my plate. (8) This had been the best birthday ever!

1. Which word in sentence 3 is a helping verb?

   A My

   B friends

   C had

   D to

2. Which other sentence contains a helping verb?

   F Sentence 2

   G Sentence 5

   H Sentence 7

   J Sentence 8

B. Read the sentences. Then answer the questions.

(1) The class _____ finished the project. (2) We all _____ helping by handing out flyers for the event. (3) Sasha _____ drawing the cover for the programs. (4) We _____ all getting ready for the audience to arrive later that week.

3. Which verb should go in the blank in sentence 1?

   A will

   B have

   C has

   D is

4. Which verb should go in the blank in sentence 2?

   F was

   G are

   H is

   J were

5. Which verb should go in the blank in sentence 3?

   A am

   B are

   C was

   D were

6. Which verb should go in the blank in sentence 4?

   F were

   G am

   H is

   J was

Copyright © McGraw Hill. Permission is granted to reproduce for classroom use.

Name _____

Fold back the paper along the dotted line. Use the blanks to write each word as it is read aloud. When you finish the test, unfold the paper. Use the list at the right to correct any spelling mistakes.

1. _____
2. _____
3. _____
4. _____
5. _____
6. _____
7. _____
8. _____
9. _____
10. _____
11. _____
12. _____
13. _____
14. _____
15. _____
16. _____
17. _____
18. _____
19. _____
20. _____

Review Words

21. _____
22. _____
23. _____

Challenge Words

24. _____
25. _____

1. center
2. once
3. scene
4. spice
5. circus
6. cement
7. police
8. certain
9. ounce
10. glance
11. germs
12. bridge
13. badge
14. strange
15. orange
16. ginger
17. wedge
18. arrange
19. sponge
20. village
21. combs
22. kneel
23. wrench
24. general
25. ceremony

Copyright © McGraw Hill. Permission is granted to reproduce for classroom use.

Name _____

The letters *c* and *g* can have a hard sound (/k/ and /g/), as in *car* and *go* or a soft sound (/s/ and /j/), as in *center* and *geography*.

When *c* comes before *i* or *e*, it usually has a /s/ sound. When a *g* comes before *i* or *e*, it often has a /j/ sound.

SPELLING TIP

The soft *g* sound can also be spelled *dge* as in *edge*.

Read the words aloud. Then write the spelling words that contain the matching spelling pattern.

orange	circus	ounce	badge	scene
once	cement	glance	strange	arrange
wedge	bridge	germs	center	sponge
ginger	village	police	spice	certain

soft *c*

1. _____
2. _____
3. _____
4. _____
5. _____
6. _____
7. _____
8. _____
9. _____
10. _____

soft *g*

11. _____
12. _____
13. _____
14. _____
15. _____
16. _____
17. _____
18. _____
19. _____
20. _____

Use the spelling rules above to write a short story. Include four words from the spelling list. Check your work for errors.

Copyright © McGraw Hill. Permission is granted to reproduce for classroom use.

Name _____

The letters *c* and *g* can have a hard sound (/k/ and /g/), as in *car* and *go*. The letters *c* and *g* can also have a soft sound (/s/ and /j/), as in *center* and *geography*.

When *c* comes before *i* or *e*, it usually has a /s/ sound. When a *g* comes before *i* or *e*, it often has a /j/ sound.

SPELLING TIP

The soft *g* sound can also be spelled *dge* as in *edge*.

Read the words aloud. Then write the spelling words that contain the matching spelling pattern.

orange	chance	ounce	change	dance
once	cement	cage	strange	arrange
pages	bridge	germs	center	sponge
ginger	village	police	nice	urge

soft *c*

1. _____
2. _____
3. _____
4. _____
5. _____
6. _____
7. _____
8. _____

soft *g*

9. _____
10. _____
11. _____
12. _____
13. _____
14. _____
15. _____
16. _____
17. _____
18. _____
19. _____
20. _____

Use the spelling rules above to write a short story. Include four words from the spelling list. Check your work for errors.

Copyright © McGraw Hill. Permission is granted to reproduce for classroom use.

Name _____

A. Write the spelling words that contain the matching spelling pattern.

orange	circus	ounce	badge	scene
difference	cement	introduce	exchange	arranged
managers	general	passage	officers	languages
gingerly	villagers	audience	decision	certain

soft c

1. _____
2. _____
3. _____
4. _____
5. _____
6. _____
7. _____
8. _____
9. _____
10. _____

soft g

11. _____
12. _____
13. _____
14. _____
15. _____
16. _____
17. _____
18. _____
19. _____
20. _____

B. Compare the words *spice* and *police*. How are they alike? How are they different?

_____

_____

_____

_____

Use the spelling rules for soft *c* and soft *g* to write a short story. Include four words from the spelling list. Check your work for errors.

Copyright © McGraw Hill. Permission is granted to reproduce for classroom use.

Name _____

center	circus	ounce	badge	wedge
once	cement	glance	strange	arrange
scene	police	germs	orange	sponge
spice	certain	bridge	ginger	village

A. Write the spelling word that belongs with the other words in each group.

1. uniform, guard, _____

2. look, see, _____

3. carnival, fair, _____

4. cooking, flavoring, _____

5. play, act, _____

6. siren, crime, _____

7. virus, sickness, _____

8. odd, unusual, _____

B. Write the spelling word that best completes each sentence.

9. I need a damp _____ to clean the kitchen counter.

10. The workers poured _____ for the new sidewalk.

11. Do you want a banana or an _____ for your snack?

12. Just one _____ of mint flavoring goes a long way!

13. The spice _____ is good for an upset stomach.

14. Are you _____ that you do not need a hat today?

15. Help me _____ the chairs for the meeting tonight.

16. The _____ of a hurricane is calm and quiet.

17. Place the _____ under the dresser to make it level.

18. You will have to pay a toll to cross the _____.

19. There were many children in the _____ we visited.

20. Did you go to the market _____ or twice this week?

Copyright © McGraw Hill. Permission is granted to reproduce for classroom use.

Name _____

Underline the six misspelled words in the paragraphs below. Write the words correctly on the lines.

Is your family thinking of getting a dog? Before you arranje to buy one, be sure to visit an animal shelter. There are many dogs there for you to fall in love with! In fact, I'm sertain that it will take just one glanse to melt your heart.

Visiting a shelter might seem stranje at first. There may be a lot of dogs barking. This sene might even seem scary. But the dogs are just looking for a good home. So the next time you think about getting a dog, think about adopting. Your new friend is sure to become the senter of your life!

1. _____   4. _____

2. _____   5. _____

3. _____   6. _____

Writing Connection

Write about another way that people can help animals. Use at least four words from the spelling list. Remember to use the spelling rules you learned as you edit your work.

_____

_____

_____

_____

_____

_____

_____

_____

_____

Copyright © McGraw Hill. Permission is granted to reproduce for classroom use.

Name _____

Remember

The letters *c* and *g* can have a hard sound (/k/ and /g/), as in *car* and *go*. The letters *c* and *g* can also have a soft sound (/s/ and /j/), as in *center* and *geography*.

When *c* comes before *i* or *e*, it usually has a /s/ sound. When a *g* comes before *i* or *e*, it often has a /j/ sound.

A. Circle the spelling word in each row that rhymes with the word in bold type. Write the spelling word on the line and read the word aloud.

1. **ridge**	ride	bridge	brought	_____
2. **bean**	scene	bone	need	_____
3. **percent**	printed	correct	cement	_____
4. **pledge**	trudge	welt	wedge	_____
5. **renter**	rater	blender	center	_____
6. **curtain**	captain	certain	crept	_____
7. **twice**	spice	spruce	stick	_____
8. **bounce**	pound	inch	ounce	_____
9. **injure**	ginger	before	jailer	_____
10. **worms**	charms	forms	germs	_____
11. **plunge**	plum	sponge	surge	_____
12. **range**	rage	store	strange	_____
13. **chance**	glance	charge	gates	_____

B. Fill in the missing letter of each word to form a spelling word.

14. poli ____ e

15. arran ____ e

16. on ____ e

17. oran ____ e

18. ____ ircus

19. villa ____ e

20. bad ____ e

Copyright © McGraw Hill. Permission is granted to reproduce for classroom use.

Name _____

Remember that **related words** have the same base word. The word meaning changes slightly with the addition of prefixes, suffixes, and inflectional endings. Examine the following related words with the base word *qualify* and think about their meanings.

disqualify   qualified   qualifies   unqualified   qualifying   qualification

Add the prefixes and suffixes in the box to the base word below to create related words. You may add more than one affix to make one word. Read the words aloud, then check your words and pronunciation in a dictionary.

dis-	en-	-ly	-ous	-ness

Courage

Write a definition for two of the words you created above. Use a dictionary if you need to.

_____

_____

_____

Copyright © McGraw Hill. Permission is granted to reproduce for classroom use.

Name _____

A hurricane has just hit! Write the vocabulary words from the box next to their meanings in parentheses to complete the sign. Not all the words are used.

organizations	mature	assigned
generosity	extraordinary	residents

ATTENTION, CORAL HILLS _____
(people who live in a place)

As you return to your homes, you will see that this _____ **(very unusual)** storm has caused extensive damage. DO NOT PANIC. Several

relief _____ **(groups joined for a purpose)**, including

the Red Cross, have been _____ **(given a task)** to help

in this area. Keep an eye on the more _____ **(showing adult qualities)** members of our community—our seniors. Lend help whenever necessary.

If you have questions, call or text the Coral Hills Community Association hotline at 555-CHCA.

Now use the words in the box to write a sign that you might see at a zoo. Use a print or digital dictionary to determine the meaning and correct pronunciation of the words. Read your sign aloud when you are finished.

poisonous	advise	cautiously	commotion	severe	unpredictable

_____

_____

_____

Copyright © McGraw Hill. Permission is granted to reproduce for classroom use.

Name _____

> - A **linking verb** does not show action. It links, or connects, the subject to a noun or an adjective in the predicate. *My dog is smelly.*
> - Linking verbs are usually forms of *be (am, is, are, was,* and *were).* Other linking verbs include *look, seem, appear, become, feel, grow, smell,* and *taste.*

Read each sentence and underline the linking verb. Write it on the line provided.

1. The refrigerator was new. _____

2. The used car seems reliable. _____

3. I feel sick today for some reason. _____

4. They are my cousins from Atlanta. _____

5. You were my best friend in kindergarten. _____

6. She appears happy in her new home. _____

Pretend that you travel to a planet with an alien civilization. Write three sentences about what you see there. Use helping verbs from the list above for all three of your sentences. Then edit your work.

_____

_____

_____

_____

_____

Copyright © McGraw Hill. Permission is granted to reproduce for classroom use.

Name _____

- A **linking verb** connects the subject to a noun or an adjective in the predicate.
- Linking verbs are usually forms of *be*, but can be other verbs.
- A linking verb must **agree** in number with the subject of the sentence.

Circle the correct linking verb in parentheses to complete the sentence. Then rewrite the sentence on the line.

1. This meat (is / are) not good anymore.

   _____

2. Some of my toys (was / were) in the yard sale.

   _____

3. The bed (feels / smells) nice and soft.

   _____

4. Your backpack (are / seems) newer than mine

   _____

Read this paragraph from "Keeping Freedom in the Family." Circle the linking verb. Then write another sentence using the same verb.

As I held on to my father's hand, we joined the line of people chanting in front of Lawrence Hospital. The year was 1965, and the hospital workers needed more money and better working conditions.

_____

_____

Copyright © McGraw Hill. Permission is granted to reproduce for classroom use.

Name _____

> - The present-tense forms of *be* are *am, is,* and *are.* The past-tense forms of *be* are *was* and *were.* The future-tense form of *be* is *will be.*
> - Use *am, was,* or *will be* with *I.* Use *is, was,* or *will be* with all singular subjects. Use *are, were,* or *will be* with all plural subjects.

A. Write *am, is,* or *are* to complete each sentence.

1. I _____ late for the birthday party.

2. The cat and dog _____ good pals.

3. My lampshade _____ old and ripped.

4. The jewelry _____ very valuable.

5. Robbie and Katrina _____ class leaders.

B. Write *was, were,* or *will be* to complete each sentence.

6. She _____ tired soon.

7. They _____ braver yesterday.

8. I _____ angry at first about what she did.

9. David _____ here later tonight.

10. June and I _____ confused until you explained it.

In your writer's notebook, describe the traits that you like most about one of your friends or family members. Include at least two present-tense linking verbs and two future-tense verbs. Circle them and correct any spelling mistakes.

Copyright © McGraw Hill. Permission is granted to reproduce for classroom use.

Name _____

> • A **linking verb** connects the subject of a sentence to a noun or adjective in the predicate. Linking verbs are usually forms of *be,* but can be other verbs.
>
> • A linking verb must **agree** in number with the subject of the sentence.
>
> • The present-tense forms of *be* are *am, is,* and *are.* The past-tense forms of *be* are *was* and *were.* The future-tense form of *be* is *will be.*
>
> • Use *am, was,* or *will be* with *I.* Use *is, was,* or *will be* with all singular subjects. Use *are, were,* or *will be* with all plural subjects.

Rewrite the paragraphs below, correcting mistakes in linking verbs and subject-verb agreement.

1. Owning a pet was a big responsibility. A pet will be a friend that will love you. But pets were also a lot of work. Some pets seems easier to take care of than they really are. For example, a puppy may look cute and cuddly, but it requires a lot of time and energy to raise.

   _____

   _____

   _____

   _____

2. Have you ever said to yourself, "I is tired of junk food!"? Well, a healthy snack was easy to make. The best part is that it tastes great, too! Carrots and celery is great to munch on when you're hungry. And a veggie sandwich will be excellent for lunch. The choices for healthy snacks were endless!

   _____

   _____

   _____

   _____

Copyright © McGraw Hill. Permission is granted to reproduce for classroom use.

Name _____

A. Read the sentences. Then answer the questions.

(1) My slippers _____ inside the drawer. (2) My broken watch _____ sitting next to the slippers.

1. Which is the correct linking verb for sentence 1?
   A am
   B are
   C appear
   D is

2. Which is the correct linking verb for sentence 2?
   F smells
   G is
   H were
   J seems

B. Read the student draft and look for any corrections that need to be made. Then choose the best answer to each question.

(1) My father were good at many things. (2) He is the best gardener in the neighborhood. (3) His roses which won a prize smells the best! (4) Sometimes he are in the garden for hours at a time! (5) I am looking forward to spending time with him in the garden this weekend.

3. What is the correct way to write sentence 1?
   A My father become good at many things.
   B My father is good at many things.
   C My father grow good at many things.
   D The sentence is correct as written.

4. What is the correct way to write sentence 2?
   F He appears the best gardener in the neighborhood.
   G He seems the best gardener in the neighborhood.
   H He are the best gardener in the neighborhood.
   J The sentence is correct as written.

5. What is the correct way to write sentence 3?
   A His roses, which won a prize, smell the best!
   B His roses winned a prize and smelled the best!
   C His roses, which won a prize, is the best!
   D The sentence is correct as written.

6. What is the correct way to write sentence 4?
   F Sometimes he is in the garden for hours at a time!
   G Sometimes he were in the garden for hours at a time!
   H Sometimes he am in the garden for hours at a time!
   J The sentence is correct as written.

Copyright © McGraw Hill. Permission is granted to reproduce for classroom use.

Name _____

Fold back the paper along the dotted line. Use the blanks to write each word as it is read aloud. When you finish the test, unfold the paper. Use the list at the right to correct any spelling mistakes.

1. _____
2. _____
3. _____
4. _____
5. _____
6. _____
7. _____
8. _____
9. _____
10. _____
11. _____
12. _____
13. _____
14. _____
15. _____
16. _____
17. _____
18. _____
19. _____
20. _____

Review Words 21. _____
22. _____
23. _____

Challenge Words 24. _____
25. _____

1. clams
2. mints
3. props
4. arches
5. dresses
6. parents
7. caves
8. glasses
9. hobbies
10. engines
11. couches
12. arrows
13. enemies
14. babies
15. ranches
16. patches
17. mistakes
18. supplies
19. mosses
20. armies
21. circus
22. germs
23. spice
24. batteries
25. compasses

Copyright © McGraw Hill. Permission is granted to reproduce for classroom use.

Name _____

Plural nouns name more than one person, place, or thing. Most follow certain spelling rules and patterns. Add -s to most singular nouns to form a plural. Add -es to form the plural if the noun ends in -s as in *lens/lenses*, -ss as in *class/classes*, -sh as in *bush/bushes*, -ch as in *lunch/lunches*, or -x as in *box/boxes*.

When a word ends in a vowel and consonant, double the consonant before adding -es: *quiz/quizzes*.

DECODING WORDS

Note that adding -es to form a plural usually adds a syllable to a word. For example, the word *glass* is one syllable, but the plural form is two: *glass/es*.

Read aloud and write the spelling words with the matching spelling patterns.

arches	dresses	hobbies	enemies	mistakes
mints	armies	engines	props	supplies
babies	caves	couches	ranches	mosses
clams	glasses	arrows	patches	parents

-s

1. _____

2. _____

3. _____

4. _____

5. _____

6. _____

7. _____

8. _____

-ies

9. _____

10. _____

11. _____

12. _____

13. _____

-es

14. _____

15. _____

16. _____

17. _____

18. _____

19. _____

20. _____

Look through this week's selection for more words to sort. Create a word sort in your writer's notebook for a partner.

Copyright © McGraw Hill. Permission is granted to reproduce for classroom use.

Name _____

A plural noun names more than one person, place, or thing. Add -s to most singular nouns to make them plural. Add -es to singular nouns that end in

- -s, as in *lens* to *lenses*
- -ch, as in *lunch* to *lunches*
- -ss, as in *class* to *classes*
- -x, as in *ax* to *axes*
- -sh, as in *bush* to *bushes*

When a word ends with a vowel followed by a consonant, double the consonant before adding -es: *quiz/quizzes*.

SPELLING TIP

If a word ends in a vowel and *y*, add -s to make it plural. If a word ends in a consonant and *y*, change *y* to *i* and add -es to make it plural.

Read aloud and write the spelling words with the matching spelling patterns.

friends	dresses	hobbies	holidays	mistakes
mints	armies	tigers	props	berries
babies	caves	couches	ranches	mosses
clams	glasses	arrows	flowers	parents

-s

1. _____
2. _____
3. _____
4. _____
5. _____
6. _____
7. _____

8. _____
9. _____
10. _____
11. _____

-es

12. _____
13. _____
14. _____

15. _____
16. _____

-ies

17. _____
18. _____
19. _____
20. _____

Look through this week's selection for more words to sort. Create a word sort in your writer's notebook for a partner.

Copyright © McGraw Hill. Permission is granted to reproduce for classroom use.

Name _____

Read aloud and write the spelling words with the matching spelling patterns.

arches	dresses	hobbies	enemies	mistakes
mints	armies	engines	belongings	supplies
babies	batteries	couches	ranches	mosses
potatoes	trophies	arrows	patches	parents

-s

1. _____
2. _____
3. _____
4. _____
5. _____
6. _____

-es

7. _____
8. _____
9. _____
10. _____
11. _____
12. _____
13. _____

-ies

14. _____
15. _____
16. _____
17. _____
18. _____
19. _____
20. _____

 **Look through this week's selection for more words to sort. Create a word sort in your writer's notebook for a partner.**

Copyright © McGraw Hill. Permission is granted to reproduce for classroom use.

Name _____

clams	dresses	hobbies	enemies	mistakes
mints	parents	engines	babies	supplies
props	caves	couches	ranches	mosses
arches	glasses	arrows	patches	armies

A. An analogy is a statement that compares sets of words. Write the spelling word that best completes each analogy below.

1. *Sons* are to *children* as *dads* are to _____.

2. *Lions* are to *tigers* as *oysters* are to _____.

3. *Chairs* are to *seats* as *sofas* are to _____.

4. *Birds* are to *nests* as *bats* are to _____.

5. *Shrubs* are to *bushes* as *farms* are to _____.

6. *Workers* are to *businesses* as *soldiers* are to _____.

7. *Men* are to *suits* as *women* are to _____.

8. *Work* is to *play* as *jobs* are to _____.

B. Write the spelling word that matches each definition below.

9. they help you see _____   15. candies _____

10. curved structures _____   16. newborns _____

11. they point the way _____   17. they make cars run _____

12. tiny plants _____   18. those against you _____

13. objects used in plays _____   19. necessary things _____

14. small pieces of fabric _____   20. errors _____

Copyright © McGraw Hill. Permission is granted to reproduce for classroom use.

Name _____

Underline the six misspelled words in the paragraphs below. Write the words correctly on the lines.

Some kids like to lie around on their couchs and watch television after school. Other kids have hobbys that they like to do. They enjoy collecting stamps or building models with real engins.

Some activities, such as cooking, may require help from parentes. But kids can do many other things by themselves. With some art supples from a craft store, countless projects are possible. And there are no such things as mistakees! Think of a mistake as creative inspiration. Take those ideas and run!

1. _____   4. _____

2. _____   5. _____

3. _____   6. _____

Write about something that you like to do after school. Use at least four words from the spelling list. Check your work to make sure you have spelled the plurals correctly.

_____

_____

_____

_____

_____

_____

_____

_____

_____

_____

Copyright © McGraw Hill. Permission is granted to reproduce for classroom use.

Name _____

Copyright © McGraw Hill. Permission is granted to reproduce for classroom use.

Remember

Plural nouns name more than one person, place, or thing. There are spelling rules and patterns to help you form plural words. Add *-s* to form most plural nouns. Add *-es* to create plural forms of nouns that end in *-s, -ss, -sh, -ch, -x,* and *-z.* If a singular noun ends in a consonant and *y,* change the *y* to an *i* and add *-es* to form the plural.

Sound out plural nouns just as you would any other word. Remember that adding *-es* usually adds a syllable. The word *watch* has one syllable, while *watches* has two syllables.

Write the missing letter or letters. Then write the word and read it aloud.

1. ranch ____ ____ _____
2. cave ____ _____
3. mistake ____ _____
4. couch ____ ____ _____
5. prop ____ _____
6. arrow ____ _____
7. arm ____ ____ ____ _____
8. engine ____ _____
9. clam ____ _____
10. dress ____ ____ _____
11. bab ____ ____ ____ _____
12. hobb ____ ____ ____ _____
13. glass ____ ____ _____
14. arch ____ ____ _____
15. suppl ____ ____ ____ _____
16. parent ____ _____
17. patch ____ ____ _____
18. mint ____ _____
19. moss ____ ____ _____
20. enem ____ ____ ____ _____

Name _____

Read the sentences below. Underline the word in the second sentence that is a synonym or an antonym of the word in bold. Then write the best definition of the word you underlined on the line.

1. Barbara Jordan's parents **encouraged** her to do well in school. She felt motivated by their support.

   _____

2. Jordan worked to improve **urban** areas. Many other state senators only focused on rural parts of the state.

   _____

3. As a congresswoman, Jordan worked to **improve** the lives of poor people. She wanted to help people better their wages and living situations.

   _____

4. Barbara Jordan gave a speech that was widely **praised**. Many people complimented her on it.

   _____

5. Several years later, Barbara Jordan retired from **public** life. She returned to private life and wrote an autobiography.

   _____

Copyright © McGraw Hill. Permission is granted to reproduce for classroom use.

Name _____

A **dictionary** lists words in alphabetical order. You use a dictionary to look up the meaning of an unfamiliar word. A **glossary** lists words and definitions related to a specific text or subject. You can find glossaries in the back of textbooks or other nonfiction books, or online.

- The **guide words** show the first and last words on the page. Words on the page appear alphabetically between guide words.

- The **entry words** show the spelling and syllables.

- The **pronunciation** of each word is shown in parentheses. **Syllabication** separates syllables by bullets and shows how many syllables a word has.

- The word's **origin**, such as the language it comes from, is often shown.

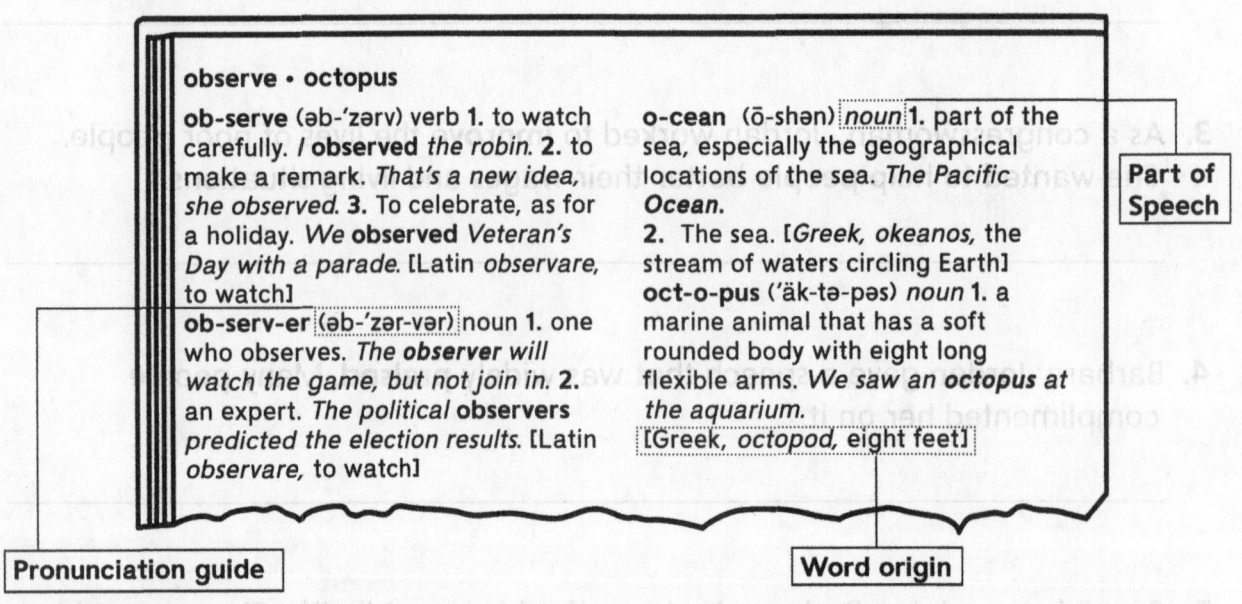

observe • octopus

ob-serve (əb-ʹzərv) verb 1. to watch carefully. *I observed the robin.* 2. to make a remark. *That's a new idea, she observed.* 3. To celebrate, as for a holiday. *We observed Veteran's Day with a parade.* [Latin *observare,* to watch]

ob-serv-er (əb-ʹzər-vər) noun 1. one who observes. *The observer will watch the game, but not join in.* 2. an expert. *The political observers predicted the election results.* [Latin *observare,* to watch]

o-cean (ō-shən) *noun* 1. part of the sea, especially the geographical locations of the sea. *The Pacific Ocean.*
2. The sea. [*Greek, okeanos,* the stream of waters circling Earth]
oct-o-pus (ʹäk-tə-pəs) noun 1. a marine animal that has a soft rounded body with eight long flexible arms. *We saw an octopus at the aquarium.*
[*Greek, octopod, eight feet*]

Part of Speech

Pronunciation guide

Word origin

Use the dictionary entry and context clues to figure out the meaning of each word in bold. Write the meaning, part of speech, and word origin on the lines.

1. I **observed** the flower's growth for a month to write my report.

_____

2. The students were eager **observers** of the scientific presentation.

_____

Read each dictionary entry aloud with a partner. Sound out each word carefully. How many syllables are in each word? How do you know?

Copyright © McGraw Hill. Permission is granted to reproduce for classroom use.

Name _____

> • Regular past-tense verbs end with -ed: *walk/walked*.
> • **Irregular past-tense verbs** do not end with -ed: *run/ran*.
> • The verbs *be* and *have* also have irregular spellings for the present and past tenses.
>
> | | **Be** | **Have** |
> |---|---|---|
> | I | was | had |
> | **You/We/They** | were | had |
> | **He/She/It** | was | had |

Read each sentence and underline the verb. On the line, write the correct past-tense form of the verb.

1. We drive all night to my cousin's house. _____

2. The child break the glass vase. _____

3. The bumblebee is on the flower. _____

4. Carlos go to school late today. _____

5. He has a book about sharks in the ocean. _____

6. The rain begin to fall outside. _____

Writing Connection Write four sentences about getting ready for school. Each sentence should include an irregular verb. After you finish check that you have used the past tense of the irregular verbs correctly.

_____

_____

_____

_____

Copyright © McGraw Hill. Permission is granted to reproduce for classroom use.

Name _____

> • Regular past-tense verbs end with -ed. **Irregular past-tense verbs**
>   **do not end with -ed.**
> • The past tense of some irregular verbs is formed with an internal
>   spelling change, such as *run* and *ran*.
> • The past tense of some irregular verbs is spelled the same as the
>   present tense, such as *read* and *read*.
> • The past form of an irregular verb that often ends with -*n* or -*en*, such
>   as *known* or *eaten*, can be used with a helping verb to tell about the
>   past (*have known, have eaten*).

**Read each sentence. Circle the verb choice
in parentheses that correctly completes the
sentence. Then write *R* on the line if it is a regular
verb. Write *I* if it is an irregular verb.**

1. The workers slowly (built / builded) the house. _____

2. She (fold / folded) the laundry before putting it away. _____

3. I (smelt / smelled) the pie baking from down the street. _____

4. My mother (set / setted) the table earlier. _____

5. Together we (drew / drawed) a picture of our family. _____

6. They had (knew / known) that this would happen. _____

 **Read this paragraph from "A New Kind of Corn." Underline all the
verbs. Then write the past-tense form of each verb below.**

> Over time, pests can build a resistance to any pesticide. A 2011 study
> shows that rootworm beetles are already developing a resistance to Bt
> corn. If these rootworms can eat Bt corn and survive, why grow it?

_____

_____

Copyright © McGraw Hill. Permission is granted to reproduce for classroom use.

Name _____

- Many irregular verbs have the same form when they are used alone or with a helping verb to tell about the past, such as *kept, was kept,* and *have kept.*
- Some irregular verbs have a different form when they are used alone than when they are used with a helping verb to tell about the past, such as *did* and *had done.*
- A **gerund** is a verbal. It is a verb ending in *-ing* that acts as a noun in a sentence. *The singing started. I like swimming.*

Rewrite each sentence with the correct past-tense form of the underlined helping verb and main verb.

1. We <u>have spended</u> too much time here already.

   _____

2. The people <u>were took</u> to their seats.

   _____

3. I <u>had forgot</u> how to braid my hair correctly.

   _____

4. My baby sister <u>has grew</u> so much!

   _____

5. The leaves <u>were shook</u> from the branches.

   _____

 **In your writer's notebook, write about the milestones in your life that you are most proud of. Make sure that each of your sentences has a helping verb and is in the past tense. Include a sentence with a gerund. Then edit your work.**

Copyright © McGraw Hill. Permission is granted to reproduce for classroom use.

Name _____

> - The past tense of irregular verbs may be formed with a spelling change or without a spelling change.
> - Many irregular verbs have the same form when they are used alone or with a helping verb to tell about the past.
> - Some irregular verbs have a different form when they are used alone than when they are used with a helping verb to tell about the past. Often, the verb will end with -*n* or -*en*, such as *shake* and *have shaken*.

Rewrite the sentences below, correcting mistakes in irregular verbs.

1. The reporter bringed his pad and taked notes while the mayor speaked.

_____

2. I cutted the paper and folded it in the shape of an animal.

_____

3. You have fell down twice while skiing this morning.

_____

4. The shirt was teared in the washing machine and ruined.

_____

5. My mother letted me play outside while she maked dinner.

_____

Copyright © McGraw Hill. Permission is granted to reproduce for classroom use.

Name _____

A. Read the paragraph. Then answer the questions.

(1) Today was a bad day. (2) Even though it was Saturday, I had to do a bunch of chores. (3) First, I _____ my room. (4) Then I _____ the grass. (5) I accidentally _____ the hose out in the yard. (6) Finally, I _____ the trash out.

1. Which past-tense verb goes in the blank in sentence 3?
   A cleaned
   B clean
   C cleanen
   D cleaning

2. Which past-tense verb goes in the blank in sentence 4?
   F cut
   G cutted
   H cutten
   J cuttened

3. Which past-tense verb goes in the blank in sentence 5?
   A leave
   B leaved
   C leaven
   D left

4. Which past-tense verb goes in the blank in sentence 6?
   F taken
   G took
   H taked
   J take

B. Read the student draft and look for any corrections that need to be made. Then choose the best answer to each question.

(1) Jared and I <u>was froze</u> after playing outside in the snow! (2) We <u>have heard</u> the school bell, so we ran inside. (3) I <u>had tried</u> so hard to warm up by rubbing my face. (4) I had to sit down and pay attention though, because the lesson <u>have started</u>.

5. Which is the correct helping verb and past-tense verb for sentence 1?
   A was frozen
   B were frozen
   C was freezed
   D Make no change.

6. Which is the correct helping verb and past-tense verb for sentence 2?
   F had heared
   G has heared
   H had heard
   J Make no change.

7. Which is the correct helping verb and past-tense verb for sentence 3?
   A were tried
   B had tryed
   C have tryed
   D Make no change.

8. Which is the correct helping verb and past-tense verb for sentence 4?
   F had start
   G had started
   H have starten
   J Make no change.

Copyright © McGraw Hill. Permission is granted to reproduce for classroom use.

Name _____

Fold back the
paper along the
dotted line. Use
the blanks to
write each word
as it is read aloud.
When you finish
the test, unfold
the paper. Use the
list at the right
to correct any
spelling mistakes.

1. _____
2. _____
3. _____
4. _____
5. _____
6. _____
7. _____
8. _____
9. _____
10. _____
11. _____
12. _____
13. _____
14. _____
15. _____
16. _____
17. _____
18. _____
19. _____
20. _____

Review Words 21. _____
22. _____
23. _____

Challenge Words 24. _____
25. _____

1. fishbowl
2. lookout
3. yardstick
4. desktop
5. campfire
6. overhead
7. waterproof
8. grandparent
9. railroad
10. snowstorm
11. loudspeaker
12. bookcase
13. bedroom
14. blindfold
15. newborn
16. bedspread
17. yourself
18. overdo
19. clothesline
20. undertake
21. dresses
22. arrows
23. babies
24. eyesight
25. paperweight

Copyright © McGraw Hill. Permission is granted to reproduce for classroom use.

Name _____

Compound words are made up of smaller words.
There are three types of compound words:

- Words with two or more words joined together,
  as in *evergreen*
- Words that are written with one or more hyphens,
  as in *left-handed*
- Words that are written as separate words, such
  as *school day*

Decoding Words

When a word
ends in a silent
e, as in *case,* the
vowel before the
consonant has a
long sound. This
is called a **vowel,
consonant,** *e*
(VCe) pattern.

**Write the compound spelling words that contain the correct number
of syllables. Then read the words aloud.**

fishbowl	campfire	railroad	bedroom	yourself
lookout	overhead	snowstorm	blindfold	overdo
yardstick	waterproof	loudspeaker	newborn	clothesline
desktop	grandparent	bookcase	bedspread	undertake

two syllables

1. _____ 8. _____
2. _____ 9. _____
3. _____ 10. _____
4. _____ 11. _____
5. _____ 12. _____
6. _____ 13. _____
7. _____ 14. _____

three syllables

15. _____
16. _____
17. _____
18. _____
19. _____
20. _____

**Look through this week's selection for more words to sort. Read the
words aloud and create a word sort in your writer's notebook for a
partner. Include words with the VCe pattern.**

Copyright © McGraw Hill. Permission is granted to reproduce for classroom use.

Name _____

Compound words are made up of smaller words. There are three types of compound words:

- Words with two or more words joined together, as in *evergreen*

- Words that are written with one or more hyphens, as in *left-handed*

- Words that are written as separate words, such as *school day*

When a word ends in a silent *e*, as in *case,* the vowel before the consonant has a long sound. This is called a **vowel, consonant,** *e* **(VCe) pattern.**

Write the compound spelling words that contain the correct number of syllables. Then read the words aloud.

fishbowl	campfire	railroad	bedroom	yourself
lookout	overhead	snowstorm	anyway	overdo
yardstick	waterproof	classroom	newborn	driveway
desktop	grandparent	airport	footstep	undertake

two syllables

1. _____
2. _____
3. _____
4. _____
5. _____
6. _____
7. _____

8. _____
9. _____
10. _____
11. _____
12. _____
13. _____
14. _____

three syllables

15. _____
16. _____
17. _____
18. _____
19. _____
20. _____

Look through this week's selection for more words to sort. Read the words aloud and create a word sort in your writer's notebook for a partner. Include words with the VCe pattern.

Copyright © McGraw Hill. Permission is granted to reproduce for classroom use.

Name _____

Write the compound spelling words that contain the correct number of syllables. Then read the words aloud.

fishbowl	campfire	teammate	skateboard	undergrowth
courtroom	overhead	snowstorm	blindfold	gentleman
yardstick	waterproof	loudspeaker	eyesight	clothesline
heartbroken	grandparent	bookcase	bedspread	undertake

two syllables   **three syllables**

1. _____   13. _____

2. _____   14. _____

3. _____   15. _____

4. _____   16. _____

5. _____   17. _____

6. _____   18. _____

7. _____   19. _____

8. _____   20. _____

9. _____

10. _____

11. _____

12. _____

 **Look through this week's selection for more words to sort. Make a word sort in your writer's notebook for a partner.**

Copyright © McGraw Hill. Permission is granted to reproduce for classroom use.

Name _____

fishbowl	campfire	railroad	bedroom	yourself
lookout	overhead	snowstorm	blindfold	overdo
yardstick	waterproof	loudspeaker	newborn	clothesline
desktop	grandparent	bookcase	bedspread	undertake

A. Write the spelling word that best completes each sentence.

1. I pulled down the _____ before getting into bed.

2. Please get a novel from the _____ for me.

3. Her _____ was piled high with papers and books.

4. Put on this _____ and spin around three times.

5. It is fun to ride trains on the _____.

6. I heard my name announced on the _____.

7. I bought a large _____ for my pet to swim in.

8. We took the dry sheets down from the _____.

9. The _____ tower is my favorite part of the clubhouse.

10. Even though it rained, I stayed dry in my _____ jacket.

B. Write the spelling word that matches each definition below.

11. to go beyond a limit _____

12. an outdoor flame _____

13. a ruler for measuring _____

14. a baby just born _____

15. hanging above _____

16. you _____

17. a place to sleep _____

18. your mother's parent _____

19. blizzard _____

20. to attempt _____

Name _____

Underline the three misspelled words in each paragraph below. Write the words correctly on the lines.

   Camping may seem like a good idea, but do your self a favor and try it at home first! Camping under the stars is a brave thing to under take. Use your backyard as a test to see if you like it. You may not be able to build a camp fire, but at least you'll see what it is like to rough it outdoors.

   To sleep outside, you'll need a water proof tent and a sleeping bag. You might also want to grab a pillow from your bed room. It is best to try it in the summer (and not in a snow storm in the middle of the winter!). Before you march outside with your flashlight, be sure to ask your parents' permission. If you're lucky, they might even join you!

1. _____   4. _____

2. _____   5. _____

3. _____   6. _____

Writing Connection | **Write about whether you would like to go camping under the stars. Use at least four words from the spelling list.**

_____

_____

_____

_____

_____

_____

_____

_____

Copyright © McGraw Hill. Permission is granted to reproduce for classroom use.

Name _____

Compound words are made up of smaller words. There are three types of compound words:
- Words with two or more words joined together, as in *evergreen*
- Words that are written with one or more hyphens, as in *left-handed*
- Words that are written as separate words, such as *school day*

fishbowl	campfire	railroad	bedroom	yourself
lookout	overhead	snowstorm	blindfold	overdo
yardstick	waterproof	loudspeaker	newborn	clothesline
desktop	grandparent	bookcase	bedspread	undertake

Fill in the missing letters to form a compound spelling word. Read the spelling word aloud, then write it on the line. Not all words will be used.

1. over _____ _____   _____
2. look _____ _____ _____   _____
3. book _____ _____ _____ _____   _____
4. _____ _____ _____ born   _____
5. _____ _____ _____ _____ fire   _____
6. rail _____ _____ _____ _____   _____
7. _____ _____ _____ _____ _____ parent   _____
8. water _____ _____ _____ _____   _____
9. _____ _____ _____ _____ head   _____
10. under _____ _____ _____   _____
11. blind _____ _____ _____   _____
12. desk _____ _____ _____   _____
13. _____ _____ _____ _____ speaker   _____
14. your _____ _____ _____ _____   _____
15. _____ _____ _____ _____ bowl   _____
16. _____ _____ _____ spread   _____
17. clothes _____ _____ _____ _____   _____

Copyright © McGraw Hill. Permission is granted to reproduce for classroom use.

Name _____

Remember that **content words** are words related to a particular field of study. For example, *pollen, crossbreeding,* and *genetically modified* are words used to describe the reproduction and growth of plants and animals. They are content words in the fields of biology, botany, food science, agriculture, and genetics.

Sometimes you can figure out what a content word means by using context clues. You can also use a dictionary to help you.

 **With a partner, look in science texts for content words related to biology, food science, and agriculture. Write the words below.**

Biology, Food Science, and Agriculture Words

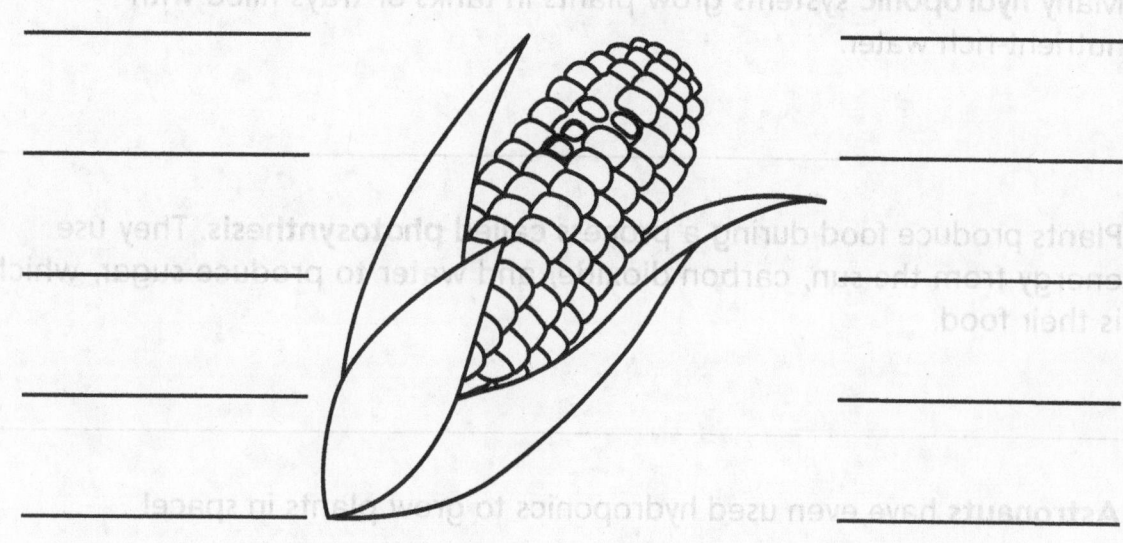

_____   _____

_____   _____

_____   _____

_____   _____

Circle two words that you were able to define by using context clues. Write the words and their meanings on the lines.

_____

_____

_____

Copyright © McGraw Hill. Permission is granted to reproduce for classroom use.

Name _____

```
┌─────────────────────────────────────────────┐
│           Greek Root Meanings                 │
│  phys – nature or body      photo - light     │
│  hydro - water              astro - stars     │
└─────────────────────────────────────────────┘
```

Read each passage below. Use the Greek roots from the box above along with context clues to find the meaning of each word in bold. Write the meaning on the line.

1. For many years, **physicists**, biologists, botanists, and other scientists have studied how we can use the awesome power of water to help humanity.

   _____

2. Many **hydroponic** systems grow plants in tanks or trays filled with nutrient-rich water.

   _____

3. Plants produce food during a process called **photosynthesis**. They use energy from the sun, carbon dioxide, and water to produce sugar, which is their food.

   _____

4. **Astronauts** have even used hydroponics to grow plants in space!

   _____

Copyright © McGraw Hill. Permission is granted to reproduce for classroom use.

Name _____

> • A **pronoun** is a word that takes the place of one or more nouns.
>
> • A **personal pronoun** refers to a person or thing, such as *I, he, she, it,* or *you.*
>
> • An **indefinite pronoun** does not name a specific person or thing, such as *anyone, everything,* or *someone.*
>
> • A **relative pronoun** is used at the beginning of a clause, such as *that, which, who, whom,* or *whose.*

Read each sentence and underline the pronoun. Write the pronoun on the line provided.

1. José was busy and could not get it for me. _____

2. My mom, who is a nurse, works long hours. _____

3. Did you see her climb the tree? _____

4. Has anyone seen a pink baseball cap? _____

5. The student in the red shirt is slightly taller than you. _____

Read this excerpt from "A World Without Rules." Circle six pronouns. Then write two sentences about an unusual experience you've had. Include at least two pronouns.

> You may sometimes wonder if rules were made to keep you from having fun and to tell you what to do. But what if we had no rules at all? Nobody would tell you what to do ever again!

_____

_____

_____

Copyright © McGraw Hill. Permission is granted to reproduce for classroom use.

Name _____

> - A **pronoun** is a word that takes the place of one or more nouns.
> - A pronoun must match its **antecedent**, or the noun it refers to, in number, gender, and case. Case refers to the form a pronoun takes depending on whether it is a subject or object in a sentence, or is showing possession. *The girl looked both ways before she crossed the road. Jobim knows we like him.*
> - Antecedents usually appear in the same sentence as their pronouns, but not always. *Stephen loves all kinds of music. He listens to it every day.*

Circle the pronoun in parentheses that agrees with the antecedent and correctly completes each sentence. Write the antecedent on the line.

1. If the people go outside, (he, they) will be very cold. _____

2. The dog wagged (its, their) tail playfully. _____

3. The mayor did (their, his) best to solve the traffic problem.

   _____

4. Both students did a great job. (Her, Their) teacher was very proud of (they, them). _____

5. When the tired woman went to bed, (he, she) fell asleep immediately.

   _____

6. Each of the airplanes had begun (its, their) descent from the sky.

   _____

 **Look back through your writer's notebook for a paragraph you wrote. Edit the paragraph for pronoun-antecedent agreement. Then check for any spelling mistakes.**

Copyright © McGraw Hill. Permission is granted to reproduce for classroom use.

Name _____

> - The pronoun *I* is always capitalized.
> - If it is not clear which noun a pronoun refers to, repeat the noun or rewrite the sentence. *The carrots and the cabbages were in the bag together. The cabbages went bad.*

Write each sentence correctly so that it is clear and uses correct capitalization.

1. Even though Hector and Henry play baseball, he is not as good at it.

   _____

2. My sister and i are both in the same elementary school.

   _____

3. Be careful with it when you put this dish in the glass case.

   _____

4. Spring has pretty flowers and green grass, which is nice.

   _____

   _____

5. When i go to self-defense class, i feel strong.

   _____

Connect to Community
Talk to a parent or trusted adult about the differences between geographical regions of the United States. Then write a paragraph about what you learned. Edit your paragraph to make sure all pronouns and antecedents agree.

Copyright © McGraw Hill. Permission is granted to reproduce for classroom use.

Name _____

- A **pronoun** is a word that takes the place of one or more nouns. There are **personal, indefinite,** and **relative** pronouns.
- An **antecedent** is the word that the pronoun refers to. A pronoun and its antecedent must match in gender and in number.
- The pronoun *I* is always capitalized.
- When a pronoun reference is unclear, repeat the noun instead or rewrite the sentence.

COMMON ERRORS

In formal writing, when a gender is unclear for a singular noun, use *his or her* so that the pronoun and antecedent still agree in number. A *citizen should always do **his or her** duty.*

Rewrite the paragraphs below, correcting mistakes in pronouns and antecedents.

1. My older sister Amy and i like to play word games. They have a lot of fun with them. Sometimes the game is too hard, so i do not like to play it. She always wins. Still, I have a lot of fun playing any game with my sister.

   _____

   _____

   _____

2. My family and i went to visit the local nature center today. There were two guides, and she showed us around the center. I saw an owl with a broken wing. Sam, my little brother, said that he had never seen it before.

   _____

   _____

   _____

Copyright © McGraw Hill. Permission is granted to reproduce for classroom use.

Name _____

Read the student draft and look for any corrections that need to be made. Then choose the best answer to each question.

(1) As she stepped out the door, Kyle wasn't surprised at the truck waiting at the curb. (2) It had been a long morning already, and Kyle was tired. (3) The truck driver got out and approached someone.

(4) "Do you need me to carry the box for you?" he asked, pointing at Kyle's box. (5) "If not, I can get the rest of the boxes." (6) Moving day was always hard on Kyle, his box packers, and the truck driver.

1. What change needs to be made in sentence 1?

   A Change *door* to **it**

   B Change *she* to **he**

   C Change *truck* to **it**

   D Change *Kyle* to **him**

2. What pronoun could best replace *Kyle* in sentence 2?

   F we

   G everyone

   H it

   J he

3. What change needs to be made in sentence 3?

   A Change *someone* to **she**

   B Change *someone* to **them**

   C Change *someone* to **him**

   D Change *someone* to **he**

4. What pronoun could replace *Kyle's box* in sentence 4?

   F they

   G them

   H it

   J everything

5. What pronoun could best replace *the boxes* in sentence 5?

   A they

   B them

   C it

   D everyone

6. What pronoun could best replace *Kyle, his box packers, and the truck driver* in sentence 6?

   F they

   G it

   H everything

   J everyone

Copyright © McGraw Hill. Permission is granted to reproduce for classroom use.

Name _____

Fold back the paper along the dotted line. Use the blanks to write each word as it is read aloud. When you finish the test, unfold the paper. Use the list at the right to correct any spelling mistakes.

1. _____
2. _____
3. _____
4. _____
5. _____
6. _____
7. _____
8. _____
9. _____
10. _____
11. _____
12. _____
13. _____
14. _____
15. _____
16. _____
17. _____
18. _____
19. _____
20. _____

Review Words 21. _____
22. _____
23. _____

Challenge Words 24. _____
25. _____

1. tasted
2. ripping
3. forced
4. flipping
5. tapped
6. flipped
7. scared
8. flagged
9. ripped
10. skipped
11. tapping
12. saved
13. skipping
14. scaring
15. flagging
16. discussed
17. saving
18. tasting
19. forcing
20. discussing
21. bedspread
22. desktop
23. snowstorm
24. outwitted
25. underscoring

Copyright © McGraw Hill. Permission is granted to reproduce for classroom use.

Name _____

> Inflectional endings *-ed* and *-ing* are added to verbs to create new verbs and tenses. The spelling for many base words does not change when adding *-ed* or *-ing*, such as when *laugh* becomes *laughed* or *laughing*.
>
> For base words ending with a consonant and *e*, drop the *e* before adding *-ed* or *-ing*. For example, *save* changes to *saved* or *saving*.

SPELLING TIP

For base words that end with a single vowel and a consonant, double the final consonant before adding *-ed* or *-ing*. *Drop* changes to *dropped* or *dropping*.

Write the spelling words that contain the matching spelling patterns. Read the words aloud.

tasted	scaring	forcing	skipping	scared
ripping	flipped	skipped	tapped	tasting
forced	saving	tapping	flagging	ripped
flipping	flagged	saved	discussed	discussing

Double consonant + -ed words

1. _____
2. _____
3. _____
4. _____
5. _____

Add -ed words

6. _____

Add -ing words

7. _____

Drop the e and add -ed words

8. _____
9. _____
10. _____
11. _____

Double consonant + -ing words

12. _____
13. _____
14. _____
15. _____
16. _____

Drop the e and add -ing words

17. _____
18. _____
19. _____
20. _____

Look through this week's selection for more words to sort. Read the words aloud and create a word sort for a partner in your writer's notebook.

Copyright © McGraw Hill. Permission is granted to reproduce for classroom use.

Name _____

> Inflectional endings *-ed* and *-ing* are added to verbs to create new verbs and tenses. The spelling for many base words does not change when adding *-ed* or *-ing*, such as when *laugh* becomes *laughed* or *laughing*.
>
> For base words ending with a consonant and *e*, drop the *e* before adding *-ed* or *-ing*. For example, *save* changes to *saved* or *saving*.

SPELLING TIP

For base words that end with a single vowel and a consonant, double the final consonant before adding *-ed* or *-ing*. Drop changes to *dropped* or *dropping*.

Write the spelling words that contain the matching spelling patterns. Read the words aloud.

tasted	caring	liking	skipping	cared
ripping	flipped	skipped	tapped	tasting
liked	saving	tapping	hopping	ripped
flipping	hopped	saved	trimmed	trimming

Double consonant + *-ed* words

1. _____
2. _____
3. _____
4. _____
5. _____
6. _____

Double consonant + *-ing* words

7. _____
8. _____
9. _____
10. _____
11. _____
12. _____

Drop the *e* and add *-ed* words

13. _____
14. _____
15. _____
16. _____

Drop the *e* and add *-ing* words

17. _____
18. _____
19. _____
20. _____

 **Look through this week's selection for more words to sort. Read the words aloud and create a word sort for a partner in your writer's notebook.**

Copyright © McGraw Hill. Permission is granted to reproduce for classroom use.

Name _____

endured	appreciating	forcing	skipping	outwitted
strumming	flipped	realized	admitted	demonstrating
exploded	demonstrated	exploding	flagging	strummed
flipping	flagged	admitting	discussed	discussing

Write the spelling words that contain the matching spelling patterns. Read the words aloud.

Double consonant + -ed words

1. _____

2. _____

3. _____

4. _____

5. _____

Drop the e and add -ed words

6. _____

7. _____

8. _____

9. _____

Add -ed words

10. _____

Double consonant + -ing words

11. _____

12. _____

13. _____

14. _____

15. _____

Drop the e and add -ing words

16. _____

17. _____

18. _____

19. _____

Add -ing words

20. _____

Look through this week's selection for more words to sort. Read the words aloud and create a word sort for a partner in your writer's notebook.

Copyright © McGraw Hill. Permission is granted to reproduce for classroom use.

Name _____

tasted	tapped	ripped	skipping	saving
ripping	flipped	skipped	scaring	tasting
forced	scared	tapping	flagging	forcing
flipping	flagged	saved	discussed	discussing

A. Write the spelling word that best completes each sentence.

1. Firefighters are good at _____ people in danger.

2. After _____ my shirt, I had to change clothes.

3. My parents _____ the idea of a vacation.

4. We were _____ down the police car to help us on the road.

5. The excited puppy's tail _____ the ground.

6. I thought the meat loaf _____ good.

7. Is the spooky show _____ you?

8. My sister _____ all the way to school.

9. The clown _____ onto his back when the pie hit him.

10. The rude man was _____ his way to the front of the line.

B. Write the spelling word that matches each definition below.

11. running and jumping _____

12. collected money _____

13. tumbling _____

14. got attention _____

15. tore _____

16. talking about _____

17. hitting lightly _____

18. frightened _____

19. using the tongue _____

20. made to do something _____

Copyright © McGraw Hill. Permission is granted to reproduce for classroom use.

Name _____

Underline the six misspelled words in the paragraphs below. Write the words correctly on the lines.

Do you hate tasteing new types of foods? Do you have to be forcd to have a dinner that does not include chicken nuggets? If so, you can stop now! There is nothing to be scareed of when trying new foods.

The world has a lot of wonderful foods to offer. If you discussd these foods with your parents, you could get an idea of what you might like. So instead of skiping that egg roll or rice ball, why not give it a whirl? You might find that you'll be flippin for it!

1. _____   4. _____

2. _____   5. _____

3. _____   6. _____

Writing Connection

Write about a food that was better than you thought it would be. Use at least four words from the spelling list. Then edit your work.

_____

_____

_____

_____

_____

_____

_____

_____

_____

Copyright © McGraw Hill. Permission is granted to reproduce for classroom use.

Name _____

Remember

Inflectional endings -*ed* and -*ing* are added to verbs to create new verb forms and tenses. The spelling for many base words does not change when adding -*ed* or -*ing*, such as when *laugh* becomes *laughed* or *laughing*.

For base words ending with a consonant and *e*, drop the final *e* before adding -*ed* or -*ing*. For example, *save* changes to *saved* or *saving*.

A. Fill in the missing letters of each word to form a spelling word. Then read the word aloud.

1. flagg ___ ___ ___
2. forc ___ ___
3. sav ___ ___ ___
4. tapp ___ ___
5. tast ___ ___
6. ripp ___ ___ ___
7. sav ___ ___
8. discuss ___ ___ ___
9. skipp ___ ___
10. flipp ___ ___ ___

11. skipp ___ ___ ___
12. flagg ___ ___
13. tapp ___ ___ ___
14. discuss ___ ___
15. flipp ___ ___
16. scar ___ ___ ___
17. ripp ___ ___
18. tast ___ ___ ___
19. forc ___ ___ ___
20. scar ___ ___

B. Write these spelling words in alphabetical order. Alphabetize them to the third letter: *tapping, skipping, tasted, scared, saved.*

21. _____
22. _____
23. _____

24. _____
25. _____

Copyright © McGraw Hill. Permission is granted to reproduce for classroom use.

Name _____

People use **content words** to speak or write about certain topics or fields of study. In this unit, you will encounter content words related to government, such as *laws, agencies, legislation,* and *democracy.* Use context clues, dictionaries, or electronic resources to help you understand the meanings and pronunciations of these words.

With a partner, search social studies texts for content words related to the history, people, and functions of the U.S. government. Write the words below.

CONNECT TO CONTENT

"A World Without Rules" makes use of content words to explore what life would be like without the laws and protections provided by our government. It explains how government agencies and rules ensure that our public spaces are maintained, our environment stays healthy, and our country is defended from invasion.

Government Words

_____

_____

_____

_____

_____

_____

_____

Circle two words that you were able to define by using context clues. Write the words and their meanings on the lines. Use a dictionary to check your work.

_____

_____

_____

Copyright © McGraw Hill. Permission is granted to reproduce for classroom use.

Name _____

Use the words in the box and the clues below to help you solve the crossword puzzle.

assigned	characteristics	agriculture	advancements
inherit	metaphor	mature	concerns
resistance	injustice	disagree	prevalent

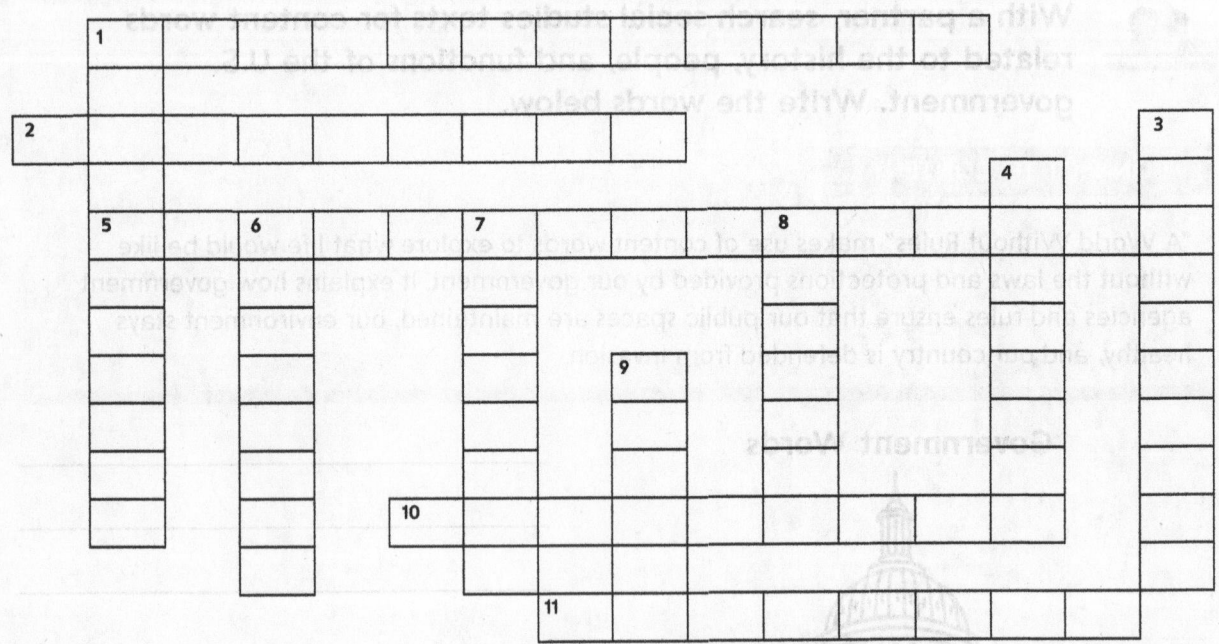

Across

1. Improvements
2. Widespread
5. Someone's qualities
10. Unfairness
11. It compares two unlike things

Down

1. Farm science
3. Fighting against
4. Have a different opinion
6. Given as a task
7. Worries
8. Receive from parents
9. Like an adult

Copyright © McGraw Hill. Permission is granted to reproduce for classroom use.

Name _____

> • A **subject pronoun** takes the place of a noun in the subject of a sentence. Subject pronouns include *I, you, he, she, it, we,* and *they. They were excited to go on vacation!*
>
> • An **object pronoun** takes the place of a noun that follows an action verb or a preposition. Object pronouns include *me, you, him, her, it, us,* and *them. Mr. Gupta handed us each a copy of the test.*

Read each sentence and circle the pronoun. Write *S* on the line if it is a subject pronoun. Write *O* if it is an object pronoun.

1. My mom does not like him. _____

2. I read a chapter every night. _____

3. Sometimes they go to the zoo together. _____

4. Will the captain say hello to us? _____

5. You can ride in the car with Jessie. _____

6. The girl did not invite them to the party. _____

Reading/Writing Connection | **Read this excerpt from "The Birth of American Democracy." Circle each pronoun you find. Then write whether each pronoun is a subject or object pronoun.**

They knew that their signatures made them traitors to Great Britain. They also knew that, if the colonies won the war, their names would go down in history.

_____

_____

Copyright © McGraw Hill. Permission is granted to reproduce for classroom use.

Name _____

> • A **subject pronoun** takes the place of a noun in the subject of a sentence. An **object pronoun** takes the place of a noun that follows an action verb or a preposition.
>
> • A **reflexive pronoun** is an object pronoun that renames the subject and ends in *-self* or *-selves*. Examples include *myself, herself, yourselves,* and *themselves.*
>
> • A reflexive pronoun is used when the subject and object of a sentence refer to the same person or thing. *Anna fixed the sentence herself.*

Circle the correct reflexive pronoun in parentheses to complete each sentence.

1. I almost hurt (myself / yourself) while walking down the stairs.

2. The cat licked (itself / themselves) after eating dinner.

3. My dad bought (herself / himself) a hot dog at the game.

4. Lila and Raul did all of the work (ourselves / themselves).

5. Did you both get (yourself / yourselves) some ice cream?

Write two sentences about what kind of food you would make for a picnic. Describe the event using reflexive pronouns. Then check that you used the reflexive pronouns correctly.

_____

_____

_____

Copyright © McGraw Hill. Permission is granted to reproduce for classroom use.

Name _____

> - Use a subject pronoun when replacing the subject of a sentence or a noun that follows a form of the verb *to be*. *The president of the linguistics club is **she**.*
>
> - Use an object pronoun after an action verb or a preposition. *He ran up to the ball and kicked it hard.*
>
> - Do not use a reflexive pronoun in place of a personal pronoun. Do not add *-self* or *-selves* to a subject pronoun.

Read each sentence. On the line, rewrite the sentence using correct subject and object pronouns.

1. I didn't realize it at first, but my cousin is him.

   _____

2. Myself am very excited to see the movie.

   _____

3. Do you want to travel with we in the car?

   _____

4. Them brought flowers in from outside.

   _____

5. It was her who scored the highest on the test.

   _____

 In your writer's notebook, write a story about a bat. Include at least two subject pronouns, two object pronouns, and two reflexive pronouns. Then check that you used all the pronouns correctly.

Copyright © McGraw Hill. Permission is granted to reproduce for classroom use.

Name _____

> • A **subject pronoun** takes the place of a sentence's subject or a noun that follows a form of the verb *to be*.
> • An **object pronoun** takes the place of a noun that follows an action verb or a preposition.
> • A **reflexive pronoun** renames the subject and ends in *-self* or *-selves*. It is used when the subject and object of a sentence refer to the same person or thing.
> • Do not use a reflexive pronoun in place of a personal pronoun. Do not add *-self* or *-selves* to a subject pronoun.

Rewrite the paragraphs below, correcting mistakes in subject and object pronouns.

COMMON ERRORS

Always check your writing to make sure you did not use a reflexive pronoun instead of an object pronoun. *The song will be sung by the choir and me.*

1. My mom and me went to the mall yesterday to buy my dad a birthday gift. Ourselves had no idea what to get him. Then I thought to myself that him really loves airplanes. I bought a model airplane at the hobby shop there and smiled the whole way home!

_____
_____
_____

2. It was sunny. My brother and me ran outside and sat in the grass while ourselves waited for my dad. Suddenly, the car pulled into the driveway. It was him! Now us could finally all go to the park.

_____
_____
_____

Copyright © McGraw Hill. Permission is granted to reproduce for classroom use.

Name _____

Read the student draft and look for any corrections that need to be made. Then choose the best answer to each question.

(1) Alice stepped off the train and waved at me. (2) She was thrilled to see me. (3) We couldn't stop ourselves from laughing. (4) I walked up to her and gave she a great big hug.

(5) "It's so good to see you!" I yelled into my ear over the noise. (6) "I thought us could get some lunch while we catch up."

(7) Alice and myself walked out of the train station. (8) We had not seen each other in two years! (9) Carrie is going to visit they next month.

1. What change, if any, should be made to sentence 1 or 2?

   A Change *Alice* to **She** in sentence 1

   B Change *She* to **Alice** in sentence 2

   C Change *me* to **myself** in sentence 2

   D Make no changes.

2. What is the correct way to write sentence 4?

   F I walked up to her and gave him a great big hug.

   G I walked up to her and gave us a great big hug.

   H I walked up to her and gave her a great big hug.

   J Make no change.

3. What change, if any, should be made to sentence 5?

   A Change *you* to **ourselves**

   B Change *I* to **we**

   C Change *my* to **his**

   D Change *my* to **her**

4. What change needs to be made in sentence 6?

   F Change *I* to **Me**

   G Change *I* to **Myself**

   H Change *us* to **we**

   J Change *we* to **ourselves**

5. What is the correct way to write sentence 7?

   A Alice and I walked out of the train station.

   B Alice and we walked out of the train station.

   C Alice and ourselves walked out of the train station.

   D Make no change.

6. What change, if any, should be made to sentence 8 or 9?

   F Change *each other* to **ourselves** in sentence 8

   G Change *they* to **us** in sentence 9

   H Change *We* to **Us** in sentence 8

   J Make no change.

Copyright © McGraw Hill. Permission is granted to reproduce for classroom use.

Name _____

Fold back the paper along the dotted line. Use the blanks to write each word as it is read aloud. When you finish the test, unfold the paper. Use the list at the right to correct any spelling mistakes.

1. _____
2. _____
3. _____
4. _____
5. _____
6. _____
7. _____
8. _____
9. _____
10. _____
11. _____
12. _____
13. _____
14. _____
15. _____
16. _____
17. _____
18. _____
19. _____
20. _____

Review Words 21. _____
22. _____
23. _____

Challenge Words 24. _____
25. _____

1. funnier
2. families
3. pennies
4. worried
5. replied
6. varied
7. marries
8. carries
9. easily
10. silliest
11. jumpier
12. emptier
13. merrier
14. applied
15. cozily
16. sorriest
17. prettily
18. lazier
19. happiest
20. dizziest
21. scaring
22. tasting
23. skipped
24. handily
25. factories

Copyright © McGraw Hill. Permission is granted to reproduce for classroom use.

Name _____

Inflectional endings -*es* and -*ed* are added to verbs to create new verb tenses, such as changing *touch* to *touches* or *touched*. The inflectional endings -*er* and -*est* are added to an adjective to create a comparative or superlative form, such as changing *tall* to *taller* or *tallest*.

SPELLING TIP

For base words that end with a consonant and a *y*, change the *y* to *i* before adding -*es*, -*ed*, -*er*, or -*est*. For example, *carry* changes to *carries* or *carried*. *Lazy* changes to *lazier* or *laziest*.

easily	silliest	funnier	merrier	prettily
marries	varied	replied	applied	lazier
emptier	families	jumpier	cozily	happiest
worried	carries	pennies	sorriest	dizziest

Write the spelling words that drop the *y* and add -*ies*.

1. _____ 2. _____ 3. _____

4. _____

Write the spelling words that drop the *y* and add -*ily*.

5. _____ 6. _____ 7. _____

Write the spelling words that drop the *y* and add -*ier*.

8. _____ 9. _____ 10. _____

11. _____ 12. _____

Write the spelling words that drop the *y* and add -*iest*.

13. _____ 14. _____ 15. _____

16. _____

Write the spelling words that drop the *y* and add -*ied*.

17. _____ 18. _____ 19. _____

20. _____

 **Use the spelling rules above to write a short tongue twister. Include four words from the spelling list and read them aloud. Check your work for errors.**

Copyright © McGraw Hill. Permission is granted to reproduce for classroom use.

Name _____

Inflectional endings -*es* and -*ed* are added to verbs to create new verb tenses, such as changing *touch* to *touches* or *touched*. The inflectional endings -*er* and -*est* are added to an adjective to create a comparative or superlative form, such as changing *tall* to *taller* or *tallest*.

SPELLING TIP

For base words that end with a consonant and a *y*, change the *y* to *i* before adding -*es*, -*ed*, -*er*, or -*est*. For example, *carry* changes to *carries* or *carried*. *Lazy* changes to *lazier* or *laziest*.

easily	silliest	funnier	copier	prettily
marries	babies	replied	cries	lazier
berries	families	flier	happier	happiest
worried	carries	pennies	sorriest	dizziest

Write the spelling words that drop the *y* and add -*ies*.

1. _____ 2. _____ 3. _____

4. _____ 5. _____ 6. _____

7. _____

Write the spelling words that drop the *y* and add -*ily*.

8. _____ 9. _____

Write the spelling words that drop the *y* and add -*ier*.

10. _____ 11. _____ 12. _____

13. _____ 14. _____

Write the spelling words that drop the *y* and add -*iest*.

15. _____ 16. _____ 17. _____

18. _____

Write the spelling words that drop the *y* and add -*ied*.

19. _____

20. _____

Use the spelling rules above to write a short tongue twister. Include four words from the spelling list and read them aloud. Check your work for errors.

Copyright © McGraw Hill. Permission is granted to reproduce for classroom use.

Name _____

easily	silliest	funnier	merrier	communities
abilities	varied	replied	societies	lazier
emptier	handily	jumpier	cozily	happiest
worried	carries	pennies	sorriest	dizziest

Write the spelling words that drop the *y* and add *-ies*.

1. _____ 2. _____ 3. _____

4. _____ 5. _____

Write the spelling words that drop the *y* and add *-ily*.

6. _____ 7. _____ 8. _____

Write the spelling words that drop the *y* and add *-ier*.

9. _____ 10. _____ 11. _____

12. _____ 13. _____

Write the spelling words that drop the *y* and add *-iest*.

14. _____ 15. _____ 16. _____

17. _____

Write the spelling words that drop the *y* and add *-ied*.

18. _____

19. _____

20. _____

Use the spelling rules you learned to write a short tongue twister. Include four words from the spelling list and read them aloud. Check your work for errors.

Copyright © McGraw Hill. Permission is granted to reproduce for classroom use.

Name _____

funnier	replied	easily	merrier	prettily
families	varied	silliest	applied	lazier
pennies	marries	jumpier	cozily	happiest
worried	carries	emptier	sorriest	dizziest

A. Write the spelling word that belongs with the other words in the group.

1. meets, dates, _____

2. answered, said, _____

3. quickly, simply, _____

4. inactive, sluggish, _____

5. different, changing, _____

6. supports, bears, _____

B. Write the spelling word that matches each definition below.

7. likelier to make laugh _____   14. less full _____

8. more nervous _____   15. most apologetic _____

9. cents _____   16. jollier _____

10. warmly and snugly _____   17. groups of relatives _____

11. most without balance _____   18. asked to be accepted _____

12. nervous _____   19. gladdest _____

13. in a lovely way _____   20. most goofy _____

Copyright © McGraw Hill. Permission is granted to reproduce for classroom use.

Name _____

Underline the six misspelled words in the paragraphs below. Write the words correctly on the lines.

Not only is Catherine my best friend, but she is also easly one of the sillyest people I know. She is merrer than the merriest elves in the North Pole!

When Catherine comes over, she thinks up the best games to play. Once, we built a giant city made out of pennyes. It was so funny. It was even funnieer when she pretended to be a giant monster and knocked all the coins down. I am happyest when I'm with my best friend, Catherine.

1. _____   4. _____

2. _____   5. _____

3. _____   6. _____

Writing Connection

Write to describe your best friend. Use at least four words from the spelling list. Then check your work for errors.

_____

_____

_____

_____

_____

_____

_____

_____

Copyright © McGraw Hill. Permission is granted to reproduce for classroom use.

Name _____

Copyright © McGraw Hill. Permission is granted to reproduce for classroom use.

Remember

Inflectional endings -es and -ed are added to verbs to create new verb forms and tenses, such as changing *touch* to *touches* or *touched*. The inflectional endings -er and -est can be added to an adjective to create a comparative or superlative form, such as changing *tall* to *taller* or *tallest*.

funnier	replied	easily	merrier	prettily
families	varied	silliest	applied	lazier
pennies	marries	jumpier	cozily	happiest
worried	carries	emptier	sorriest	dizziest

A. Fill in the missing letters to form a spelling word. Read each word aloud.

1. empt ____ ____ ____
2. prett ____ ____ ____
3. famil ____ ____ ____
4. merr ____ ____ ____
5. sill ____ ____ ____ ____
6. var ____ ____ ____
7. carr ____ ____ ____
8. dizz ____ ____ ____
9. worr ____ ____ ____
10. coz ____ ____ ____

11. happ ____ ____ ____ ____
12. funn ____ ____ ____
13. appl ____ ____ ____
14. marr ____ ____ ____
15. sorr ____ ____ ____ ____
16. penn ____ ____ ____
17. jump ____ ____ ____
18. eas ____ ____ ____
19. repl ____ ____ ____
20. laz ____ ____ ____

B. Write these spelling words in alphabetical order. Alphabetize them to the second letter: *merrier, easiest, funnier, families, marries.*

21. _____   24. _____
22. _____   25. _____
23. _____

Name _____

Knowing **Greek roots** can help you figure out the meanings of unfamiliar words. Take a look at these Greek roots and their meanings:

astr – star   **bio** – life   **cardi** – heart   **hepta** – seven
deca – ten   **derm** – skin   **logy** – study of

Identify the Greek roots in each sign below. Write the words and their definitions on the lines. Check your answers in a dictionary.

Cedar Grove Hospital
Medical Building A
272 S. Coral Street

Center for Dermatology
Department of Cardiology

North Hills University
Franklin D. Roosevelt Hall

Department of Astronomy
Dr. Anika Kapoor, Chair

Department of Biology
Dr. Kenneth Tinibu, Chair

_____   _____

_____   _____

_____   _____

Association of Northern Colleges
Regional Track and Field Meet
Saturday, June 5th – Events

• 9:00 – Men's Decathlon
• 11:00 – 100-Meter Dash
• 1:00 – Women's Heptathlon
• 2:00 – 100-Meter Hurdles
• 3:00 – Long Jump
• 4:00 – Javelin Throw

_____

_____

Copyright © McGraw Hill. Permission is granted to reproduce for classroom use.

Name _____

Latin Roots

commun – common   *port* – carry

mem – remember   *spect* – look

dent – tooth

A. Look at each word below and identify the Latin root. Circle the roots and write the meaning of each word. Use the information above to help you.

1. community _____

2. portable _____

3. spectacles _____

4. dental _____

5. memorizing _____

6. inspected _____

B. Using what you know about the roots *spect* and *dent,* write the meaning of each word below. Use a dictionary to check your work.

7. spectator

_____

8. dentist

_____

Copyright © McGraw Hill. Permission is granted to reproduce for classroom use.

Name _____

- A subject pronoun and a present-tense verb must **agree** in number.

- Add -s or -es to most verbs when using the subject pronouns *he, she,* and *it*. Remember, when a verb ends in a *y*, you usually drop the *y* and add *-ies*. *He runs. It chases him. She watches. She worries.*

- Do not add -s or -es to verbs when using the subject pronouns *I, we, you,* and *they. I run. You chase me. They watch.*

Complete each sentence by writing the correct form of the present-tense verb in parentheses.

1. It (flash) _____ on and off.

2. They (howl) _____ at the moon.

3. At first, we don't (remember) _____ the story.

4. I think he (carry) _____ too many bags.

5. You (listen) _____ carefully for the sound of the car.

Writing Connection **Write about a problem and a solution. Choose the genre that you will write in, and try freewriting to help you get your ideas on paper. Then revise your draft. Use only present-tense verbs in your piece. After you finish, check your work.**

_____

_____

_____

_____

_____

Copyright © McGraw Hill. Permission is granted to reproduce for classroom use.

Name _____

- A subject pronoun and a present-tense verb must **agree** in number.
- Use subject pronouns with the present-tense forms of *have* in the following ways: *I have, you have, he/she/it has, we have,* and *they have.*
- Use subject pronouns with the present-tense forms of *be* in the following ways: *I am, you are, he/she/it is, we are,* and *they are.*

A. Read each sentence. Complete the sentence with *have* **or** *has,* **based on the subject pronoun.**

1. They _____ gone to the supermarket.

2. I think it _____ melted in the glass.

3. Do you know that we _____ twenty marbles?

B. Read each sentence. Complete the sentence with *am, are,* **or** *is,* **based on the subject pronoun.**

4. I _____ so lucky to know you!

5. The teacher said she _____ giving a test.

6. I think they _____ older than they look.

 **Read this excerpt from "A Telephone Mix-Up." Find the sentence that uses the present form of** *have* **or** *be* **with a pronoun. Underline the** *have* **or** *be* **form used, and circle the pronoun. Then write three sentences about some things that are happening in school today in your writer's notebook. Use at least two instances of** *have* **and** *be* **with a pronoun. Then edit your work.**

> ...Her father was smiling broadly while tinkering with the shiny brass bells on top. "Isn't she a beauty?" he asked. "Have you ever seen such magnificence?"

Copyright © McGraw Hill. Permission is granted to reproduce for classroom use.

Name _____

- Use quotation marks at the beginning and end of a speaker's exact words. Begin a quotation with a capital letter. *Tony said, "Come back."*
- **Commas** and **periods** always go inside quotation marks. *"I can't believe," she began, "that I got an A on that hard test."*
- A question mark or an exclamation mark goes inside quotation marks when it is part of the quotation. *He asked, "How much is this tomato?"*
- A question mark or an exclamation mark goes outside quotation marks when it is not part of the quotation. *Did Toria say, "I am going to the store"?*

Rewrite each sentence correctly by adding quotation marks and using correct capitalization and punctuation.

1. Jane said, I like to read about unusual animals.

   _____

2. My teacher asked, do you know who the president is?

   _____

3. Ms. Mendez exclaimed, close that window quickly!

   _____

4. I rushed inside and shouted, quick! Where is my camera?

   _____

5. My family at home includes my mother, father, sister, and me, I said.

   _____

 **In your writer's notebook, write a story about a conversation with a friend. Include at least four quotations. Then pair up with a classmate. Read the conversations out loud and check for correct capitalization and punctuation, including quotation marks.**

Copyright © McGraw Hill. Permission is granted to reproduce for classroom use.

Name _____

- A subject pronoun and a present-tense verb must **agree** in number.
- Follow specific rules for using subject pronouns with the present-tense forms of *have* and *be*.
- Use quotation marks around someone's exact words.
- Follow specific punctuation and capitalization rules for quotation marks.

Rewrite the sentences below, correcting mistakes in present-tense pronoun-verb agreement and quotation marks.

COMMON ERRORS

Use quotations only when directly quoting what someone has said or stating the title of something. Do not use quotation marks unnecessarily.

1. I asks, "What is your favorite season"?

_____

2. Let's eat before we finish the puzzle, I suggests.

_____

3. You has more balloons than I do.

_____

4. They is very happy to let us has the prize.

_____

5. What am you doing? I asks worriedly.

_____

6. It rock back and forth in a noisy way.

_____

Copyright © McGraw Hill. Permission is granted to reproduce for classroom use.

Name _____

Read the selection. Then choose the best answer to each question.

(1) We _____ sure that this is the correct place. (2) I _____ two parties to go to this weekend. (3) I _____ most excited about this party. (4) My friend _____ a party after the school play tomorrow.

(5) My mom looks at me, and she honk loudly. (6) She reminds me that I need to leave the party early tonight. (7) She are helping me with my book report tonight! (8) I wave goodbye to her and walk through the front door.

1. What word goes in the blank in sentence 1?

   A have

   B has

   C is

   D are

2. What word goes in the blank in sentence 2?

   F have

   G is

   H are

   J am

3. What word goes in the blank in sentence 3?

   A have

   B am

   C are

   D is

4. What word goes in the blank in sentence 4?

   F have

   G has

   H am

   J is

5. What is the correct verb for sentence 5?

   A lookes

   B look

   C honk

   D honks

6. What is the correct verb for sentence 6?

   F remind

   G reminds

   H needs

   J needes

7. What is the correct verb for sentence 7?

   A am

   B is

   C are

   D have

8. What is the correct verb for sentence 8?

   F wave

   G waves

   H walkes

   J walks

Copyright © McGraw Hill. Permission is granted to reproduce for classroom use.

Name _____

Fold back the paper along the dotted line. Use the blanks to write each word as it is read aloud. When you finish the test, unfold the paper. Use the list at the right to correct any spelling mistakes.

1. _____ 1. mood
2. _____ 2. stoop
3. _____ 3. zoom
4. _____ 4. crew
5. _____ 5. stew
6. _____ 6. ruler
7. _____ 7. produce
8. _____ 8. issue
9. _____ 9. tutor
10. _____ 10. truth
11. _____ 11. bruised
12. _____ 12. juicy
13. _____ 13. suits
14. _____ 14. group
15. _____ 15. you'll
16. _____ 16. huge
17. _____ 17. crook
18. _____ 18. wool
19. _____ 19. used
20. _____ 20. should

Review Words 21. _____ 21. pennies
22. _____ 22. prettily
23. _____ 23. funnier
Challenge Words 24. _____ 24. barbeque
25. _____ 25. crooked

Name _____

The /ü/ sound, as in *spoon*, may be spelled *oo, ew, u_e, ue, u, ui,* and *ou* (*soon, blew, rude, clue, July, fruity,* and *through*).

The /ū/ sound in *cube* may be spelled *u, u_e,* and *ew* (*pupil, huge,* and *fewer*).

The /ů/ sound in *book* may be spelled *oo* and *ou* (*cooking* and *could*).

DECODING WORDS

Retune begins with the prefix *re-*. Prefixes often form the first syllable in a word. Final *e* vowel spellings like *u_e* must stay in the same syllable. Blend the syllables: *re-tune*.

Read aloud and write the words with matching spelling patterns.

suits	stew	crook	bruised	should
issue	ruler	crew	group	wool
zoom	produce	used	you'll	mood
truth	juicy	stoop	huge	tutor

/ü/ spelled *oo* (as in *food*)

1. _____
2. _____
3. _____

/ü/ spelled *u/u_e/ue* (as in *July/rude/clue*)

4. _____
5. _____
6. _____
7. _____
8. _____

/ü/ spelled *ui* (as in *fruit*)

9. _____
10. _____
11. _____

/ü/ spelled *ou* (as in *soup*)

12. _____
13. _____

/ü/ spelled *ew* (as in *blew*)

14. _____
15. _____

/ů/ spelled *oo* (as in *book*)

16. _____
17. _____

/ů/ spelled *ou* (as in *would*)

18. _____

/ū/ spelled *u_e* (as in *cube*)

19. _____
20. _____

Look through this week's selection for more words to sort. Create a word sort in your writer's notebook for a partner.

Copyright © McGraw Hill. Permission is granted to reproduce for classroom use.

Name _____

> The /ü/ sound, as in *spoon*, may be spelled *oo, ew, u_e, ue, u, ui,* and *ou* (*soon, blew, rude, clue, July, fruity,* and *through*).
>
> The /ū/ sound in *cube* may be spelled *u, u_e,* and *ew* (*pupil, huge,* and *fewer*).
>
> The /ù/ sound in *book* may be spelled *oo* and *ou* (*cooking* and *could*).

DECODING WORDS

Retune begins with the prefix *re-*. Prefixes often form the first syllable in a word. Final *e* vowel spellings like *u_e* must stay in the same syllable. Blend the syllables: *re-tune*.

Read aloud and write the words with the matching spelling patterns.

suit	stew	cookie	fruit	should
tunes	used	spool	group	wool
zoom	new	grew	you'll	tooth
due	July	food	huge	true

/ü/ spelled *oo* (as in *mood*)

1. _____
2. _____
3. _____
4. _____

/ü/ spelled *u/u_e/ue* (as in *tutor/rude/clue*)

5. _____
6. _____
7. _____
8. _____

/ü/ spelled *ui* (as in *bruised*)

9. _____
10. _____

/ü/ spelled *ou* (as in *soup*)

11. _____
12. _____

/ü/ spelled *ew* (as in *blew*)

13. _____
14. _____
15. _____

/ü/ spelled *oo* (as in *book*)

16. _____
17. _____

/ù/ spelled *ou* (as in *would*)

18. _____

/ū/ spelled *u_e* (as in *cube*)

19. _____
20. _____

Look through this week's selection for more words to sort. Create a word sort in your writer's notebook for a partner.

Copyright © McGraw Hill. Permission is granted to reproduce for classroom use.

Name _____

Read aloud and write the words with the matching spelling patterns.

suits	smooth	crooked	bruised	should
tissue	shrewd	crew	parachute	communication
zoom	produce	mute	you'll	boost
truthful	juicy	doodle	huge	tutor

/ü/ spelled oo (as in food)

1. _____

2. _____

3. _____

4. _____

/ü/ spelled u/u_e/ue (as in July/rude/clue)

5. _____

6. _____

7. _____

8. _____

9. _____

/ü/ spelled ui (as in fruit)

10. _____

11. _____

12. _____

/ü/ spelled ou (as in soup)

13. _____

/ü/ spelled ew (as in blew)

14. _____

15. _____

/ù/ spelled oo (as in book)

16. _____

/ù/ spelled ou (as in would)

17. _____

/ū/ spelled u/u_e (as in pupil/cube)

18. _____

19. _____

20. _____

 **Look through this week's selection for more words to sort. Create a word sort in your writer's notebook for a partner.**

Copyright © McGraw Hill. Permission is granted to reproduce for classroom use.

Name _____

mood	stew	tutor	suits	crook
stoop	ruler	truth	group	wool
zoom	produce	bruised	you'll	used
crew	issue	juicy	huge	should

A. Write the spelling word that belongs with the other words in the group.

1. injured, hurt, _____

2. zip, fast, _____

3. moist, slushy, _____

4. he'll, she'll, _____

5. thief, robber, _____

6. would, could, _____

7. many, together, _____

8. market, groceries, _____

B. Write the spelling word that best completes each sentence.

9. Leaving the lights on is a _____ waste of energy.

10. Mom cooked the _____ slowly for many hours.

11. Did you see the latest _____ of this magazine?

12. I am in a great _____ today!

13. My grandfather has two good _____ that he wears.

14. Use your _____ to measure how tall the plant is.

15. I am an English _____ for kids after school.

16. She _____ the towel to dry her hands.

17. We put a welcome mat on our front _____.

18. That warm sweater is made of _____.

19. The _____ of workers got the job done early.

20. I always tell the _____.

Copyright © McGraw Hill. Permission is granted to reproduce for classroom use.

Name _____

Underline the six misspelled words in the paragraphs below. Write the words correctly on the lines.

    I decided to help my aunt make her famous stue. We made a list and decided that we shood head over to the market. Once inside, we went straight to the produice department.

    After picking up some carrots and onions, we looked at a groop of potatoes. All of them were brused! Aunt Wendy was not happy. She spoke to a clerk who brought out a fresh bag for us. As we left, we both knew that the meal would be a hewge success!

1. _____   4. _____

2. _____   5. _____

3. _____   6. _____

Writing Connection

Write about a meal that you prepared with someone. Use at least four words from the spelling list. Use a dictionary or an online resource to check that you have spelled the spelling words and high-frequency words correctly.

_____

_____

_____

_____

_____

_____

_____

_____

_____

_____

Copyright © McGraw Hill. Permission is granted to reproduce for classroom use.

Name _____

Copyright © McGraw Hill. Permission is granted to reproduce for classroom use.

Remember

The /ü/ sound, as in *spoon*, may be spelled *oo, ew, u_e, ue, u, ui*, and *ou* (*soon, blew, rude, clue, July, fruity,* and *through*).

The /ū/ sound in *cube* may be spelled *u, u_e,* and *ew* (*pupil, huge,* and *fewer*).

The /u̇/ sound in *book* may be spelled *oo* and *ou* (*cooking* and *could*).

Circle the spelling word in each row that rhymes with the word in bold type. Write the spelling word on the line. Then read the word aloud.

1. **roots**	rants	sports	suits	_____
2. **hood**	should	had	word	_____
3. **stool**	sold	look	you'll	_____
4. **full**	fail	wool	while	_____
5. **new**	crew	crow	pull	_____
6. **book**	break	crook	fluke	_____
7. **scooter**	sweater	tutor	flutter	_____
8. **luge**	high	look	huge	_____
9. **room**	zoom	took	rule	_____
10. **tissue**	scissor	issue	amiss	_____
11. **rude**	mood	made	rug	_____
12. **goosey**	grassy	furry	juicy	_____
13. **blue**	groom	hook	stew	_____
14. **moose**	produce	mister	erase	_____
15. **soup**	stop	stoop	pup	_____
16. **cooler**	caller	ruler	stroller	_____
17. **fused**	used	cried	stood	_____
18. **loop**	good	loom	group	_____
19. **youth**	south	troop	truth	_____
20. **oozed**	bruised	based	dozed	_____

Name _____

Expand your vocabulary by adding or removing inflectional endings, prefixes, or suffixes to a base word to create different forms of a word.

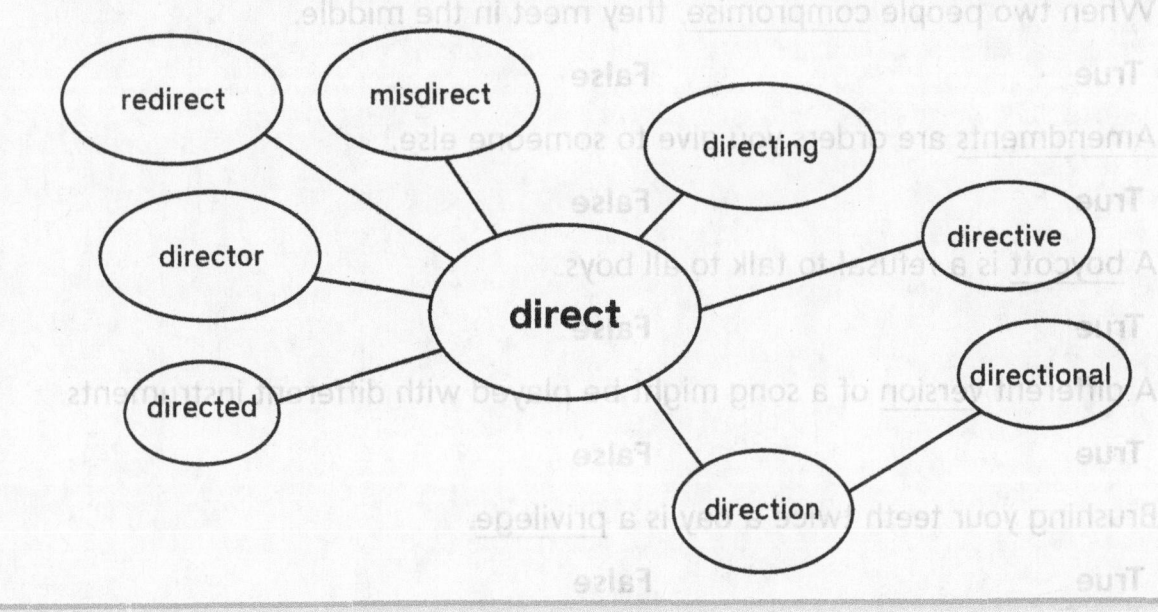

redirect   misdirect   directing   directive   director   **direct**   directional   directed   direction

Choose a base word from "A Telephone Mix-Up" and write it below the telephone. Then add prefixes, suffixes, and inflectional endings to make as many related words as you can. Use a dictionary to help you.

_____

_____

_____

Copyright © McGraw Hill. Permission is granted to reproduce for classroom use.

Name _____

Each sentence below contains an underlined vocabulary word. Circle *True* if the statement is true. Circle *False* if the statement is false.

1. When two people <u>compromise</u>, they meet in the middle.

   True   False

2. <u>Amendments</u> are orders you give to someone else.

   True   False

3. A <u>boycott</u> is a refusal to talk to all boys.

   True   False

4. A different <u>version</u> of a song might be played with different instruments.

   True   False

5. Brushing your teeth twice a day is a <u>privilege</u>.

   True   False

6. Green, leafy trees are <u>prevalent</u> in the world's deserts.

   True   False

7. A <u>democracy</u> is a form of government in which one ruler has all the power.

   True   False

8. You must wait for something that will happen <u>eventually</u>.

   True   False

9. <u>Legislation</u> is carried out by senators and representatives in Congress.

   True   False

10. A dentist is <u>qualified</u> to examine teeth and fill cavities.

    True   False

11. <u>Agriculture</u> is something that annoys or bothers people.

    True   False

12. Promising to be someone's friend is an example of a <u>commitment</u>.

    True   False

Copyright © McGraw Hill. Permission is granted to reproduce for classroom use.

Name _____

- A **possessive pronoun** takes the place of a possessive noun. It does not have an apostrophe. *Brian's dog is brown. His dog is brown.*

- A possessive pronoun must match the noun it replaces in number and gender. Use *my* for first-person singular nouns, *your* for second-person singular nouns, and *his/her/its* for third-person singular nouns. For plural nouns, use *our* for first-person, *your* for second-person, and *their* for third-person point of view.

Read each sentence and rewrite the underlined word or words using a possessive pronoun or a possessive pronoun and a noun.

1. I left <u>the book that belongs to me</u> at home. _____

2. <u>Lisa's</u> telephone is broken. _____

3. The mechanic said that <u>the car's</u> wheels are brand new. _____

4. <u>The bedroom that belongs to you and me</u> needs to be cleaned.

   _____

5. May I borrow <u>the necklace that belongs to you?</u> _____

6. <u>Maya and Lucy's</u> parrot says "Hello." _____

Read this paragraph from "Star Parties." Find the sentence that includes a possessive pronoun. Underline the possessive pronoun and circle the subject that the possessive pronoun is replacing.

Observatories have powerful technology that astronomers use to do their research.

Then, in your writer's notebook, write a story about a group that goes into space. What do they bring? Whom do they meet? Use at least four possessive pronouns. Edit your work.

Copyright © McGraw Hill. Permission is granted to reproduce for classroom use.

Name _____

- A **stand-alone possessive pronoun** is not used directly before a noun. *That leftover sandwich is mine.*

- Add *-s* to most pronouns that are used after a noun to form a stand-alone possessive pronoun, such as *yours, hers, his, ours,* and *theirs.*

- *Mine* is a stand-alone possessive pronoun. *His* and *its* are the same when used before a noun or as a stand-alone possessive pronoun.

Circle the correct possessive pronoun in parentheses to complete the sentence. Then rewrite the sentence on the line.

1. I think that this skateboard is (his / its).

   _____

2. This is (hers / her) and that is (your / yours).

   _____

3. I will watch your dog if you watch (my / mine).

   _____

Write a paragraph about your favorite character from a book, movie, TV show, or song. Include at least two possessive pronouns and one stand-alone possessive pronoun.

   _____

   _____

   _____

   _____

Copyright © McGraw Hill. Permission is granted to reproduce for classroom use.

Name _____

- Add an apostrophe and *-s* to a singular noun to make it possessive: *dog/dog's*.
- Add an apostrophe to make most plural nouns possessive: *dogs/dogs'*.
- Add an apostrophe and *-s* to form the possessive of plural nouns that do not end in *-s: women/women's*.
- Possessive pronouns do not have apostrophes. They should agree in number and gender with the possessive nouns they replace.

Rewrite each sentence. Correct the punctuation of possessive nouns and pronouns.

1. My little sisters favorite game is hide-and-seek.

   _____

2. The childrens dog ate it's food too quickly.

   _____

3. Five truck's horns made an overpowering noise.

   _____

4. Sometimes the ocean waves power can destroy the beach.

   _____

5. The subject of the report was our's to choose.

   _____

 **In your writer's notebook, describe the houses in your neighborhood and who lives in them. Include at least five possessive nouns. Circle them. Then edit your work to make sure you used the apostrophes correctly.**

Copyright © McGraw Hill. Permission is granted to reproduce for classroom use.

Name _____

- A **possessive pronoun** takes the place of a possessive noun and does not include an apostrophe. It must match the noun it replaces in number and gender.
- A **stand-alone possessive pronoun** is not used directly before a noun. Add -s to most pronouns that are used before a noun to form a stand-alone possessive pronoun.
- *Mine* is a stand-alone possessive pronoun. *His* and *its* are the same when used before a noun or as a stand-alone possessive pronoun.

Rewrite the paragraphs below, correcting mistakes in possessive nouns and pronouns.

1. Me name is Robert, and this is mine wife, Florence.
   That's her' given name, but she prefers to be called
   Flossy. Let us show you around our's home. Down
   the hall we have ours offices. The one on the left is
   mines, and the one on the right is Flossys.

   _____

   _____

   _____

   _____

2. The rancher watched hi's horses as they ran around theirs paddock. They
   all looked happy except for one. It's leg was lifted, and it was limping. The
   rancher frowned and told his' daughter to get hers lasso. He would have to
   bring this horse in to give it time to rest.

   _____

   _____

   _____

   _____

Copyright © McGraw Hill. Permission is granted to reproduce for classroom use.

Name _____

Read the selection. Then choose the best answer to each question.

(1) I love this town because _____ family has lived here for years. (2) Every morning, neighbors walk to the diner to have _____ breakfast and chat. (3) Mrs. Taggart's dog always waits outside the diner wagging _____ tail. (4) When I try to steal my friend's bacon to give to the dog, she tells me that it's _____!

(5) _____ town has interesting events, too. (6) _____ sister's favorite is the picnic basket auction in the summer. (7) My dad says the sledding contest in winter is _____. (8) My brothers say that the toy boat race in spring is _____.

1. Which word best completes sentence 1?
   A mine
   B its
   C ours
   D our

2. Which word best completes sentence 2?
   F his
   G their
   H our
   J they're

3. Which word best completes sentence 3?
   A its
   B her's
   C hers
   D it's

4. Which word best completes sentence 4?
   F hers
   G her
   H our
   J its

5. Which word best completes sentence 5?
   A Their
   B Mine
   C His
   D Our

6. Which word best completes sentence 6?
   A Hers
   B Ours
   C My
   D Mine

7. Which word best completes sentence 7?
   F her
   G his
   H my
   J theirs

8. Which word best completes sentence 8?
   A there's
   B theirs
   C they'res
   D theres

Name _____

Fold back the
paper along the
dotted line. Use
the blanks to
write each word
as it is read aloud.
When you finish
the test, unfold
the paper. Use the
list at the right
to correct any
spelling mistakes.

1. _____   1. noises
2. _____   2. voices
3. _____   3. rejoice
4. _____   4. annoy
5. _____   5. destroy
6. _____   6. voyage
7. _____   7. mound
8. _____   8. south
9. _____   9. pound
10. _____   10. hound
11. _____   11. pouch
12. _____   12. thousand
13. _____   13. wound
14. _____   14. grouch
15. _____   15. cowboy
16. _____   16. gown
17. _____   17. frown
18. _____   18. howling
19. _____   19. flower
20. _____   20. tower

Review Words
21. _____   21. crook
22. _____   22. zoom
23. _____   23. group

Challenge Words
24. _____   24. drought
25. _____   25. downtown

Copyright © McGraw Hill. Permission is granted to reproduce for classroom use.

Name _____

> A diphthong occurs when two vowels are blended into a single syllable, making the vowel sound change.
>
> The diphthong /oi/ is spelled *oy* and *oi*, as in *boy* and *oil*. The diphthong /ou/ is spelled *ou* and *ow*, as in *ground* and *now*.

DECODING WORDS

Some vowel teams, like *oy* and *ow*, have a consonant that acts as a vowel. These vowel teams must stay in the same syllable. For example: *boy-cott*.

Read aloud and write the spelling words with the matching spelling patterns.

pound	cowboy	noises	wound	rejoice
grouch	voyage	hound	voices	tower
frown	annoy	howling	thousand	flower
mound	south	destroy	gown	pouch

ou

1. _____
2. _____
3. _____
4. _____
5. _____
6. _____
7. _____
8. _____

oy

9. _____
10. _____
11. _____

ow

12. _____
13. _____
14. _____
15. _____
16. _____

oi

17. _____
18. _____
19. _____

ow and oy

20. _____

 Use the spelling patterns above to write a short tongue twister. Include four words from the spelling list. Check your work for errors.

Copyright © McGraw Hill. Permission is granted to reproduce for classroom use.

Name _____

> A diphthong occurs when two vowels are blended into a single syllable, making the vowel sound change.
>
> The diphthong /oi/ is spelled *oy* and *oi*, as in *boy* and *oil*. The diphthong /ou/ is spelled *ou* and *ow*, as in *ground* and *now*.

DECODING WORDS

Some vowel teams, like *oy* and *ow*, have a consonant that acts as a vowel. These vowel teams must stay in the same syllable. For example: *boy-cott*.

Read aloud and write the spelling words with the matching spelling patterns.

pound	cowboy	noise	wound	coin
grouch	brown	hound	voices	tower
frown	loyal	howl	thousand	flower
mound	south	cloud	gown	pouch

ou

1. _____
2. _____
3. _____
4. _____
5. _____
6. _____
7. _____
8. _____
9. _____

oy

10. _____

ow

11. _____
12. _____
13. _____
14. _____
15. _____
16. _____

oi

17. _____
18. _____
19. _____

ow and oy

20. _____

 **Use the spelling patterns above to write a short tongue twister. Include four words from the spelling list. Check your work for errors.**

Copyright © McGraw Hill. Permission is granted to reproduce for classroom use.

Name _____

A. Read aloud and write the spelling words with the matching spelling patterns.

trouser	cowboy	void	wound	rejoice
grouch	voyage	encounter	hardboiled	empower
downtown	annoyance	howling	thousand	prowl
mound	southpaw	destroy	nowadays	announce

ou

1. _____

2. _____

3. _____

4. _____

5. _____

6. _____

7. _____

8. _____

oy

9. _____

10. _____

11. _____

12. _____

13. _____

14. _____

oi

ow

15. _____

16. _____

17. _____

18. _____

19. _____

ow and *oy*

20. _____

B. Compare the words *noises* and *voices*. How are they alike? How are they different?

_____

_____

 Use the spelling patterns you've learned to write a short tongue twister. Include four words from the spelling list. Check your work for errors.

Copyright © McGraw Hill. Permission is granted to reproduce for classroom use.

Name _____

noises	destroy	pound	wound	frown
voices	voyage	hound	grouch	howling
rejoice	mound	pouch	cowboy	flower
annoy	south	thousand	gown	tower

A. Write the spelling word that matches each synonym below.

1. bag _____

7. blossom _____

2. grump _____

8. 16 ounces _____

3. wrangler _____

9. celebrate _____

4. 1,000 _____

10. tall building _____

5. sounds _____

11. scowl _____

6. turned _____

B. Write the spelling word to complete each analogy below.

12. *Jet* is to *airplane* as *trip* is to _____

13. *Give* is to *take* as *please* is to _____

14. *Hole* is to *hollow* as *hill* is to _____

15. *Shirt* is to *blouse* as *dress* is to _____

16. *Remember* is to *forget* as *create* is to _____

17. *Giggling* is to *laughing* as *barking* is to _____

18. *Up* is to *down* as *north* is to _____

19. *Cat* is to *kitty* as *dog* is to _____

20. *Band* is to *instruments* as *choir* is to _____

Copyright © McGraw Hill. Permission is granted to reproduce for classroom use.

Name _____

Underline the six misspelled words in the paragraphs below. Write the words correctly on the lines.

People take trips all over the world, but a voiage out West is like no other. Taking a trip to the western United States may mean traveling for a thowsand miles, but it is well worth it. There is beauty behind every hill and mownd.

The West brings back the old days. If you travel there, you are sure to see cowbois and horses on the open plains. You may even hear wolves houling at the moon at night. Consider taking a trip to the West and rejoyce in all the wonders it has to offer!

1. _____   4. _____

2. _____   5. _____

3. _____   6. _____

Writing Connection

Write about a place that you would like to see one day. Use at least four words from the spelling list. Then check your work to make sure you have spelled the high-frequency words correctly.

_____

_____

_____

_____

_____

_____

_____

Copyright © McGraw Hill. Permission is granted to reproduce for classroom use.

Name _____

Copyright © McGraw Hill. Permission is granted to reproduce for classroom use.

Remember

A diphthong occurs when two vowels are blended into a single syllable. If a vowel sound changes in a single syllable, it is a diphthong.

The diphthong /oi/ is spelled *oy* and *oi,* as in *boy* and *oil.* The diphthong /ou/ is spelled *ou* and *ow,* as in *ground* and *now.*

A. Circle the word that rhymes with the word in bold type. Read aloud and write the word.

1. **shower**	shoulder	tower	toiled	_____
2. **choices**	cases	voices	vices	_____
3. **couch**	grouch	rich	cake	_____
4. **sound**	sour	pound	proud	_____
5. **town**	gown	grow	tow	_____
6. **enjoy**	away	joyful	destroy	_____
7. **found**	fried	food	mound	_____
8. **ouch**	pooch	pouch	lunch	_____
9. **clown**	clue	own	frown	_____
10. **mouth**	south	youth	mount	_____
11. **sound**	hound	should	hood	_____
12. **ground**	gold	bind	wound	_____
13. **employ**	annoy	before	empty	_____
14. **scowling**	bowling	howling	going	_____
15. **hour**	flower	fire	tour	_____

B. Write these spelling words in reverse alphabetical order:
thousand, noises, voyage, rejoice, cowboy.

16. _____   18. _____   20. _____

17. _____   19. _____

Name _____

> **Context clues** are other words in the text that help you figure out the meaning of an unfamiliar or multiple-meaning word. Context clues can be found in the same sentence as the unfamiliar word or in the same paragraph.
>
> There are different kinds of context clues to look for. The author may include a definition of the word. You might find a synonym, restatement, or antonym that reveals the word's meaning.

Read each passage. Underline the context clues that help you understand the word in bold and write the word's meaning on the line.

1. Scientists knew that pressure in the atmosphere was a reliable indicator of weather changes. If they could measure that air pressure and its changes, they could be better weather forecasters. Luckily, Evangelista Torricelli's **barometer**, invented in 1643, made this possible.

   _____

2. Many inventors only develop one or two ideas or devices in their lifetime. Thomas Edison, however, was a **prolific** inventor who received patents for over a thousand different inventions.

   _____

3. In the 1800s, a number of contraptions were invented to help people get to where they were going faster. One example is the **velocipede**, an early form of the bicycle with one or more wheels propelled by pedals.

   _____

   _____

4. **Cranes** have been around since the sixth century B.C. These simple machines used for lifting and transporting heavy objects were invented by the ancient Greeks to help construct tall buildings.

   _____

Copyright © McGraw Hill. Permission is granted to reproduce for classroom use.

Name _____

Read each selection from "Leonardo's Mechanical Knight." Underline the synonym that helps you figure out the meaning of each word in bold. Then write the definition of the word in bold on the line.

1. For months Leonardo had begged and **pleaded** with his father to get him a suit of armor.

   _____

2. He began working on the new invention in the barn that day. It wasn't long before the barn was overflowing with notes, tools, and equipment as he **toiled** away on the knight.

   _____

3. High atop a rickety ladder, Leonardo was deep in **concentration**. All his focus was on fixing the mechanical knight's arm, but it wasn't easy work.

   _____

4. No matter what he did, the knight's arm refused to lift! Leonardo frowned and **scowled** at it.

   _____

5. "It's a simple system of pulleys and cables," he said in a **humble** voice. "Don't be so modest. I've never seen anything like it before!"

   _____

Copyright © McGraw Hill. Permission is granted to reproduce for classroom use.

Name _____

> • **Homophones** are words that sound alike but have different spellings and meanings, such as *see* and *sea*.
>
> • Some frequently confused homophones are the possessive pronoun *their* and the contraction *they're*.

Read each sentence. Circle the correct word in parentheses and write it on the line to complete the sentence.

1. **(their / there)** The boys put on _____ coats and ran outside.

2. **(your / you're)** Did you drop _____ letter in the mailbox?

3. **(there / they're)** Did you go _____ last Saturday?

4. **(your / you're)** _____ lucky to be in the school play.

5. **(their / they're)** I think _____ coming to my party.

6. **(its / it's)** The log is slippery because _____ wet.

Write a paragraph about your pet, real or imaginary. Describe what it looks like and how it acts. Include at least three pronouns. Then edit your work.

_____

_____

_____

_____

Copyright © McGraw Hill. Permission is granted to reproduce for classroom use.

Name _____

> • **Homophones** are words that sound alike but have different spellings and meanings. Some pronouns are also homophones.
>
> • **Subject pronouns** are often used in conjunction with verbs to form contractions: *they are/they're*.
>
> • **Contractions** and **possessive pronouns** can be homophones, such as the contraction *it's* and the possessive pronoun *its*.

A. Read each sentence and circle the subject pronoun. On the line, write a contraction for the subject pronoun and verb.

1. They are about to get on the bus. _____

2. You are early for the movie. _____

3. It is in the box on the floor. _____

B. Underline the homophone that correctly completes each sentence.

4. Do you think (their / they're / there) at the park right now?

5. Is this (your / you're) backpack?

6. The cat licked (its / it's) paw over and over again.

Read this excerpt from "Genius." Circle the contraction. Then write your own sentence using the possessive pronoun homophone of the contraction you circled. Edit your work to make sure you used the correct homophone.

> The spiral notebook in my hand provides her quick relief.
> It tells her there's no danger of a break-in by a thief.
> "Okay," she says, then, props herself up vertically in bed.

_____

_____

Copyright © McGraw Hill. Permission is granted to reproduce for classroom use.

Name _____

- An apostrophe is used in a contraction to take the place of the missing letter or letters: *it is/it's*.
- An apostrophe should not be used with a possessive pronoun.

Rewrite each sentence. Correct any incorrect contractions and possessive pronouns.

1. I put my bag here and my parents stored their's at their feet.

_____

2. Youre going to love this new book that just came out.

_____

3. Do you think theyre going to be late for the show?

_____

4. I picked up the small suitcase by it's handle.

_____

5. Is that you'r aunt sitting with your mother in the audience?

_____

6. I think its funny that you and I have the same first name.

 **Go back through your writer's notebook and search for any possessive nouns or contractions you may have used. Check to make sure you have used the correct form. Correct any mistakes you may have made.**

Copyright © McGraw Hill. Permission is granted to reproduce for classroom use.

Name _____

- **Subject pronouns** are often used with verbs to form contractions.
- **Contractions** and **pronouns** can be homophones.
- An apostrophe is used in a contraction to take the place of the missing letter or letters.
- An apostrophe should not be used with a possessive pronoun.

Rewrite the paragraphs below, correcting mistakes in contractions and pronouns.

HANDWRITING CONNECTION

Remember to write legibly, with clear capital letters at the beginning of sentences and clear punctuation at the ends.

1. If your afraid of heights, do not go to the top of the Empire State Building in New York City. Its one of the tallest buildings in the world. Millions of people go there every year. They say theyre not afraid, but once they see how high it is they change there minds!

_____

_____

_____

2. Ana is happy today. Shes going to meet her pen pal, Marco. He's visiting with his family from Brazil. There good friends and write all the time. Ana thinks its exciting to finally meet Marco face to face! She can't wait to talk to him in person.

_____

_____

_____

Copyright © McGraw Hill. Permission is granted to reproduce for classroom use.

Name _____

Read the selection. Then choose the best answer to each question.

(1) _____ almost eight o'clock in the morning when my mom looks in my bedroom. (2) "Aren't you going to the park with _____ friends this morning? (3) You have to hurry because _____ waiting in the car!"

(4) The park is beautiful with _____ many lakes and trees. (5) We watch an alligator from a distance as it moves _____ tail back and forth. (6) I thought we brought snacks to eat, but _____ missing from the cooler. (7) _____ is a trail nearby, so we go on a long hike. (8) " _____ going to be so sore tomorrow!" my friends all say.

1. Which word best completes sentence 1?
   A It's
   B Its
   C They're
   D Their

2. Which word best completes sentence 2?
   F it's
   G its
   H your
   J you're

3. Which word best completes sentence 3?
   A they're
   B its
   C it's
   D there

4. Which word best completes sentence 4?
   F they're
   G it's
   H their
   J its

5. Which word best completes sentence 5?
   A they're
   B it's
   C there
   D its

6. Which word best completes sentence 6?
   A they're
   B its
   C their
   D it's

7. Which word best completes sentence 7?
   F They're
   G There
   H Their
   J Theirs

8. Which word best completes sentence 8?
   A Your
   B Theirs
   C You're
   D Theres

Copyright © McGraw Hill. Permission is granted to reproduce for classroom use.

Name _____

Fold back the paper along the dotted line. Use the blanks to write each word as it is read aloud. When you finish the test, unfold the paper. Use the list at the right to correct any spelling mistakes.

1. _____
2. _____
3. _____
4. _____
5. _____
6. _____
7. _____
8. _____
9. _____
10. _____
11. _____
12. _____
13. _____
14. _____
15. _____
16. _____
17. _____
18. _____
19. _____
20. _____

Review Words 21. _____
22. _____
23. _____

Challenge Words 24. _____
25. _____

1. caught
2. laws
3. drawn
4. strawberry
5. straw
6. awe
7. shawl
8. alter
9. halt
10. talking
11. walker
12. chalk
13. stalk
14. small
15. caller
16. squall
17. cough
18. fought
19. thought
20. false
21. south
22. pouch
23. annoy
24. wallpaper
25. awkward

Copyright © McGraw Hill. Permission is granted to reproduce for classroom use.

Name _____

The /ô/ vowel is pronounced *aw*, as in *awesome*. It can be spelled in the following ways: *augh*, as in *daughter*; *ough*, as in *sought*; *aw*, as in *claw*; *al*, as in *salt*; *all*, as in *tall*.

SPELLING TIP

The variant vowel /ô/ is **most often** spelled *aw*, as in *hawk*, and *au*, as in *haul*.

Read aloud and write the spelling words that contain each spelling pattern.

caught	straw	halt	stalk	cough
laws	awe	talking	small	fought
drawn	shawl	walker	caller	thought
strawberry	alter	chalk	squall	false

the *aw* sound spelled *augh*

1. _____

the *aw* sound spelled *ough*

2. _____

3. _____

4. _____

the *aw* sound spelled *aw*

5. _____

6. _____

7. _____

8. _____

9. _____

10. _____

the *aw* sound spelled *al*

11. _____

12. _____

13. _____

14. _____

15. _____

16. _____

17. _____

the *aw* sound spelled *all*

18. _____

19. _____

20. _____

 **Look through this week's selection for more words to sort. Create a word sort in your writer's notebook for a partner.**

Copyright © McGraw Hill. Permission is granted to reproduce for classroom use.

Name _____

The /ô/ vowel is pronounced *aw*, as in *awesome*. It can be spelled in the following ways: *augh*, as in *daughter*; *ough*, as in *sought*; *aw*, as in *claw*; *al*, as in *salt*; *all*, as in *tall*.

SPELLING TIP

The variant vowel /ô/ is **most often** spelled *aw*, as in *hawk*, and *au*, as in *haul*.

Read aloud and write the spelling words that contain each spelling pattern.

fault	straw	halt	awful	cough
laws	awe	talking	small	tall
draw	thaw	walk	caller	saw
taught	alter	chalk	raw	false

the *aw* sound spelled *ough*

1. _____

the *aw* sound spelled *au*

2. _____

the *aw* sound spelled *aw*

3. _____
4. _____
5. _____
6. _____
7. _____
8. _____
9. _____
10. _____

the *aw* sound spelled *al*

11. _____
12. _____
13. _____
14. _____
15. _____
16. _____

the *aw* sound spelled *all*

17. _____
18. _____
19. _____

the *aw* sound spelled *augh*

20. _____

Look through this week's selection for more words to sort. Create a word sort in your writer's notebook for a partner.

Copyright © McGraw Hill. Permission is granted to reproduce for classroom use.

Name _____

A. Read aloud and write the spelling words that contain each spelling pattern.

caught	applauded	halted	stalk	wallpaper
daughter	clause	because	malt	fought
dinosaur	shawl	vault	alteration	thoughtful
strawberry	audiences	sprawling	squall	sought

the *aw* sound spelled *augh*

1. _____

2. _____

the *aw* sound spelled *ough*

3. _____

4. _____

5. _____

the *aw* sound spelled *aw*

6. _____

7. _____

8. _____

the *aw* sound spelled *al*

9. _____

10. _____

11. _____

12. _____

the *aw* sound spelled *all*

13. _____

14. _____

the *aw* sound spelled *au*

15. _____

16. _____

17. _____

18. _____

19. _____

20. _____

B. Compare the words *caught* and *cough*. How are they alike? How are they different?

_____

_____

Look through this week's selection for more words to sort. Create a word sort in your writer's notebook for a partner.

Copyright © McGraw Hill. Permission is granted to reproduce for classroom use.

Name _____

caught	straw	halt	stalk	cough
laws	awe	talking	small	fought
drawn	shawl	walker	caller	thought
strawberry	alter	chalk	squall	false

A. Write the spelling word that is the antonym, or opposite, of each word below.

1. large _____

2. listening _____

3. agreed _____

4. stillness _____

5. violations _____

6. disinterest _____

7. receiver _____

8. remain _____

B. Write the spelling word that best completes each sentence.

9. The fishermen _____ a lot of fish today.

10. The teacher used _____ to write on the board.

11. I have a _____ even though my cold is gone.

12. The _____ does not use a car to get places.

13. I disagree with that _____ summary of what happened!

14. It is chilly outside, and I need a _____.

15. The old plant _____ was brown and dry.

16. A _____ tastes delicious with whipped cream.

17. The cars must _____ at red stoplights.

18. The picture of me was _____ to be funny-looking.

19. I _____ this book was very entertaining.

20. There was _____ on the floor in the barn.

Copyright © McGraw Hill. Permission is granted to reproduce for classroom use.

Name _____

Underline the six misspelled words in the paragraphs below. Write the words correctly on the lines.

"Be the first coller to answer our question correctly, and you'll win the jackpot!" the radio announcer said. I called in, and the announcer asked who was tawking. I gave him my name. He told me that to win I would have to answer a true or folse question.

I thouht I knew the answer, but they cought me off guard with a trick question. Even though I didn't win the jackpot, I got a smawl gift for playing. It was a gift certificate to my favorite movie theater. All in all, things turned out all right!

1. _____   4. _____

2. _____   5. _____

3. _____   6. _____

Writing Connection

Write about a goal or dream you would like to achieve. Use at least four words from the spelling list. Then use a dictionary to check your spelling of the high-frequency and spelling words.

_____

_____

_____

_____

_____

_____

_____

_____

Copyright © McGraw Hill. Permission is granted to reproduce for classroom use.

Name _____

Remember

The /ô/ vowel is pronounced *aw*, as in *awesome*. It can be spelled in the following ways: *augh*, as in *daughter*; *ough*, as in *sought*; *aw*, as in *claw*; *al*, as in *salt*; *all*, as in *tall*.

The variant vowel /ô/ is **most often** spelled aw, as in *hawk*, and *au*, as in *haul*.

A. Circle the spelling word in each row that rhymes with the word in bold type. Write the spelling word on the line. Then read the word aloud.

1. **hawk**	rake	chalk	black	_____
2. **thaw**	straw	that	stew	_____
3. **bought**	thought	moat	cot	_____
4. **yawn**	span	caw	drawn	_____
5. **taller**	filler	caller	tanner	_____
6. **off**	muff	tough	cough	_____
7. **gauze**	buzz	laws	says	_____
8. **walk**	wick	make	stalk	_____
9. **mall**	shawl	bill	malt	_____
10. **call**	toll	squall	tail	_____
11. **taught**	tough	fought	boat	_____
12. **saw**	awe	blew	bar	_____
13. **brought**	beet	crate	caught	_____
14. **crawl**	paw	small	pal	_____
15. **fault**	halt	hurt	heart	_____

B. Write these spelling words in reverse alphabetical order:
talking, false, alter, walker, strawberry.

16. _____   18. _____   20. _____

17. _____   19. _____

Copyright © McGraw Hill. Permission is granted to reproduce for classroom use.

Name _____

> Remember that **related words** have the same base word. The meaning of the word is changed slightly with the addition of prefixes, suffixes, and inflectional endings. Examine the following related words with the base word *note* and their meanings.
>
> **noted:** *noticed for a particular reason*
>
> **denoting:** *to be a name for; mean*
>
> **notable:** *worthy of notice*
>
> **notation:** *a quick note to assist memory*

How many words can you make with the base word *attain*? Use your knowledge of prefixes, suffixes, and inflectional endings to help you. Read your words aloud and try to guess what your words might mean. Then look up the meanings of your words in a print or online dictionary.

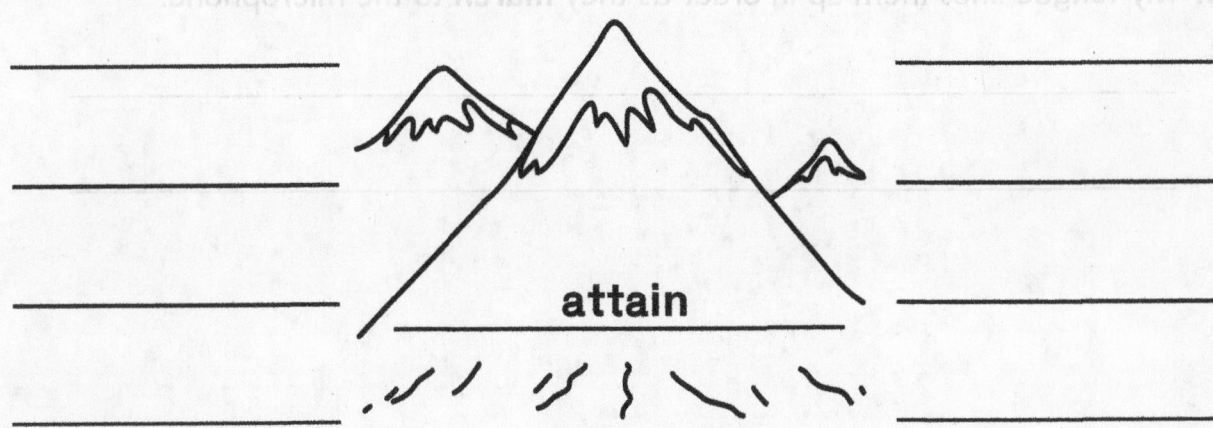

_____   _____

_____   _____

_____   attain   _____

_____   _____

Copyright © McGraw Hill. Permission is granted to reproduce for classroom use.

Name _____

Read each passage. Each word in bold has a different connotation in the poem than its usual denotation. Explain the connotation on the lines.

1. Letters **trip** over each other as they race to leave my mouth.

    _____

    _____

2. One last kid **sags** with his head in his hands. He is mouthing each letter as I say it.

3. My tongue lines them up in order as they **march** to the microphone:

    _____

    _____

    _____

Copyright © McGraw Hill. Permission is granted to reproduce for classroom use.

Name _____

> • An **adjective** is a word that describes a noun or a pronoun. It modifies, or limits or adds to, the meaning of the noun or pronoun: *blue car.*
>
> • An adjective usually comes before the noun or pronoun it describes. It also may follow a linking verb. *Anna seems sleepy.*
>
> • Adjectives are usually placed in order of *opinion, size, age,* and then *color*: *a good, large, old, yellow dog.*

Read each sentence and find the adjective or adjectives. Write all of the adjectives in the sentence on the line provided.

1. The garden has red roses. _____

2. Our playful friends play many games. _____

3. The waves looked dangerous. _____

4. Have you seen my little dog? _____

5. The big red truck drove down the busy road. _____

Read these sentences from "Your World Up Close." Circle two adjectives and underline the nouns they describe. Using the sentences as a model, write three sentences describing your favorite object. Review your work to make sure you have used adjectives correctly.

The light microscopes you use in school are weak and do not show much detail. An electron microscope is a much more powerful tool, and it allows scientists to see things we can't see with our own eyes.

_____

_____

_____

_____

Copyright © McGraw Hill. Permission is granted to reproduce for classroom use.

Name _____

- An **adjective** is a word that describes a noun or a pronoun. It can be formed from a noun.

- A **proper adjective** is formed from a proper noun. It begins with a capital letter: *The Franklin Science Museum.*

- Proper adjectives may describe languages, races, or nationalities: *Greek language, African American, Filipino.*

- Brand names are often proper adjectives: *Travel Right Luggage.*

Circle the proper adjective that is incorrectly written in each sentence. Write the proper adjective correctly on the line.

1. I ordered french fries with my hamburger. _____

2. She visited the jefferson Library yesterday. _____

3. There is nothing like the warm feel of florida sunshine. _____

4. It is an italian custom that has been in my family for years.

_____

5. The chinese exchange student spoke English well. _____

6. Her mother and father are both hispanic. _____

7. My favorite brand of socks is red Hot Socks. _____

8. The four Peaks Water company made a huge profit last year.

_____

 **In your writer's notebook, write a short paragraph describing a favorite place in your community. Include two proper adjectives. Check your work to make sure that you have used all the adjectives correctly.**

Name _____

> - Use **quotation marks** at the beginning and end of a direct quotation. *My mother called out to me, "Come downstairs for dinner!"*
>
> - Use a comma before the opening quotation mark if a sentence begins before the quote. Use a comma before the ending quotation mark if a sentence continues after the quote. *She said, "I made your favorite dish," as she stirred the pot.*
>
> - Use quotation marks before and after the titles of short works. *I read about it in an article called "Massaging Your Dog."*

Write each sentence correctly by adding commas and quotation marks where they belong.

1. My teacher just read us a short story called My Pet Gorilla.

   _____

2. My friend said, I can walk home with you after school.

   _____

3. "She is a good pet rabbit" my dad said about Lila.

   _____

4. My favorite short story is Under the Blue Sky.

   _____

5. He asked Can I go with you to the supermarket?

   _____

 **In your writer's notebook, write a short story that includes a conversation between two or more characters. Then edit your work for correct use of quotation marks and commas.**

Copyright © McGraw Hill. Permission is granted to reproduce for classroom use.

Name _____

- An **adjective** is a word that describes a noun or a pronoun. It can be formed from a noun.

- A **proper adjective** is formed from a proper noun. It begins with a capital letter.

- Use **quotation marks** at the beginning and end of a direct quotation and before and after the titles of short works.

Rewrite the paragraphs below, correcting mistakes in adjectives and quotations.

1. Next week, I will go to my first spanish class. It will be at the riverwood Center in town. My mom said I'm so proud of you for learning a new language. I am worried though, since there are still many english words that I don't understand!

COMMON ERRORS
Remember that only short works need quotation marks. Longer works, such as books or newspapers, need to be underlined or italicized.

_____

_____

_____

_____

2. I love the japanese bookstore that just opened in the mall. It is Small, but it has interesting books. I bought a book of short stories there. My favorite story in the book is The Warrior. "That is my favorite one, too" said the manager of the bookstore.

_____

_____

_____

_____

Copyright © McGraw Hill. Permission is granted to reproduce for classroom use.

Name _____

Read the paragraph. Then choose the best answer to each question.

(1) Do you live near the _____ coast? (2) My family and I visited there once one _____ summer. (3) We were all so _____ to be going on a trip! (4) The _____ beaches were pink and white. (5) The trees were _____ ! (6) We heard so many languages being spoken around us, like _____ . (7) Dad insisted that we stop by a _____ restaurant for sausages.

(8) I think next summer, we are going to go to _____ .

1. Which word fits best in sentence 1?

   A left

   B Pacific

   C Left

   D pacific

2. Which word fits best in sentence 2?

   F National

   G red

   H hot

   J July

3. Which word fits best in sentence 3?

   A vacation

   B terrible

   C excited

   D long

4. Which word fits best in sentence 4?

   F sandy

   G pink

   H white

   J summer

5. Which word fits best in sentence 5?

   A enormous

   B Enormous

   C eastern

   D Eastern

6. Which word fits best in sentence 6?

   F spanish and mandarin

   G Spanish and mandarin

   H spanish and Mandarin

   J Spanish and Mandarin

7. Which word fits best in sentence 7?

   A chinese

   B German

   C french

   D Open

8. Which word fits best in sentence 8?

   F new England

   G new england

   H New England

   J New england

Copyright © McGraw Hill. Permission is granted to reproduce for classroom use.

Name _____

Fold back the paper along the dotted line. Use the blanks to write each word as it is read aloud. When you finish the test, unfold the paper. Use the list at the right to correct any spelling mistakes.

1. _____
2. _____
3. _____
4. _____
5. _____
6. _____
7. _____
8. _____
9. _____
10. _____
11. _____
12. _____
13. _____
14. _____
15. _____
16. _____
17. _____
18. _____
19. _____
20. _____

Review Words
21. _____
22. _____
23. _____

Challenge Words
24. _____
25. _____

1. blanket
2. blossom
3. dipper
4. distant
5. foggy
6. fossil
7. member
8. nodded
9. planner
10. plastic
11. rumbles
12. slender
13. summer
14. swallow
15. tablet
16. thriller
17. traffic
18. welcome
19. willow
20. witness
21. talking
22. drawn
23. shawl
24. cupboard
25. friendly

Copyright © McGraw Hill Permission is granted to reproduce for classroom use.

Name _____

Look at the word *chin. Chin* is one syllable with one vowel sound. The syllable ends in a consonant, the letter *n.* Syllables ending in a consonant are called **closed syllables**. Most closed syllables have a short vowel sound.

DECODING WORDS

When a word has two consonants in the middle, divide the word between the consonants to sound it out. For example, *bas-ket.*

Read aloud and write each word under its spelling pattern.

blanket	foggy	planner	summer	traffic
blossom	fossil	plastic	swallow	welcome
dipper	member	rumbles	tablet	willow
distant	nodded	slender	thriller	witness

words with double consonants

1. _____
2. _____
3. _____
4. _____
5. _____
6. _____
7. _____
8. _____
9. _____
10. _____
11. _____

words with different consonants

12. _____
13. _____
14. _____
15. _____
16. _____
17. _____
18. _____
19. _____
20. _____

Work with a partner to find more words that contain closed syllables. Record the words you find in your writer's notebook.

Copyright © McGraw Hill. Permission is granted to reproduce for classroom use.

Name _____

> Look at the word *chin. Chin* is one syllable with one vowel sound. The syllable ends in a consonant, the letter *n.* Syllables ending in a consonant are called **closed syllables**. Most closed syllables have a short vowel sound.

DECODING WORDS

When a word has two consonants in the middle, divide the word between the consonants to sound it out. For example, *bas-ket.*

Read aloud and write each word under its spelling pattern.

dinner	foggy	planner	summer	traffic
finger	fossil	plastic	swallow	welcome
dipper	member	kitten	pillow	willow
hello	holly	lesson	thriller	problem

words with double consonants

1. _____   6. _____   11. _____

2. _____   7. _____   12. _____

3. _____   8. _____   13. _____

4. _____   9. _____   14. _____

5. _____   10. _____   15. _____

words with different consonants

16. _____   19. _____

17. _____   20. _____

18. _____

Work with a partner to find more words that contain closed syllables. Record the words you find in your writer's notebook.

Copyright © McGraw Hill. Permission is granted to reproduce for classroom use.

Name _____

A. Read aloud and write each word under its spelling pattern.

blanket	foggy	planner	magnet	traffic
blossom	fossil	plastic	swallow	windows
dipper	canyon	rumbles	palmetto	willow
distant	comfort	slender	perhaps	witness

words with double consonants

1. _____

2. _____

3. _____

4. _____

5. _____

6. _____

7. _____

8. _____

9. _____

words with different consonants

10. _____

11. _____

12. _____

13. _____

14. _____

15. _____

16. _____

17. _____

18. _____

19. _____

20. _____

B. Compare the words *blossom* and *fossil*. How are they alike and different?

_____

_____

_____

 **Work with a partner to find more words that contain closed syllables. Record the words you find in your writer's notebook.**

Copyright © McGraw Hill. Permission is granted to reproduce for classroom use.

Name _____

blanket	foggy	planner	summer	traffic
blossom	fossil	plastic	swallow	welcome
dipper	member	rumbles	tablet	willow
distant	nodded	slender	thriller	witness

A. An *analogy* is a statement that compares sets of words. Write the spelling word to complete each analogy below.

1. *Builder* is to *maker* as *organizer* is to _____

2. *Curvy* is to *straight* as *clear* is to _____

3. *Up* is to *down* as *goodbye* is to _____

4. *Jet* is to *roars* as *truck* is to _____

5. *Coat* is to *jacket* as *flower* is to _____

6. *Empty* is to *full* as *near* is to _____

7. *Dog* is to *poodle* as *tree* is to _____

8. *Sea* is to *ocean* as *quilt* is to _____

B. Write the spelling word that matches each definition below.

9. part of a group _____

15. thin _____

10. something to write on _____

16. a suspenseful story _____

11. a warm or hot season _____

17. moved head up and down _____

12. manmade material _____

18. many vehicles in one area _____

13. to move throat muscles _____

19. remains from the past _____

14. one who sees something _____

20. a cuplike scoop _____

Copyright © McGraw Hill. Permission is granted to reproduce for classroom use.

Name _____

Underline the six misspelled words in the paragraphs below. Write the words correctly on the lines.

Lucy read the poster with great interest. It said, "Wellcome to the Habitat Museum! We hope you will join us this sumer. We will meet every Saturday under the wilow tree in front of the library."

Lucy was excited to become a new memmber of the museum club. The poster said that there would be a movie at the museum next Saturday. It is about a hiker who is a wittnes to a robbery. The stolen item is a dinosaur fosil. Lucy couldn't wait to see it!

1. _____   **4.** _____

2. _____   **5.** _____

3. _____   **6.** _____

Writing Connection

Write about a club that you have joined or would like to join. Use at least four words from the spelling list. As you check your work, be sure that you have spelled the high-frequency words correctly.

_____

_____

_____

_____

_____

_____

_____

_____

_____

_____

Copyright © McGraw Hill. Permission is granted to reproduce for classroom use.

Name _____

Remember

Syllables that end in a consonant are called **closed syllables**. Most closed syllables have a short vowel sound.

blanket	foggy	planner	summer	traffic
blossom	fossil	plastic	swallow	welcome
dipper	member	rumbles	tablet	willow
distant	nodded	slender	thriller	witness

Fill in the missing letters to form a spelling word. Write the word on the line. Then read the word aloud.

1. sle __ __ er _____

2. tra __ __ ic _____

3. fo __ __ il _____

4. bla __ __ et _____

5. wi __ __ ow _____

6. pla __ __ er _____

7. swa __ __ ow _____

8. di __ __ ant _____

9. we __ __ ome _____

10. pla __ __ ic _____

11. fo __ __ y _____

12. thri __ __ er _____

13. no __ __ ed _____

14. su __ __ er _____

15. ru __ __ __ es _____

16. wi __ __ ess _____

17. blo __ __ om _____

18. ta __ __ et _____

19. me __ __ er _____

20. di __ __ er _____

Copyright © McGraw Hill. Permission is granted to reproduce for classroom use.

Name _____

Content words are used to write about fields of study. In this unit, you will find content words related to science and technology, such as *electron microscope, magnification,* and *photomicrograph.* Use context clues, dictionaries, electronic resources, and your knowledge of Greek and Latin roots to help you understand the meanings of these words.

Search classroom texts, newspapers, and magazines for content words related to the tools scientists use. Write the words below.

Science and Technology Words

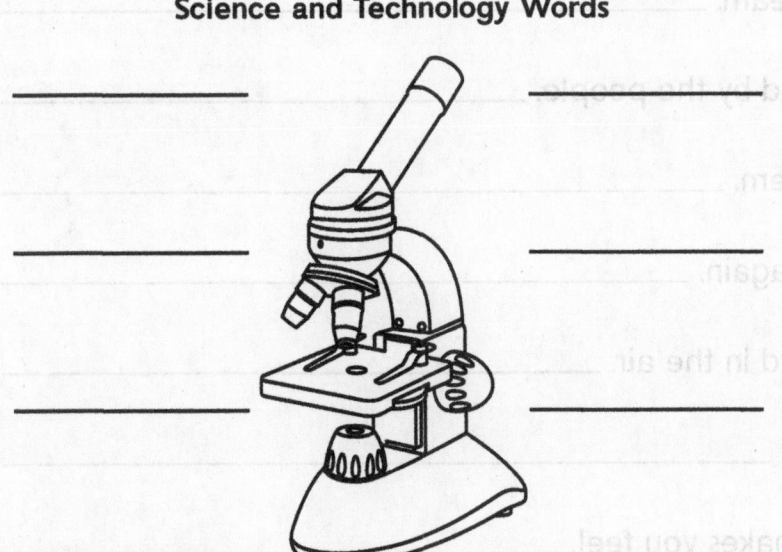

_____ _____

_____ _____

_____

_____

_____ _____

CONNECT TO CONTENT

"Your World Up Close" describes the technology used to magnify objects, such as snowflakes, fingerprints, and skin cells, to thousands of times their actual size. It also explains how scientists use these magnified images. The author uses content words to tell about these topics.

Circle two words that you were able to define by using context clues. Write the words and their meanings on the lines.

_____

_____

_____

_____

_____

Copyright © McGraw Hill. Permission is granted to reproduce for classroom use.

Name _____

Write the vocabulary word from the box that answers each riddle below.

attain	commitment	hovering	connotation
gleaming	democracy	triumph	denotation
dangling	technology	stanza	repetition

1. You'll find me in a dictionary. _____

2. I'm felt by the winning team. _____

3. I'm a government for and by the people. _____

4. I'm a paragraph in a poem. _____

5. I'm done over and over again. _____

6. I describe a hummingbird in the air. _____

7. I'm a promise you make. _____

8. I describe how a word makes you feel. _____

9. I'm a new kind of phone. _____

10. I'm something you hope to do with a goal. _____

11. I describe polished silver or gold. _____

12. I'm what an acrobat does high above. _____

Copyright © McGraw Hill. Permission is granted to reproduce for classroom use.

Name _____

- An **article** is a type of adjective. It comes before the noun it describes.

- The article *the* identifies a particular person, place, or thing. It refers to both singular and plural nouns: *the kitten, the kittens.*

- The articles *a* and *an* refer to a general person, place, or thing. They refer to singular nouns only. Use *a* before a noun that begins with a consonant, such as *a carrot*. Use *an* before a noun that begins with a vowel, such as *an eagle*.

Read each sentence and circle the article. On the line, write S if the related noun is singular. Write P if the noun is plural.

1. We saw a film in science class today. _____

2. These are the people I was telling you about. _____

3. Did you go to see the movie that I suggested? _____

4. I ate an omelet this morning. _____

5. My sisters are the captains of their cheerleading squad. _____

Reading/Writing Connection

Read this excerpt from "The Incredible Shrinking Potion." Underline the articles. Then write two sentences about a science experiment you would like to do. Include at least three articles. Then check your work.

It began as a simple science project. It was only one week ago that Isabel, Mariela, and Hector were working on a shrinking potion that would amaze everyone at the science fair.

_____

_____

_____

Copyright © McGraw Hill. Permission is granted to reproduce for classroom use.

Name _____

> • The words *a, an,* and *the* are special adjectives called **articles**. They identify people, places, or things.
>
> • *This, that, these,* and *those* are **demonstrative adjectives**. They show whether the related noun is singular or plural. They also show if an object is close to or far from the speaker or writer: *this chair, that desk, these pencils.*
>
> • *This* and *that* refer to singular nouns, such as *this car* and *that truck. These* and *those* refer to plural nouns, such as *these books* and *those rulers.*

Circle the correct demonstrative adjective in parentheses to complete each sentence. On the line, write *S* if the related noun is singular. Write *P* if the noun is plural.

1. I took (this / these) napkin for myself. _____

2. Are (that / those) your mother's earrings? _____

3. Put this crate here and put (that / those) crate there. _____

4. Get me placemats that look like (that / these) two. _____

5. What type of material is (that / those) scarf made from?

_____

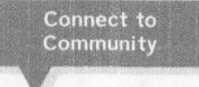

Talk to a parent or another trusted adult about a special hobby they have. Then write a paragraph in your writer's notebook about the conversation. Include at least three articles and two demonstrative adjectives. Then check your work for adjective-noun agreement.

Copyright © McGraw Hill. Permission is granted to reproduce for classroom use.

Name _____

- Use *a* before a word if the word begins with a consonant sound. Use *an* before a word if the word begins with a vowel sound.

- Do not use *a* or *an* before a plural noun.

- *This* and *that* refer to singular nouns. *These* and *those* refer to plural nouns.

Read each sentence. Circle the article or demonstrative adjective that is incorrect. Explain why it is incorrect on the line.

1. Did you read a books I lent you for the weekend?

   _____

2. Remi did not pick those apple from the tree.

   _____

3. She is a eager student who wants to learn.

   _____

4. Give these cards to me and put that flowers over there.

   _____

5. I have an oboe and an flute in my bedroom.

   _____

 **In your writer's notebook, write about a hobby you are interested in learning more about. Include at least three articles and two demonstrative adjectives. Underline the articles and circle the demonstrative adjectives. After you have completed writing, pair up with a partner. Write down these instructions in your writer's notebook. Take turns reading the instructions aloud. Then restate them in your own words. Did you follow all the instructions?**

Copyright © McGraw Hill. Permission is granted to reproduce for classroom use.

Name _____

- The words *a*, *an*, and *the* are special adjectives called **articles**. They identify people, places, or things. Use *a* and *an* for singular nouns. Use *the* for singular or plural nouns.

- Use *a* before a word if the word begins with a consonant sound. Use *an* before a word if the word begins with a vowel sound.

- *This*, *that*, *these*, and *those* are **demonstrative adjectives**. Use *this* and *that* for singular nouns. Use *these* and *those* for plural nouns.

Rewrite the sentences below, correcting mistakes in articles and demonstrative adjectives.

HANDWRITING CONNECTION

Be sure not to press down too hard when writing so that your strokes are smooth and sure.

1. I will paint an picture of that clouds in the sky.

   _____

2. This grades show that he is an bright student.

   _____

3. I watched the bird fly over those hill.

   _____

4. The elephant is a largest land mammal.

   _____

5. Can I order this doughnuts for an party on Saturday?

   _____

6. I have to walk these dog after school when I get off a bus.

   _____

Copyright © McGraw Hill. Permission is granted to reproduce for classroom use.

Name _____

Read the student draft. Then choose the best answer to each question.

(1) "Where are these items in the store?" she asked the clerk as she pointed to a list in her hand. (2) Sabrina watched <u>an</u> wheels of the clerk's mind work quickly to plan a response.

(3) She was planning to buy an headphones today, along with a loaf of bread. (4) Then the clerk led her to <u>the</u> umbrellas she needed. (5) <u>That</u> gloves over there were her favorite color!

(6) As she loaded an bag into her car, she was glad she had found everything she wanted.

1. How many articles are in sentence 1?

   A one

   B two

   C three

   D four

2. What is the best word to use in place of the underlined word in sentence 2?

   F a

   G those

   H the

   J Make no change.

3. Which word is an error in sentence 3?

   A a

   B an

   C was

   D with

4. What is the best word to use in place of the underlined word in sentence 4?

   F an

   G these

   H those

   J Make no change.

5. What is the best word to use in place of the underlined word in sentence 5?

   A This

   B These

   C Those

   D Make no change.

6. What is the best way to write the beginning of sentence 6?

   F As she loaded a bag into . . .

   G As she loaded this bag into . . .

   H As she loaded that bag into . . .

   J Make no change.

Copyright © McGraw Hill. Permission is granted to reproduce for classroom use.

Name _____

Fold back the paper along the dotted line. Use the blanks to write each word as it is read aloud. When you finish the test, unfold the paper. Use the list at the right to correct any spelling mistakes.

1. _____
2. _____
3. _____
4. _____
5. _____
6. _____
7. _____
8. _____
9. _____
10. _____
11. _____
12. _____
13. _____
14. _____
15. _____
16. _____
17. _____
18. _____
19. _____
20. _____

Review Words 21. _____
22. _____
23. _____

Challenge Words 24. _____
25. _____

1. famous
2. radar
3. razor
4. vacancy
5. beside
6. beyond
7. defend
8. delay
9. demand
10. prevent
11. secret
12. veto
13. bison
14. diver
15. cider
16. silence
17. clover
18. spoken
19. stolen
20. tulip
21. swallow
22. plastic
23. rumbles
24. request
25. sequence

Copyright © McGraw Hill. Permission is granted to reproduce for classroom use.

Name _____

> Look at the syllable *mo* in the word *motor. Mo* is one syllable with one vowel sound. It ends with a vowel. Syllables ending in a vowel are called **open syllables**. Most open syllables have a long vowel sound.

DECODING WORDS

> *Veto* has two open syllables: *ve-to.* An open syllable ends in a vowel and has a long vowel sound. So, blend /vē/ /tō/.

Write and read aloud spelling words that contain matching first-syllable sounds.

clover	cider	tulip	vacancy	secret
radar	stolen	prevent	diver	spoken
bison	defend	famous	beside	beyond
demand	delay	veto	silence	razor

long *e* sound

1. _____
2. _____
3. _____
4. _____
5. _____
6. _____
7. _____
8. _____

long *a* sound

9. _____
10. _____
11. _____
12. _____

long *o* sound

13. _____
14. _____
15. _____

long *i* sound

16. _____
17. _____
18. _____
19. _____

long *u* sound

20. _____

Work with a partner to find more words that contain open syllables. Record the words you find in your writer's notebook.

Copyright © McGraw Hill. Permission is granted to reproduce for classroom use.

Name _____

> Look at the syllable *mo* in the word *motor. Mo* is one syllable with one vowel sound. It ends with a vowel. Syllables ending in a vowel are called **open syllables**. Most open syllables have a long vowel sound.

DECODING WORDS

Veto has two open syllables: *ve-to.* An open syllable ends in a vowel and has a long vowel sound. So, blend /vē/ /tō/.

Write and read aloud spelling words that contain matching first-syllable sounds.

music	ruby	tulip	major	secret
radar	stolen	spicy	tiny	spoken
spider	fever	basic	paper	return
meter	delay	pilot	truly	razor

long *e* sound

1. _____
2. _____
3. _____
4. _____
5. _____

long *a* sound

6. _____
7. _____
8. _____
9. _____
10. _____

long *i* sound

13. _____
14. _____
15. _____
16. _____

long *o* sound

11. _____
12. _____

long *u* sound/*ü* sound

17. _____
18. _____
19. _____
20. _____

Work with a partner to find more words that contain open syllables. Record the words you find in your writer's notebook.

Copyright © McGraw Hill. Permission is granted to reproduce for classroom use.

Name _____

Write the spelling words that contain the matching sounds in the first syllable. Then read the word aloud.

rehearse	cider	humid	vacancy	secretive
radar	finance	prevention	decay	spoken
bison	defense	famous	weasel	basic
demanding	delayed	vetoed	silence	razor

long e sound

1. _____

2. _____

3. _____

4. _____

5. _____

6. _____

7. _____

8. _____

9. _____

long a sound

10. _____

11. _____

12. _____

13. _____

14. _____

long o sound

15. _____

long i sound

16. _____

17. _____

18. _____

19. _____

long u sound

20. _____

 **Work with a partner to find more words that contain open syllables. Record the words you find in your writer's notebook.**

Copyright © McGraw Hill. Permission is granted to reproduce for classroom use.

Name _____

famous	beside	demand	bison	clover
radar	beyond	prevent	diver	spoken
razor	defend	secret	cider	stolen
vacancy	delay	veto	silence	tulip

A. Write the spelling word that has the same meaning as each word or phrase below.

1. next to _____

2. juice _____

3. refuse _____

4. opening _____

5. to stop _____

6. unknown _____

7. to pause _____

8. outside the limits _____

9. to request firmly _____

10. a lack of noise _____

B. Write the spelling word that best completes each sentence.

11. The detectives searched for the diamond that was _____.

12. Be careful that you do not cut yourself with that sharp _____.

13. We watched the _____ swim under the surface of the water.

14. The _____ is a sign of spring in many parts of the world.

15. The police officer used _____ to find out who was speeding.

16. Huge herds of _____ used to fill the plains of the Old West.

17. Those were the greatest words ever _____!

18. The guard dog's purpose was to _____ the property.

19. A four-leaf _____ is a sign of good luck.

20. The _____ singer wore a floppy hat as a disguise.

Name _____

Underline the six misspelled words in the paragraphs below. Write the words correctly on the lines.

Dear Ms. Fisher,

    I know you are a faymous actress, but I hope you'll read my letter. I wanted to tell you that I love your movies. Your acting is beeyond belief! I bet that everyone would love to know what your seecret is to such great acting.

    I just saw your last movie in which you were a deep sea divver. It must have been hard to prepare for that role. Not only did you have to swim, but you had to deefend yourself against the bad guys. I really liked the undersea raddar that you used to catch them! Please continue to make great movies!

Sincerely,

Tamika Green

1. _____ 4. _____

2. _____ 5. _____

3. _____ 6. _____

Imagine that you are acting in a movie. Write to describe the movie. Use at least four words from the spelling list.

_____

_____

_____

_____

_____

Copyright © McGraw Hill. Permission is granted to reproduce for classroom use.

Name _____

Remember

Syllables that end in a vowel are called **open syllables**. Most open syllables have a long vowel sound.

famous	beside	demand	bison	clover
radar	beyond	prevent	diver	spoken
razor	defend	secret	cider	stolen
vacancy	delay	veto	silence	tulip

A. Fill in the missing letters of each word to form a spelling word. Then read the word aloud.

1. s __ __ ence

2. b __ __ ond

3. cl __ __ er

4. r __ __ or

5. d __ __ er

6. t __ __ ip

7. v __ __ o

8. b __ __ ide

9. pr __ __ ent

10. st __ __ en

11. f __ __ ous

12. c __ __ er

13. d __ __ ay

14. r __ __ ar

15. s __ __ __ et

16. d __ __ end

17. sp __ __ en

18. v __ __ ancy

19. d __ __ and

20. b __ __ on

B. Write these spelling words in alphabetical order. Alphabetize them to the third letter: *clover, delay, cider, defend, demand.*

21. _____

22. _____

23. _____

24. _____

25. _____

Copyright © McGraw Hill. Permission is granted to reproduce for classroom use.

Name _____

> **Homophones** are words that sound the same but have different spellings and meanings. Pay attention to how a homophone is used to help figure out its meaning. Below are some examples. What is the meaning of each of these words?
>
> **bored/board**　　**lesson/lessen**　　**dough/doe**　　**base/bass**

This box of crackers contains ten homophones with the wrong spelling. Cross out each word and write the correct homophone. Use a dictionary to check your spelling.

Crunchy Oat Crisps

Now with 50% moor crisps!

We make our healthy crisps with oat flower and other hole grains. Then we bake them in the son until they have just the write crunch!

Enjoy our grate new flavors!

Cheerful Cheddar will satisfy all yore cheesy cravings—and put a smile on your face.

Happy Herbs has a delightful blend of rosemary, basil, and time that will tickle your taste buds.

Sunny Salted Caramel gives you the best of both worlds. Can't decide between salty and suite? Now you don't have to!

150 Calories Per Serving　　Net Wait: 9 ounces

Copyright © McGraw Hill. Permission is granted to reproduce for classroom use.

Name _____

A. Draw lines to match each word in Column 1 with an antonym in Column 2.

Column 1   **Column 2**

1. identical   a. simple

2. reliable   b. maintain

3. entire   c. different

4. alter   d. part

5. specific   e. general

6. detailed   f. unsteady

B. Rewrite each sentence below using an antonym for the underlined word.

1. We stayed to watch the **entire** movie.

_____

2. My mother did **not alter** the soup recipe.

_____

3. The math lesson was so **detailed** that I had to take notes.

_____

Copyright © McGraw Hill. Permission is granted to reproduce for classroom use.

Name _____

> • **Comparative adjectives** compare two things. They usually end in *-er* or include the word *more* or *less*: *smarter, more famous.*
>
> • **Superlative adjectives** compare more than two things. They usually end in *-est* or include the word *most* or *least*: *tallest, most wonderful.*

Complete each sentence by circling the correct comparative or superlative adjective in parentheses.

1. My hair is (longer, longest) than yours.

2. This flower is the (prettier, prettiest) of all of them.

3. The turtle in the back is the (slower, slowest) in the group.

4. My father is (stronger, strongest) than I am.

5. This lake is the (more, most) peaceful place I have ever been.

6. I am (happier, happiest) to go here than my brother is.

7. It is (less, least) sunny today than yesterday.

8. The summer is (warmer, warmest) than the winter.

9. This is the (heavier, heaviest) piece of furniture in the house.

10. She is the (smarter, smartest) girl in our school.

Read this excerpt from "Sadie's Game." Then rewrite the sentence so that it contains a superlative adjective.

She had never seen a crowd express such disappointment before.

_____

_____

Copyright © McGraw Hill. Permission is granted to reproduce for classroom use.

Name _____

> • **Comparative** and **superlative adjectives** compare things. They usually end in -er or -est, or they include the words more/most or less/least.
>
> • The comparative form of good is better: a better job. The superlative form of good is best: the best restaurant.
>
> • The comparative form of bad is worse: a worse headache than yesterday. The superlative form of bad is worst: the worst day.

A. Complete each sentence with better or best, based on whether a comparative or superlative form is needed.

1. This meal was _____ than the last one we ate.

2. You are the _____ friend I could ever have.

3. He had the _____ score in the entire class.

4. Tomorrow's weather will be _____ than today's.

B. Complete each sentence with worse or worst, based on whether a comparative or superlative form is needed.

5. That is the _____ smell in the world!

6. I did _____ on the test than I thought.

7. Khalil is _____ at English than math.

8. This photo is the _____ of the three.

> In your writer's notebook, write about a genre of books that you enjoy reading. Include at least five comparative or superlative adjectives. Then review your work to make sure that you used the correct forms of the adjectives.

Copyright © McGraw Hill. Permission is granted to reproduce for classroom use.

Name _____

> • A **greeting** is a polite way to start a letter. Greetings are capitalized and followed by a comma or a colon. Titles such as *Mr.* and *Mrs.* are abbreviated : *Dear Mr. Edwards.*
>
> • A **closing** is a word or phrase that ends a letter. It is usually followed by a comma and the letter writer's signature: *Sincerely, Elsie.*

Rewrite each letter greeting and closing using correct capitalization and punctuation.

1. To Whom It May concern: _____

2. sincerely, _____

3. Dear Mister Edwards _____

4. to the Store Manager; _____

5. Love always _____

Writing Connection

Write a letter to your best friend about any topic you choose. Edit your work to make sure that your greeting is capitalized and followed by a comma or a colon. Check to see that you have included a closing phrase followed by a comma and your signature.

_____

_____

_____

_____

_____

_____

_____

Copyright © McGraw Hill. Permission is granted to reproduce for classroom use.

Name _____

- **Comparative** and **superlative adjectives** compare things. They usually end in *-er* or *-est*, or they include the words *more/most* or *less/least*.

- The comparative and superlative forms of *good* are *better* and *best*. The comparative and superlative forms of *bad* are *worse* and *worst*.

- A **greeting** is a polite way to start a letter. It is capitalized and followed by a comma or a colon. A **closing** is a word or phrase that ends a letter. It is usually followed by a comma and the letter writer's signature.

Rewrite the letter below, correcting mistakes in comparative and superlative adjectives as well as in the letter's greeting and closing.

Dear Mister woodhouse

I am writing to say that I love your garden. My garden is much worst. Your tomatoes are redder and your cucumbers are biggest. How do you do it? I'm sure you know the goodest gardening secrets in the world! You are the nicer person I know. Could you help me with my garden?

Your neighbor,

Jeremy

> **HANDWRITING CONNECTION**
>
> Be sure to write your answer legibly in cursive. Remember to leave appropriate spaces between words.

_____

_____

_____

_____

_____

_____

_____

Copyright © McGraw Hill. Permission is granted to reproduce for classroom use.

Name _____

Read the student draft and look for any corrections that need to be made. Then choose the best answer to each question.

(1) These are the worse pancakes I have ever eaten. (2) They are flat than my mother's pancakes. (3) My mom's pancakes are the fluffiest I have ever seen!

(4) I think that breakfast time is the better time of all three meals. (5) But with these terrible pancakes, it's looking like the worst! (6) Maybe tomorrow I will make more betterer pancakes.

1. What change, if any, needs to be made in sentence 1?

   A Change *worse* to **badder**

   B Change *worse* to **worst**

   C Change *worse* to **worser**

   D Make no change.

2. What is the correct way to write sentence 2?

   F They are flatter than my mother's pancakes.

   G They are flattest than my mother's pancakes.

   H They are flatterest than my mother's pancakes.

   J Make no change.

3. What change, if any, should be made in sentence 3?

   A Change *fluffiest* to **fluffier**

   B Change *fluffiest* to **fluffy**

   C Change *fluffiest* to **best fluffy**

   D Make no change.

4. What is the correct way to write sentence 4?

   F I think that breakfast time is the bestest time of all three meals.

   G I think that breakfast time is the better time of all three meals.

   H I think that breakfast time is the goodest time of all three meals.

   J I think that breakfast time is the best time of all three meals.

5. What change, if any, needs to be made to sentence 5?

   A Change *worst* to **worse**

   B Change *worst* to **baddest**

   C Change *worst* to **worser**

   D Make no change.

6. What change, if any, should be made in sentence 6?

   F Change *more betterer* to **best**

   G Change *more betterer* to **better**

   H Change *more betterer* to **more good**

   J Make no change.

Copyright © McGraw Hill. Permission is granted to reproduce for classroom use.

Name _____

Fold back the paper along the dotted line. Use the blanks to write each word as it is read aloud. When you finish the test, unfold the paper. Use the list at the right to correct any spelling mistakes.

1. _____
2. _____
3. _____
4. _____
5. _____
6. _____
7. _____
8. _____
9. _____
10. _____
11. _____
12. _____
13. _____
14. _____
15. _____
16. _____
17. _____
18. _____
19. _____
20. _____

Review Words 21. _____
22. _____
23. _____

Challenge Words 24. _____
25. _____

1. brain
2. staircase
3. domain
4. praise
5. trainer
6. oatmeal
7. beneath
8. repeat
9. reveal
10. increase
11. sneak
12. boast
13. afloat
14. croak
15. compound
16. discount
17. speed
18. sleeve
19. sheep
20. baboon
21. secret
22. diver
23. spoken
24. employee
25. reindeer

Copyright © McGraw Hill. Permission is granted to reproduce for classroom use.

Name _____

> When two vowels appear together in a word such as *lean*, they often form one vowel sound. In the word *lean*, the vowels *e* and *a* make a team to form the long *e* sound. These are called **vowel teams**. A syllable that includes a vowel team is a **vowel-team syllable**.

DECODING WORDS

> *Eighteen* has two vowel team spellings--*eigh* and *ee*. Vowel team spellings, like the digraph *ee*, must stay in the same syllable. Blend the syllables together: *eigh-teen*, /ā/ /tēn/.

Read aloud and write the spelling words that contain the matching vowel team.

croak	oatmeal	beneath	domain	repeat
brain	speed	praise	reveal	sneak
baboon	staircase	sheep	compound	afloat
sleeve	discount	boast	increase	trainer

ea

1. _____
2. _____
3. _____
4. _____
5. _____

oo

6. _____

ai

7. _____
8. _____
9. _____
10. _____
11. _____

oa

12. _____
13. _____
14. _____

ee

15. _____
16. _____
17. _____

ou

18. _____
19. _____

oa and ea

20. _____

Work with a partner to find multisyllabic words that contain vowel teams. Record the words you find in your writer's notebook. Separate vowel-team syllable words from multisyllabic VV syllables.

Copyright © McGraw Hill. Permission is granted to reproduce for classroom use.

Name _____

When two vowels appear together in a word such as *lean*, they often form one vowel sound. In the word *lean*, the vowels *e* and *a* make a team to form the long *e* sound. These are called **vowel teams**. A syllable that includes a vowel team is a **vowel-team syllable**.

DECODING WORDS

Eighteen has two vowel team spellings--*eigh* and *ee*. Vowel team spellings, like the digraph *ee*, must stay in the same syllable. Blend the syllables together: *eigh-teen*, /ā/ /tēn/.

Read aloud and write the spelling words that contain the matching vowel team.

discount	balloon	repeat	oatmeal	remain
tree	bait	speed	between	sneak
beneath	compound	trainer	reveal	brain
domain	staircase	boat	steam	defeat

ea

1. _____
2. _____
3. _____
4. _____
5. _____
6. _____

ai

8. _____
9. _____
10. _____
11. _____
12. _____
13. _____

ee

15. _____
16. _____
17. _____

ou

18. _____
19. _____

oo

7. _____

oa

14. _____

oa and ea

20. _____

Work with a partner to find multisyllabic words that contain vowel teams. Record the words you find in your writer's notebook. Separate vowel-team syllable words from multisyllabic VV syllables.

Copyright © McGraw Hill. Permission is granted to reproduce for classroom use.

Name _____

Read aloud and write the spelling words that contain the matching vowel team.

afraid	trainer	revealing	afloat	speeding
maintain	oatmeal	defeat	croaking	accountable
quail	beneath	sneaker	woeful	sheepish
sprain	repeated	boast	discounted	baboon

ea   **ai**   **ee**

1. _____   7. _____   15. _____

2. _____   8. _____   16. _____

3. _____   9. _____

4. _____   10. _____   **oe**

5. _____   11. _____   17. _____

oo   **oa**   **ou**

6. _____   12. _____   18. _____

                     13. _____   19. _____

                     14. _____

                                            oa and ea

                                            20. _____

 **Work with a partner to find multisyllabic words that contain vowel teams. Record the words you find in your writer's notebook. Separate vowel-team syllable words from multisyllabic VV syllables.**

Copyright © McGraw Hill. Permission is granted to reproduce for classroom use.

Name _____

brain	trainer	reveal	afloat	speed
staircase	oatmeal	increase	croak	sleeve
domain	beneath	sneak	compound	sheep
praise	repeat	boast	discount	baboon

A. Write the spelling word that best completes each sentence.

1. What is the _____ limit on this highway?

2. My parents' _____ made me feel good about myself.

3. This _____ includes some strange chemicals.

4. He did not _____ when he won the game.

5. Would you please _____ the question?

6. Use your _____ to think and solve problems.

7. My shirt _____ was torn in the clothes dryer.

8. The raft stayed _____ because it was filled with air.

9. Please _____ the oven temperature.

10. The wool in those pants came from _____.

B. Write the spelling word that belongs with each group below.

11. steps, handrail, _____

12. under, below, _____

13. coach, teacher, _____

14. monkey, ape, _____

15. cry, utter, _____

16. show, uncover, _____

17. yogurt, cereal, _____

18. land, area, _____

19. crawl, creep, _____

20. coupon, sale, _____

Copyright © McGraw Hill. Permission is granted to reproduce for classroom use.

Name _____

Underline the six misspelled words in the text below. Write the words correctly on the lines.

Nature clubs often have camping weekends that they repeet every year. Some even have a discownt that they offer to their members. You can increise your chances of enjoying yourself if you follow these tips:

- Take plenty of food and water.
- Remember that you are in the animals' domane. Leave it just like you found it.
- Stay with the group leader. Do not try to sneek away from the group.
- Wear warm clothes and dress in layers.

If you follow these rules, you will be able to bowst about a wonderful camping experience!

1. _____   4. _____

2. _____   5. _____

3. _____   6. _____

Write about a trip that you have taken to a park or other natural area. Use at least four words from the spelling list.

_____

_____

_____

_____

_____

_____

Copyright © McGraw Hill. Permission is granted to reproduce for classroom use.

Name _____

Copyright © McGraw Hill. Permission is granted to reproduce for classroom use.

Remember

When two vowels appear together in a word, they often work as a team to form one vowel sound. In the word *lean*, the vowels *e* and *a* make a team to form the long *e* sound. These are called **vowel teams**. A syllable that includes a vowel team is a **vowel-team syllable**.

brain	trainer	reveal	afloat	speed
staircase	oatmeal	increase	croak	sleeve
domain	beneath	sneak	compound	sheep
praise	repeat	boast	discount	baboon

Fill in the missing letters to form a spelling word. Write the word on the line.

1. br __ __ n _____
2. cr __ __ k _____
3. ben __ __ th _____
4. sp __ __ d _____
5. tr __ __ ner _____
6. sn __ __ k _____
7. bab __ __ n _____
8. pr __ __ se _____
9. disc __ __ nt _____
10. rev __ __ l _____
11. sl __ __ ve _____
12. st __ __ rcase _____
13. comp __ __ nd _____
14. b __ __ st _____
15. rep __ __ t _____
16. sh __ __ p _____
17. oatm __ __ l _____
18. afl __ __ t _____
19. dom __ __ n _____
20. incr __ __ se _____

Name _____

Expand your vocabulary by adding or removing inflectional endings, prefixes, or suffixes to a base word to create different forms of a word.

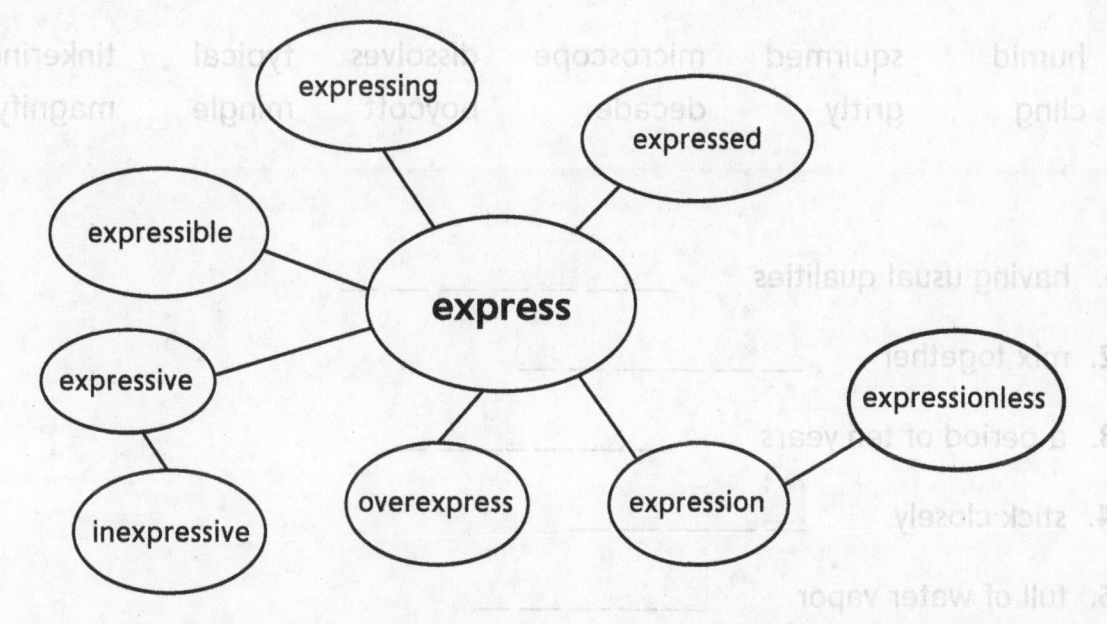

The base word *emote* can be found in "Sadie's Game." Add prefixes, suffixes, and inflectional endings to write as many related words for *emote* as you can. Use a dictionary to help you.

Copyright © McGraw Hill. Permission is granted to reproduce for classroom use.

Name _____

Write each vocabulary word next to its meaning. Then write the letters from the boxes to answer the trivia question.

humid	squirmed	microscope	dissolves	typical	tinkering
cling	gritty	decade	boycott	mingle	magnify

1. having usual qualities __ __ [□] __ __ __

2. mix together __ __ __ __ [□] __

3. a period of ten years __ __ __ [□] __ __

4. stick closely [□] __ __ __ __

5. full of water vapor [□] __ __ __ __

6. planned refusal to buy something [□] __ __ __ __ __

7. make something look bigger __ __ __ __ [□] __ __

8. disappears in liquid __ __ __ __ __ __ __ __

9. working on aimlessly __ __ [□] __ __ __ __ __

10. twisted the body __ __ __ __ __ [□] __ __

11. containing small bits of sand __ __ __ [□] __ __

12. device for looking at tiny things __ __ __ __ [□] __ __ __ __

James Naismith invented the game of basketball in 1891. What did he use to make the hoops?

__ __ __ __ __ __ __ __ __ __ __

Copyright © McGraw Hill. Permission is granted to reproduce for classroom use.

Name _____

> • For most adjectives with two or *more* syllables, add more to compare two nouns. *The cat is more silent than the dog.*
>
> • Add *most* to compare more than two nouns. *Of carrots, peas, and kale, carrots are the most popular in the cafeteria.*

Write *more* or *most* to correctly complete each sentence.

1. This book is _____ exciting than the last one I read.

2. I am _____ nervous about the race than you are.

3. Which city is the _____ crowded of all?

4. I am _____ talented in art than in music.

5. That is the _____ ridiculous thing I have ever seen.

Write about three of your favorite foods using the words *more* or *most*. Check your work. Then share your sentences with a partner. Identify where your partner used the words *more* and *most*. Then identify the nouns they have compared.

_____

_____

_____

_____

_____

_____

_____

_____

Copyright © McGraw Hill. Permission is granted to reproduce for classroom use.

Name _____

- For most adjectives with two or more syllables, add *more* to compare two nouns. Add *most* to compare more than two nouns.

- Use *-er* or *-est* with many two-syllable adjectives, but not all. If you are unsure whether to use *-er/-est* or *more/most*, look in a dictionary.

- When you add *more* or *most*, do not use the *-er* or *-est* form of the adjective.

Rewrite each sentence. Use the correct form of the adjective.

1. The roller coaster is the most thrillingest ride in the entire theme park!

_____

2. I think this pattern is more ugly than the last one we saw.

_____

_____

3. She was the carefullest volunteer at the shelter.

_____

4. This is the most hungry I've been all day.

_____

This sentence from "What If It Happened to You?" is changed so it has an error. Circle the error. Then write the corrected sentence below.

"Well, I've sort of been saving for a more new bracelet," she answered, looking away.

_____

_____

Copyright © McGraw Hill. Permission is granted to reproduce for classroom use.

Name _____

- Use a comma before the coordinating conjunction when you combine two simple sentences to form a compound sentence. *Jacob ran around the block, but he stretched his muscles first.*

- **Appositives** and **appositive phrases** rename nouns or give more information about them. They can be used to combine two sentences that explain or refer to the same thing.

- **Commas** are used to set off many **appositives** from the rest of the sentence. *My mother, a tall woman, runs very fast.*

- **Adjectives, adverbs,** and **correlative conjunctions** may also be used to combine sentences.

Combine each pair of sentences. Write the new sentence on the line.

1. I want to go to the movies. I don't want to go ice skating.

    _____

2. The dog ran around the backyard. It was a playful pup.

    _____

3. I am late for school. I am almost ready to leave.

    _____

4. He finished his homework. He was quick.

    _____

 **In your writer's notebook, write about a time that you had to be brave. What did you do? Then go back through your work and try to combine two of the sentences you wrote. Edit your work for spelling, punctuation, and subject-verb agreement.**

Copyright © McGraw Hill. Permission is granted to reproduce for classroom use.

Name _____

- For most long adjectives, use *more* or *most* to compare people, places, or things.
- If you are unsure whether to use *-er/-est* or *more/most,* look in a dictionary.
- Use a comma before the coordinating conjunction when you combine two simple sentences to form a compound sentence.
- **Appositives, adjectives, adverbs,** and **correlative conjunctions** may be used to combine sentences.

Rewrite the sentences below, correcting mistakes in adjectives and combining sentences.

COMMON ERRORS

Remember that two independent clauses combined with a comma is a run-on sentence. Don't forget to add the coordinating conjunction!

1. I think you are more thirstier than I am.

   _____

2. The cat is black. The dog is white.

   _____

3. She is the creativest person I know.

   _____

4. My coat is very warm. It is red.

   _____

5. He is a talenteder singer than I am.

   _____

6. She was the interestingest person at the party.

   _____

Name _____

Read the paragraphs. Then choose the best answer to each question.

(1) I have the _____ friends and family! (2) Of my friends, Maria is the _____; she's always telling the best jokes. (3) Luiz is the _____ of all of us. (4) He gets the _____ grades.

(5) As far as my family goes, my sister is _____ than I am at fixing things around the house. (6) Maybe it's because her arms are _____ than mine, so she can reach more things!

1. What word fits best in the blank in sentence 1?

   A cooler
   B coolest
   C most cool
   D more cool

2. What word fits best in the blank in sentence 2?

   F hilariouser
   G more hilarious
   H most hilarious
   J most hilariousest

3. What word fits best in the blank in sentence 3?

   A most smart
   B smarter
   C more smart
   D smartest

4. What word fits best in the blank in sentence 4?

   A highest
   B most high
   C higher
   D more high

5. What word fits best in the blank in sentence 5?

   F talenteder
   G talentedest
   H most talented
   J more talented

6. What word fits best in the blank in sentence 6?

   A more longer
   B most long
   C longer
   D longest

Copyright © McGraw Hill. Permission is granted to reproduce for classroom use.

Name _____

Fold back the
paper along the
dotted line. Use
the blanks to
write each word
as it is read aloud.
When you finish
the test, unfold
the paper. Use
the list at the
right to correct
any spelling
mistakes.

1. _____   1. grocer
2. _____   2. pepper
3. _____   3. barber
4. _____   4. grader
5. _____   5. polar
6. _____   6. tanker
7. _____   7. singer
8. _____   8. enter
9. _____   9. odor
10. _____   10. collar
11. _____   11. zipper
12. _____   12. powder
13. _____   13. danger
14. _____   14. cheddar
15. _____   15. popular
16. _____   16. harbor
17. _____   17. anchor
18. _____   18. elevator
19. _____   19. daughter
20. _____   20. victor

Review Words   21. _____   21. increase
22. _____   22. oatmeal
23. _____   23. sleeve

Challenge Words   24. _____   24. conductor
25. _____   25. waiter

Copyright © McGraw Hill. Permission is granted to reproduce for classroom use.

Name _____

Look at the syllable *mar*. It has one vowel sound and ends in *r*. When a vowel is followed by the letter *r*, the two letters act as a team to form a special vowel sound. A syllable having this kind of letter team is called an **r-controlled vowel syllable**.

Copyright © McGraw Hill. Permission is granted to reproduce for classroom use.

DECODING WORDS

When a vowel is followed by *r*, the team must stay together in the same syllable when decoding. For example: *bar-ber, har-bor.*

Write and read aloud words with matching *r*-controlled vowel syllables.

zipper	odor	victor	tanker	popular
anchor	grocer	cheddar	elevator	collar
daughter	polar	powder	singer	enter
barber	pepper	grader	harbor	danger

-or

1. _____
2. _____
3. _____
4. _____
5. _____

-ar

6. _____
7. _____
8. _____
9. _____

-er

10. _____
11. _____
12. _____
13. _____
14. _____
15. _____
16. _____
17. _____
18. _____
19. _____
20. _____

Use the spelling patterns above to write a short story. Include four words from the spelling list. Read the story aloud and check your work for errors.

Name_____

Look at the syllable *mar*. It has one vowel sound and ends in *r*. When a vowel is followed by the letter *r*, the two letters act as a team to form a special vowel sound. A syllable having this kind of letter team is called an **r-controlled vowel syllable**.

DECODING WORDS

When a vowel is followed by *r*, the team must stay together in the same syllable when decoding. For example: *bar-ber, har-bor.*

Write and read aloud words with matching *r*-controlled vowel syllables.

actor	danger	enter	skater	cleaner
barber	zipper	powder	odor	victor
pepper	collar	singer	trainer	grader
dollar	tanker	polar	solar	motor

-or

1. _____
2. _____
3. _____
4. _____

-ar

5. _____
6. _____
7. _____
8. _____

-er

9. _____
10. _____
11. _____
12. _____
13. _____
14. _____
15. _____
16. _____
17. _____
18. _____
19. _____
20. _____

Use the spelling patterns above to write a short story. Include four words from the spelling list. Read the story aloud and check your work for errors.

Copyright © McGraw Hill. Permission is granted to reproduce for classroom use.

Name _____

A. Write the spelling words with *r*-controlled vowel syllables that contain the matching spelling pattern. Then read the word aloud.

grocery	polar	odor	danger	anchor
professor	tractor	collar	cheddar	elevator
barbershop	composer	waiter	popular	daughter
grammar	ranger	powder	harbor	victor

-or

1. _____
2. _____
3. _____
4. _____
5. _____
6. _____
7. _____

-ar

8. _____
9. _____
10. _____
11. _____
12. _____

-er

13. _____
14. _____
15. _____
16. _____
17. _____
18. _____
19. _____
20. _____

B. Compare the words *enter* and *victor*. How are they alike? How are they different?

_____

_____

_____

 Use the spelling patterns you learned to write a short story. Include four words from the spelling list. Read the story aloud and check your work for errors.

Copyright © McGraw Hill. Permission is granted to reproduce for classroom use.

Name _____

grocer	polar	odor	danger	anchor
pepper	tanker	collar	cheddar	elevator
barber	singer	zipper	popular	daughter
grader	enter	powder	harbor	victor

A. Write the spelling word that belongs with each group of words.

1. dog, leash, _____

2. swiss, cream, _____

3. haircut, shop, _____

4. actor, dancer _____

5. child, girl, _____

6. hull, oars, _____

7. come, arrive, _____

8. tomato, cucumber, _____

9. oil, ship, _____

10. harm, risk, _____

B. Write the spelling word that best completes each sentence.

11. I like to watch the ships come into the _____.

12. That fifth-_____ won the science prize at school.

13. The _____ on my winter jacket is stuck.

14. We will ride the _____ to the top of the building.

15. Many flowers have a pleasant _____.

16. The _____ boy was voted "friendliest" at school.

17. The mother put _____ on the baby after his bath.

18. I am the _____ because I won the game!

19. The _____ areas of the world are very cold.

20. The kind _____ helped me find the canned corn.

Copyright © McGraw Hill. Permission is granted to reproduce for classroom use.

Name _____

Underline the six misspelled words in the paragraphs below.
Write the words correctly on the lines.

An oil tankor is a ship that carries oil from one place to another. It often travels through poler regions that have a lot of ice. This can be a dangor to the hull, or bottom, of the ship. If the hull were to be damaged, oil could leak into the ocean and harm sea life.

There have been reports of ships that have leaked oil. But many ships travel every day. Most are able to entor safely into a harbar and drop the ancher. People are looking for other types of clean fuel to use, but for now we count on these ships to help us live our lives.

1. _____   4. _____

2. _____   5. _____

3. _____   6. _____

Writing Connection

Write about something that we count on to live our lives every day. Use at least four words from the spelling list. Check your work with a dictionary and be sure that you have spelled any high-frequency words correctly.

_____

_____

_____

_____

_____

_____

_____

_____

Copyright © McGraw Hill. Permission is granted to reproduce for classroom use.

Name _____

Remember

When a vowel is followed by the letter *r*, the two letters act as a team to form a special vowel sound. A syllable that contains this kind of letter team is called an *r-controlled vowel syllable*.

grocer	polar	odor	danger	anchor
pepper	tanker	collar	cheddar	elevator
barber	singer	zipper	popular	daughter
grader	enter	powder	harbor	victor

A. Fill in the missing letters of each word to form a spelling word.

1. har __ __ __

2. tank __ __

3. ched __ __ __

4. en __ __ __

5. vic __ __ __

6. gro __ __ __

7. col __ __ __

8. an __ __ __ __

9. bar __ __ __

10. pow __ __ __

11. eleva __ __ __

12. grad __ __

13. zip __ __ __

14. popu __ __ __

15. pep __ __ __

16. o __ __ __

17. daugh __ __ __

18. sing __ __

19. po __ __ __

20. dan __ __ __

B. Write these spelling words in alphabetical order. Alphabetize them to the third letter: *grocer, pepper, powder, popular, grader.*

21. _____ 23. _____ 25. _____

22. _____ 24. _____

Name _____

> Remember that **idioms** are well-known phrases that have a specific figurative meaning in a certain language. You should not consider the literal meanings of the words when defining an idiom. Read this example: Alicia and her sister are opposites who never <u>see eye to eye</u>. The sentence is not literally about the sisters' eyes. It means that they never agree on anything.

Read each passage and examine the underlined idiom. Then circle the correct meaning.

1. Zander had never been on a skateboard before. He felt <u>like a fish out of water</u>.

   A Zander would rather be fishing than skateboarding.

   B Zander felt very unfamiliar and out of place.

   C Zander was a good swimmer but not a good skateboarder.

2. Kacey was going to make her first jump off the high diving board. But then she <u>got cold feet</u> and decided not to risk it.

   A Kacey was suddenly too scared to jump off the diving board.

   B The pool made Kacey's feet so cold that she had to leave.

   C Kacey's injured feet prevented her from jumping off the diving board.

3. Pedro was already happy to have passed his math test. The B+ he received was simply <u>icing on the cake.</u>

   A Pedro was going to celebrate his passing grade with a cake.

   B Pedro thought that doing math problems is like icing a cake.

   C Pedro's B+ was an extra good thing in addition to passing his test.

4. Regan laughed at her friend, who had stepped in mud. Her glee faded, however, when she saw her own shoes and realized she was <u>in the same boat.</u>

   A Regan and her friend were both riding in the same boat.

   B Regan and her friend had both stepped in mud.

   C Regan realized that her shoes were as big as a boat.

5. Yoshi asked his father to listen to his speech. "<u>I'm all ears</u>," said Mr. Hamada.

   A Yoshi was giving a speech about the ear.

   B Mr. Hamada was ready to listen to Yoshi's speech.

   C Mr. Hamada has very big ears.

Copyright © McGraw Hill. Permission is granted to reproduce for classroom use.

Name _____

Read each passage from "The Stray Dog." Find and underline the simile or metaphor. Then identify what is being compared and if it is a simile or a metaphor.

1. Joon bent down for a closer look, but he certainly didn't recognize the animal from any of the families in the neighborhood. The dog was a big fluffy ball of dirt and had no tags, so there could be little doubt that the animal was a stray.

    Simile or metaphor? _____

    What is being compared? _____

    _____

2. Uncle Bae was Joon's least favorite relative, mainly because he was always grumpy. He was about as warm as a block of ice.

    Simile or metaphor? _____

    What is being compared? _____

    _____

3. He plopped the loafers right in Uncle Bae's lap. Uncle Bae's face lit up like the sun. It was the first time in a long time that Joon had seen his uncle smile.

    Simile or metaphor? _____

    What is being compared? _____

    _____

Copyright © McGraw Hill. Permission is granted to reproduce for classroom use.

Name _____

> - The adjective *good* becomes *better* or *best* when it is used to compare. *This soup is good, but that soup is better.*
> - Use *better* to compare two people, places, or things. *An A is a better grade than a B.*
> - Use *best* to compare more than two. *Of all my friends, I am the best at gymnastics.*

Write *better* or *best* to correctly complete each sentence.

1. This is a _____ meal than the one we had last night.

2. This painting has the _____ frame in the art gallery.

3. Michael is the _____ singer of everyone in the chorus.

4. Tigers are _____ swimmers than lions.

5. That is the _____ movie I've seen in a long time.

Writing Connection Write a paragraph comparing your favorite things to do on the weekend. Include and underline at least three instances of *better* or *best*. Then edit your work for correct grammar and spelling.

_____

_____

_____

_____

_____

_____

Copyright © McGraw Hill. Permission is granted to reproduce for classroom use.

Name _____

> - The adjective *bad* becomes *worse* or *worst* when it is used to compare. *This TV show is bad, but that TV show is worse.*
> - Use *worse* to compare two people, places, or things. *Missing an exam is worse than forgetting your homework.*
> - Use *worst* to compare more than two. *I think purple is the worst of all the colors.*

Write *worse* or *worst* to correctly complete each sentence.

1. The rainy weather created _____ conditions than before.

2. Monday is always the _____ day of the week for me.

3. I am a _____ cook than my mother.

4. The plant has a _____ fungus than I thought.

5. Finally, the _____ part of the test was over.

6. These are the _____ seats in the theater.

7. This is _____ traffic than it was this morning.

8. Our house has the _____ damage from the storm.

9. Yours is a _____ excuse than mine!

10. Her _____ fear was that she would be late.

Read this sentence from "The Founding of Jamestown." Then write a sentence using the words *better* or *best* about another attitude the colonists could have instead.

> Smith knew that an attitude of every man for himself would endanger the colony.

_____

_____

Name _____

Adjectives, participial phrases, appositives, adverbs, and prepositional phrases can be used to combine two sentences into one longer sentence.

- *My friend is creative. She enjoys cooking. She cooks new foods. / My creative friend enjoys cooking new foods.*

- *That poodle belongs to my neighbor. The poodle is chewing on a stick. / That poodle, the one chewing on a stick, belongs to my neighbor.*

Combine each pair of sentences. Write the new sentence on the lines.

1. This school has students who like to build things. They are creative.

_____

_____

2. The girl was the winner of the spelling bee. She spelled a difficult word.

_____

_____

3. My brother is a clumsy kid. He always bumps into things.

_____

_____

4. The geese flew upward toward the clouds. They flew quickly.

_____

_____

 **In your writer's notebook, write a simple description about a pet you know. Then look back through your sentences to see if any can be combined. Write the combined sentences below your first description.**

Copyright © McGraw Hill. Permission is granted to reproduce for classroom use.

Name _____

> - The adjective *good* becomes *better* or *best* when it is used to compare.
> - The adjective *bad* becomes *worse* or *worst* when it is used to compare.
> - Adjectives, participial phrases, appositives, adverbs, and prepositional phrases can all be used to combine two sentences into one longer sentence.

Rewrite the sentences below, correcting mistakes in adjectives and combining sentences.

1. This is a good song than the last one, but the first song is the better.

   _____

2. I am the worse gardener in my entire family.

   _____

3. The sun set below the horizon. The sun moved slowly

   _____

4. The student got a gold star in class. He got the better score on the test.

   _____

   _____

5. The bad day I ever had was when I was in the third grade.

   _____

6. Ramon is a worst soccer player than Andrew, but Kyle is bad of all.

Copyright © McGraw Hill. Permission is granted to reproduce for classroom use.

Name _____

Read the student draft and look for any corrections that need to be made. Then choose the best answer to each question.

(1) This is the _____ dinner I have ever had! (2) Of the mashed potatoes and macaroni, I like the mashed potatoes _____. (3) But the Brussels sprouts are the _____ part of the meal!

(4) "You guys are the _____ cooks ever," I say to Mom and Dad.

(5) It was the complete opposite of the meal I had last week, which was the _____ meal ever. (6) The only thing _____ than the green beans was the ham, which was dry and hard.

1. What word fits best in the blank in sentence 1?

   A best
   B better
   C bestest
   D bester

2. What word fits best in the blank in sentence 2?

   F worst
   G best
   H worstest
   J better

3. What word fits best in the blank in sentence 3?

   A bestest
   B worser
   C worse
   D best

4. What word fits best in the blank in sentence 4?

   F worse
   G worst
   H better
   J best

5. What word fits best in the blank in sentence 5?

   A better
   B best
   C worst
   D worse

6. What word fits best in the blank in sentence 6?

   F better
   G best
   H worse
   J worst

Copyright © McGraw Hill. Permission is granted to reproduce for classroom use.

Name _____

Fold back the paper along the dotted line. Use the blanks to write each word as it is read aloud. When you finish the test, unfold the paper. Use the list at the right to correct any spelling mistakes.

1. _____
2. _____
3. _____
4. _____
5. _____
6. _____
7. _____
8. _____
9. _____
10. _____
11. _____
12. _____
13. _____
14. _____
15. _____
16. _____
17. _____
18. _____
19. _____
20. _____

Review Words 21. _____
22. _____
23. _____

Challenge Words 24. _____
25. _____

1. pebble
2. humble
3. double
4. gamble
5. trouble
6. uncle
7. needle
8. fiddle
9. cuddle
10. cradle
11. jungle
12. single
13. marble
14. ramble
15. tackle
16. ankle
17. freckle
18. buckle
19. hustle
20. tangle
21. barber
22. anchor
23. cheddar
24. staple
25. stifle

Copyright © McGraw Hill. Permission is granted to reproduce for classroom use.

Name _____

> The syllable *ple* has one vowel sound. Notice that the syllable ends in -*le*. When a word ends in -*le*, the consonant before it plus the letters -*le* form the last syllable. This is called a **consonant + *le* syllable**. (or **final stable syllable**).

DECODING WORDS

The word *apple* ends with the consonant + *le* syllable, -*ple*. Blend the sounds of the word *apple* and read the word aloud: *ap-ple*.

Read aloud and write the spelling words with consonant + *le* syllables that contain the following spelling patterns.

pebble	uncle	tackle	marble	freckle
needle	trouble	cuddle	single	double
buckle	humble	jungle	cradle	hustle
gamble	fiddle	ramble	ankle	tangle

-dle

1. _____

2. _____

3. _____

4. _____

-gle

5. _____

6. _____

7. _____

-tle

8. _____

-cle

9. _____

-kle

10. _____

11. _____

12. _____

13. _____

-ble

14. _____

15. _____

16. _____

17. _____

18. _____

19. _____

20. _____

 **Work with a partner to find multisyllabic words that contain consonant + *le* syllables. Read aloud and record the words you find in your writer's notebook.**

Copyright © McGraw Hill. Permission is granted to reproduce for classroom use.

Name _____

> Look at the syllable *ple*. *Ple* is one syllable and has one vowel sound. Notice that the syllable ends in -*le*. When a word ends in -*le*, the consonant before it plus the letters -*le* form the last syllable. This is called a **consonant + *le* syllable**.

Copyright © McGraw Hill. Permission is granted to reproduce for classroom use.

DECODING WORDS

The word *apple* ends with the consonant + *le* syllable, -*ple*. Blend the sounds of the word *apple* and read the word aloud: *ap-ple*.

Read aloud and write the spelling words with consonant + *le* **syllables that contain the following spelling patterns.**

pebble	uncle	tackle	couple	turtle
candle	bundle	cuddle	juggle	double
battle	able	waffle	cradle	hustle
table	fiddle	maple	ankle	bottle

-dle
1. _____
2. _____
3. _____
4. _____
5. _____

-kle
6. _____
7. _____

-tle
8. _____
9. _____
10. _____
11. _____

-cle
12. _____

-fle
13. _____

-ble
14. _____
15. _____
16. _____
17. _____

-gle
18. _____

-ple
19. _____
20. _____

Work with a partner to find multisyllabic words that contain consonant + *le* **syllables. Read aloud and record the words you find in your writer's notebook.**

Name _____

Read aloud and write the spelling words with consonant + *le* syllables that contain the following spelling patterns.

pebble	bicycle	wrinkle	marble	freckle
needle	trouble	struggle	single	scribble
buckle	humble	jungle	cradle	hustle
gamble	ruffle	scramble	ankle	stifle

-dle

1. _____

2. _____

-fle

3. _____

4. _____

-kle

5. _____

6. _____

7. _____

8. _____

-tle

9. _____

-cle

10. _____

-ble

11. _____

12. _____

13. _____

14. _____

15. _____

16. _____

17. _____

-gle

18. _____

19. _____

20. _____

 **Work with a partner to find multisyllabic words that contain consonant + *le* syllables. Read aloud and record the words you find in your writer's notebook.**

Copyright © McGraw Hill. Permission is granted to reproduce for classroom use.

Name _____

pebble	trouble	cuddle	marble	freckle
humble	uncle	cradle	ramble	buckle
double	needle	jungle	tackle	hustle
gamble	fiddle	single	ankle	tangle

A. Write the spelling word that matches each definition below.

1. problem _____

2. move quickly _____

3. your father's brother

   _____

4. wander _____

5. handle or solve

   _____

6. snuggle _____

7. a little stone _____

8. only one _____

9. violin _____

10. modest or not proud

    _____

B. Write the spelling word that best completes each sentence.

11. The monkeys swung on the vines through the _____

12. The _____ helped to keep the backpack closed.

13. It was a _____ to go because it might not be fun.

14. The baby-sitter placed the baby in his _____.

15. My foot is connected to my _____.

16. The house had a beautiful _____ floor.

17. This _____ has a very sharp point!

18. I want to _____ the amount of money I have.

19. You have a _____ on your nose.

20. Your hair will _____ if you do not brush it often.

Copyright © McGraw Hill. Permission is granted to reproduce for classroom use.

Name _____

Underline the three misspelled words in each paragraph below. Write the words correctly on the lines.

Many people think doctors are great, but I say that nurses should be praised. They tacle many problems every day. Most nurses do not rest until every singel task is done. This can be doublle the work of a normal person!

Nurses do many different tasks. They may use a needil to help someone feel better. They may also use their arms as a cradele for a baby. Most nurses are humbal about their work and say they are just doing their job. I say, "Thank you!" because they do it so well!

1. _____ 4. _____

2. _____ 5. _____

3. _____ 6. _____

Writing Connection Write about another important job. Use four words from the spelling list. Use a dictionary to be sure you have spelled the high-frequency words correctly.

_____

_____

_____

_____

_____

_____

_____

Copyright © McGraw Hill. Permission is granted to reproduce for classroom use.

Name _____

Remember

Look at the syllable *ple. Ple* is one syllable and has one vowel sound. Notice that the syllable ends in *-le.* When a word ends in *-le,* the consonant before it plus the letters *-le* form the last syllable. This is called a **consonant + *le* syllable**.

pebble	trouble	cuddle	marble	freckle
humble	uncle	cradle	ramble	buckle
double	needle	jungle	tackle	hustle
gamble	fiddle	single	ankle	tangle

A. Fill in the missing letters of each word to form a spelling word.

1. hus _____ _____ _____
2. un _____ _____ _____
3. mar _____ _____ _____
4. gam _____ _____ _____
5. sin _____ _____ _____
6. frec _____ _____ _____
7. peb _____ _____ _____
8. an _____ _____ _____
9. fid _____ _____ _____
10. jun _____ _____ _____
11. dou _____ _____
12. tan _____ _____ _____
13. nee _____ _____ _____
14. trou _____ _____ _____
15. ram _____ _____ _____
16. tac _____ _____ _____
17. cud _____ _____ _____
18. hum _____ _____ _____
19. cra _____ _____
20. buc _____ _____ _____

B. Use the lines below to write the spelling words in alphabetical order. Alphabetize them to the third letter. Then read the words aloud.

1. _____
2. _____
3. _____
4. _____
5. _____
6. _____
7. _____
8. _____
9. _____
10. _____
11. _____
12. _____
13. _____
14. _____
15. _____
16. _____
17. _____
18. _____
19. _____
20. _____

Name _____

When you read informational texts about sciences, government, sports, or other specific topics, pay attention to the **content words** used by the author. For example, an article about an event in American history might contain the words *colony, fort, expedition,* or *settlement.* To fully understand the text, use context clues, word analysis, dictionaries, or electronic resources to clarify the meanings of these content words.

With a partner, look in social studies texts for content words related to people, places, and events in early American history. Write the words below.

American History Words

CONNECT TO CONTENT

"The Founding of Jamestown" uses content words to describe the establishment of Jamestown in 1607, the relationship of the English and the tribe of Powhatan, and the roles of John Smith and Pocahontas in this early settlement. The selection also addresses the work archaeologists have done to unearth artifacts from this period.

_____   _____

_____   _____

_____   _____

_____   _____

Circle two words that you were able to define by using context clues. Write the words and their meanings on the lines.

_____

_____

Copyright © McGraw Hill. Permission is granted to reproduce for classroom use.

Name _____

Read each group of sentences below. Underline the context clues that help you understand the meaning of the proverb or adage in bold. Then write the meaning of the proverb or adage in bold.

1. In the search for gold, it was **every man for himself**. The people looking for gold increased. Gold became harder to find.

   _____

2. At first, it was easy to find gold. But **all good things must come to an end**. People had to turn to other methods of making money in order to make a living.

   _____

3. I stayed up late every night for a week to study for the exam. But I showed that **hard work pays off**. I got the highest grade in the class.

   _____

4. At first I didn't believe my dad when he said that an alligator had gotten into the swimming pool. But **seeing is believing**. My eyes were wide as I watched from the window as animal control took the alligator away.

   _____

5. Tanya played the piano for many years. **Practice makes perfect**, and she had become an expert.

   _____

Copyright © McGraw Hill. Permission is granted to reproduce for classroom use.

Name _____

> • An **adverb** modifies, or tells more about, a verb, such as *how, when,* or *where.* Most end in *-ly* and usually tell *how.* Some adverbs describe *how often* or *how intensely* something happens, such as *annually* or *enough.*
>
> • Adverbs can be written before or after the verbs they describe. *We* *nicely* *asked if we could stay. We asked* *nicely* *if we could stay.*

Read each sentence and underline the adverb. Write it on the line provided.

1. She slept late on Tuesday morning. _____

2. We leaned carefully over the fence. _____

3. My dad and I tried hard to fix the car. _____

4. The baby loudly cried for her mother. _____

5. He always wanted to see the national park. _____

Read this sentence from "The Great Energy Debate." Underline the adverb. Using the sentences above as a model, write three sentences about a time you got into an argument with someone. Then check your work to make sure that you have used the adverbs correctly.

> Because fossil fuels are non-renewable resources, if we keep using them, eventually there will be none left.

_____

_____

_____

_____

Copyright © McGraw Hill. Permission is granted to reproduce for classroom use.

Name _____

- An **adverb** is a word that tells more about a verb. It can be written before or after the verb it describes. Some adverbs tell *where* an action takes place. *There are birds **everywhere**.*

- Some adverbs tell *when* an action takes place. These adverbs may describe how often an action takes place. *I'm going to school **now**.*

- Some adverbs tell *how* an action takes place. These adverbs may describe how frequently or how completely an action is performed. *The man walked his dog **daily**. / The man **briskly** walked his dog.*

- Relative adverbs (*where, when, how*) begin adjective clauses that modify nouns.

Circle the adverb in each sentence. On the line, write if the adverb tells *where*, *when*, or *how* the action takes place.

1. The little bird flew away. _____

2. The student clearly wrote her name. _____

3. That man entered the room last _____

4. We joyfully sang our favorite song. _____

5. Remember to not look down! _____

6. I never see my cousins in Europe. _____

7. She spoke angrily to the naughty children. _____

8. I will get ready for bed now. _____

 **In your writer's notebook, write a paragraph about the last time someone surprised you. Include at least five adverbs that tell how often and how completely and then check that you have used them correctly.**

Copyright © McGraw Hill. Permission is granted to reproduce for classroom use.

Name _____

> • *Good* is an adjective and is used only to modify a noun. *She is a good dog.*
>
> • *Well* is an adverb when it is used to modify a verb. It tells *how* about a verb. *The woman has always done her job well.*
>
> • Do not confuse the adjective *good* with the adverb *well.*

Complete each sentence by writing *good* or *well* on the line.

1. You completed that task very _____.

2. Do you know him _____?

3. This is a _____ example of what I mean.

4. You have written a very _____ book review.

5. The girl spoke _____ even though she was tired.

6. You have received a _____ score.

Copyright © McGraw Hill. Permission is granted to reproduce for classroom use.

Writing Connection

Write two sentences about something good. Then write two sentences about something you do well. Include the words *good* and *well* in your sentences. Then check your work.

_____

_____

_____

_____

_____

_____

Name _____

- An **adverb** is a word that tells more about a verb.

- Adverbs tell *where, when,* or *how* an action takes place.

- *Good* is an adjective used to modify a noun.

- *Well* is an adverb when it is used to modify a verb. It tells *how* about a verb.

COMMON ERRORS

Not all words that end in *-ly* are adverbs. Some words ending in *-ly* are adjectives. Determine whether the word is describing a noun or a verb to identify it correctly.

Rewrite the sentences below, correcting mistakes in adverbs and adjectives.

1. We mistaken thought that there would be enough chairs for everyone.

   _____

2. Did you search good enough for the missing shoe?

   _____

3. I shut the door very quiet so that I would not wake the baby.

   _____

4. The horse jumped overly the hay bale in the pasture.

   _____

5. She did good on the difficult test.

   _____

6. She said her name soft, and I did not hear it.

   _____

Copyright © McGraw Hill. Permission is granted to reproduce for classroom use.

Name _____

Read the paragraphs. Then choose the best answer to each question.

(1) _____ I went to a baseball game. (2) The batter walked out of the dugout, stretching lazy. (3) He stopped there on the plate, swinging his bat and waiting for the pitcher to throw the ball. (4) The batter _____ hit the ball, and it sailed over the fence. (5) I looked up to the sky and watched the arc of the ball.

(6) Next, my family and I went out to a café for lunch. (7) We walked _____ and sat down at a booth. (8) We excited talked about the game as we waited for our food.

1. What word goes in the blank in sentence 1?
   A Today
   B Wisely
   C Here
   D Terribly

2. What change, if any, should be made in sentence 2?
   F Change *out* to **outly**.
   G Change *lazy* to **terribly**.
   H Change *lazy* to **lazily**.
   J Make no change.

3. Which word is an adverb in sentence 3?
   A stopped
   B there
   C swinging
   D throw

4. What word fits best in the blank in sentence 4?
   F endlessly
   G now
   H delicately
   J easily

5. Which word is an adverb in sentence 5?
   A looked
   B up
   C watched
   D arc

6. How does the adverb describe the verb in sentence 6?
   F It tells where.
   G It tells when.
   H It tells how.
   J There are no adverbs in sentence 6.

7. What word fits best in the blank in sentence 7?
   A outside
   B really
   C inside
   D last

8. What change, if any, should be made in sentence 8?
   F Change *excited* to **excitedly**.
   G Change *talked* to **talkingly**.
   H Change *waited* to **waitly**.
   J Make no change.

Copyright © McGraw Hill. Permission is granted to reproduce for classroom use.

Name _____

Fold back the paper along the dotted line. Use the blanks to write each word as it is read aloud. When you finish the test, unfold the paper. Use the list at the right to correct any spelling mistakes.

1. _____
2. _____
3. _____
4. _____
5. _____
6. _____
7. _____
8. _____
9. _____
10. _____
11. _____
12. _____
13. _____
14. _____
15. _____
16. _____
17. _____
18. _____
19. _____
20. _____

Review Words 21. _____
22. _____
23. _____
Challenge Words 24. _____
25. _____

1. shaken
2. sunken
3. eleven
4. woven
5. widen
6. ridden
7. proven
8. often
9. robin
10. cousin
11. raisin
12. muffin
13. penguin
14. button
15. reason
16. cotton
17. wagon
18. dragon
19. common
20. skeleton
21. uncle
22. double
23. paddle
24. toughen
25. vitamin

Copyright © McGraw-Hill. Permission is granted to reproduce for classroom use.

Name _____

Some words end with a vowel + *n*. The final syllable in these words is not accented. These word endings sound like *on* in *person*. The spelling of the word ending may differ, but the /ən/ pronunciation does not change.

SPELLING TIP

Possible spellings for vowel + *n* endings include *-in, -an, -en,* and *-on.*

Read aloud and write the spelling words with the following spelling patterns.

shaken	widen	often	penguin	ridden
robin	wagon	cousin	raisin	muffin
skeleton	proven	reason	button	common
woven	sunken	dragon	cotton	eleven

-in

1. _____
2. _____
3. _____
4. _____
5. _____

-on

6. _____
7. _____
8. _____
9. _____
10. _____
11. _____
12. _____

-en

13. _____
14. _____
15. _____
16. _____
17. _____
18. _____
19. _____
20. _____

Use words with the spelling patterns above to write a short rhyming poem. Include four words from the spelling list. Check your work for errors.

Copyright © McGraw Hill. Permission is granted to reproduce for classroom use.

Name _____

Some words end with a vowel + *n*. The final syllable in these words is not accented. These word endings sound like *on* in *person*. The spelling of the word ending may differ, but the /ən/ pronunciation does not change.

SPELLING TIP

Possible spellings for vowel + *n* endings include *-in, -an, -en,* and *-on*.

Read aloud and write the spelling words with the following spelling patterns.

shaken	widen	eleven	season	wagon
dragon	cotton	person	open	woman
robin	button	garden	reason	common
ripen	cousin	muffin	kitten	lemon

-in

1. _____

2. _____

3. _____

-on

4. _____

5. _____

6. _____

7. _____

8. _____

9. _____

10. _____

11. _____

12. _____

-en

13. _____

14. _____

15. _____

16. _____

17. _____

18. _____

19. _____

-an

20. _____

 Use words with the spelling patterns above to write a short rhyming poem. Include four words from the spelling list. Check your work for errors.

Copyright © McGraw Hill. Permission is granted to reproduce for classroom use.

Name _____

A. Read aloud and write the spelling words with the following spelling patterns.

fasten	straighten	certain	penguin	raisin
cousin	muffin	sunken	woven	mountain
eleven	common	oxygen	salmon	proven
pardon	often	kitchen	mistaken	skeleton

-in

1. _____

2. _____

3. _____

4. _____

-on

5. _____

6. _____

7. _____

8. _____

-en

9. _____

10. _____

11. _____

12. _____

13. _____

14. _____

15. _____

16. _____

17. _____

18. _____

-ain

19. _____

20. _____

B. Compare the words *robin* and *cotton*. How are they alike? How are they different?

_____

_____

 Use words with the spelling patterns above to write a short rhyming poem. Include four words from the spelling list. Check your work for errors.

Name _____

shaken	widen	robin	penguin	wagon
sunken	ridden	cousin	button	dragon
eleven	proven	raisin	reason	common
woven	often	muffin	cotton	skeleton

A. Write the spelling word that belongs with the other words in the group.

1. prune, date, _____

2. zipper, buckle, _____

3. whale, seal, _____

4. knight, fire, _____

5. lowered, buried, _____

6. rarely, sometimes, _____

7. stirred, blended, _____

8. cupcake, pastry, _____

B. Write the spelling word that best completes each sentence.

9. The _____ they went shopping was to buy milk.

10. She had never _____ on a train before today.

11. Is this shirt made out of _____?

12. It was _____ that the man was innocent.

13. My older brother is _____ years old.

14. We put the puppies in a _____ and pulled it.

15. The _____ basket was made of straw.

16. It is _____ to see a lot of cars on the highway.

17. The _____ made a nest in the oak tree.

18. They need to _____ the opening for the truck to fit.

19. My _____ is my aunt's son.

20. The human _____ has many bones.

Copyright © McGraw Hill. Permission is granted to reproduce for classroom use.

Name _____

Underline the six misspelled words in the paragraphs below. Write the words correctly on the lines.

It was elevin o'clock when the package arrived at the doorstep. It looked commen enough, except for the big red bow on top. I ran to get it because it wasn't ofton that I received a gift. Today was special, though. It was my birthday!

When I looked at the return address, I saw that the package was from my cousen, Ally. I ripped off the paper and opened the box. Inside was the most beautiful sweater I ever saw! It was wovon with my favorite colors and made with the softest cottin. I was so excited that I ran inside to call Ally right away.

1. _____   4. _____

2. _____   5. _____

3. _____   6. _____

Write about a wonderful gift that you or someone you know received. Use four words from the spelling list. Use a dictionary or electronic resource to make sure you have spelled the high-frequency words correctly.

_____

_____

_____

_____

_____

_____

_____

_____

_____

Copyright © McGraw Hill. Permission is granted to reproduce for classroom use.

Name _____

Remember

Some words end with a vowel + *n*. The final syllable in these words is not accented. These word endings sound like *on* in *person*. The spelling of the word ending may differ, but the /ən/ pronunciation does not change.

shaken	widen	robin	penguin	wagon
sunken	ridden	cousin	button	dragon
eleven	proven	raisin	reason	common
woven	often	muffin	cotton	skeleton

Fill in the missing letters of each word to form a spelling word. Write the word on the line. Then read the word aloud.

1. shak ____ ____   _____

2. reas ____ ____   _____

3. muff ____ ____   _____

4. comm ____ ____   _____

5. wov ____ ____   _____

6. rob ____ ____   _____

7. prov ____ ____   _____

8. wag ____ ____   _____

9. pengu ____ ____   _____

10. skelet ____ ____   _____

11. rais ____ ____   _____

12. wid ____ ____   _____

13. sunk ____ ____   _____

14. cott ____ ____   _____

15. oft ____ ____   _____

16. drag ____ ____   _____

17. ridd ____ ____   _____

18. elev ____ ____   _____

19. cous ____ ____   _____

20. butt ____ ____   _____

Copyright © McGraw Hill. Permission is granted to reproduce for classroom use.

Name _____

Use context clues, word analysis, dictionaries, and online sources to help you understand the meanings, pronunciation, and syllabification of **content words** you encounter while reading. This unit features content words related to the study of energy resources and our environment, including *renewable, nonrenewable, fossil fuels*, and *wind turbines*.

Search science texts for content words related to energy use and how humans affect the environment. Write the words below.

Energy and Environment Words

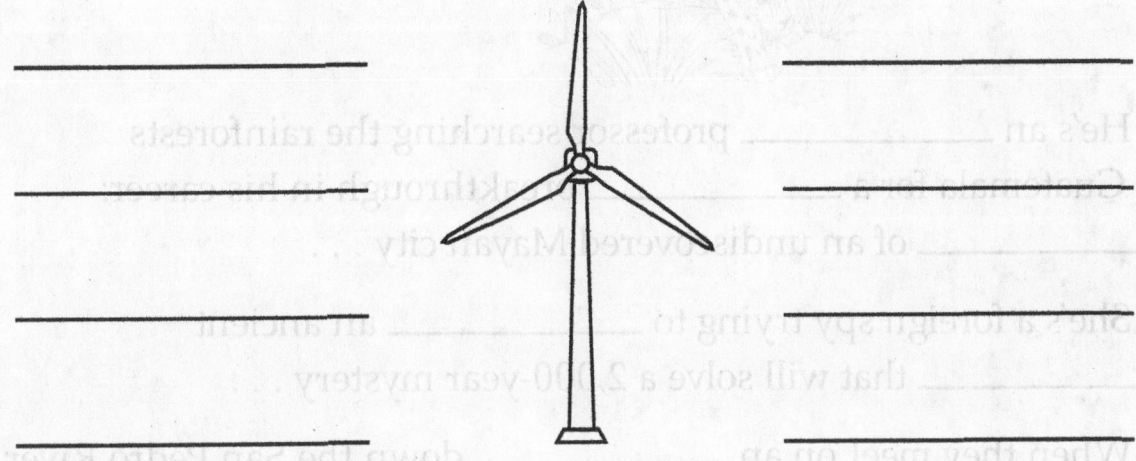

_____   _____

_____   _____

_____   _____

_____   _____

Circle two words that you were able to define by using context clues. Write the words and their meanings on the lines.

_____

_____

_____

_____

_____

Copyright © McGraw Hill. Permission is granted to reproduce for classroom use.

Name _____

The movie poster below is missing some words. Write the correct vocabulary word from the box in each blank to complete the text.

permanent	triumph	document	expedition
typical	express	era	uncover
tremendous	evidence	archaeology	emotion

Now in Theaters!

Secrets of the Jungle

He's an _____ professor searching the rainforests of Guatemala for a _____ breakthrough in his career: _____ of an undiscovered Mayan city . . .

She's a foreign spy trying to _____ an ancient _____ that will solve a 2,000-year mystery . . .

When they meet on an _____ down the San Pedro River, will they become friends or bitter rivals?

This film is a _____! Words cannot _____ how much I love it! Four Stars! –Robert Eagan, *The West Bay Times*

Secrets of the Rainforest deserves a _____ and lasting place among the best films of our _____. – Isabel Fuertes, *The Chronicle*

Not a _____ movie. I experienced every _____, from joy to despair. –David Rashad, *Fort Russell Daily News*

Copyright © McGraw Hill. Permission is granted to reproduce for classroom use. McGraw-Hill Education

Name _____

- Adverbs can be used to compare two or more actions.

- Add *-er* or *-est* to most short adverbs to compare actions. *I was the fastest runner in my class.*

- Use *more* or *most* with long adverbs and a few short adverbs to compare actions. *I jumped up and down more excitedly than my brother.*

Complete each sentence by circling the correct adverb in parentheses.

1. I swim the (faster, fastest) in my team.

2. She stroked the kitten (more, most) gently than her sister did.

3. The patient arrived (sooner, soonest) than expected.

4. My mother acted (more, most) elegantly than my father.

5. She stumbled over the log the (more, most) awkwardly of everyone.

6. The baseball player threw the ball (farther, farthest) than I could.

7. This plane flew the (closer, closest) to the tower of all the planes.

8. Out of everyone, she behaved (more, most) lovingly toward me.

 **Read this excerpt from "Of Fire and Water." Underline the adverb. Then write a sentence using the same adverb to compare. Then check your sentence.**

He tricked Zeus into choosing a cleverly disguised sacrificial dish rather than a richer dish for his offering.

_____

_____

Copyright © McGraw Hill. Permission is granted to reproduce for classroom use.

Name _____

> • Add *-er/-est* or *more/most* to most adverbs to compare actions.
>
> • Use *better* and *best* to make comparisons using the adverb *well*. *Sara did the **best** job on the project.*
>
> • Use *worse* and *worst* to make comparisons using the adverb *badly*. *Devon was worse than Teri at baseball.*

A. Complete each sentence with *better* or *best* to compare.

1. She did the _____ of all the students in the class.

2. A dog can hear _____ than a human being.

3. I performed _____ in the race than my brother.

B. Complete each sentence with *worse* or *worst* to compare.

4. I scored _____ on the test than my friend.

5. Harry plays the piano _____ when he does not practice.

6. He sounds the _____ of all when his voice is hoarse.

Writing Connection — **Write a paragraph about what superhero powers you wish you could have. Include comparisons using *better, best, worse,* and *worst*.**

_____
_____
_____
_____
_____
_____

Copyright © McGraw Hill. Permission is granted to reproduce for classroom use.

Name _____

> - Use a comma before coordinating conjunctions, after a beginning dependent clause, and to separate three or more items in a series.
>
> - Capitalize sentence beginnings, proper adjectives, proper nouns, and the first word in a quotation that is a full sentence.
>
> - A comma or period always goes inside closing quotation marks. A question mark or exclamation mark goes inside when it is part of the quotation.
>
> - Use a comma in direct address after the name of a person being spoken to: *Janelle, I like your poem!*

Write each sentence correctly by fixing capitalization and punctuation errors.

1. My father had a german shepherd when he was a boy.

_____

2. Dad can we go to the movies on Saturday?

_____

3. I shouted at my friends, "I'm over here"!

_____

4. There were big medium and small sizes available.

_____

5. "Get me some sugar from the pantry" my mother requested.

_____

In your writer's notebook, write a short story about any topic you wish. Choose a genre, take notes, and plan out your story. As you write, include a direct quote, a dependent clause, and three items in a series. Then edit your work.

Copyright © McGraw Hill. Permission is granted to reproduce for classroom use.

> • Add *-er/-est* or *more/most* to adverbs to compare actions.
> • Make comparisons using *better/best* for the adverb *well* and *worse/worst* for the adverb *badly*.
> • Follow correct punctuation rules for commas and quotation marks.
> • Follow correct capitalization rules.

Rewrite the sentences below, correcting mistakes in adverbs, capitalization, and punctuation.

HANDWRITING CONNECTION

Use the lines to keep your writing straight, relax your grip, and take your time!

1. When I was, rehearsing I acted weller then I did on stage.

   _____

2. "She laughed happilyer when she saw the clown" my aunt explained.

   _____

3. Does the canada goose fly most fast of all geese?

   _____

4. She drew worst than she thought she would.

   _____

5. The man stood most close to the fire hydrant.

   _____

6. Trying not to wake anyone he tiptoed the quietliest of everyone.

   _____

Copyright © McGraw Hill. Permission is granted to reproduce for classroom use.

Name _____

Read the student draft. Then choose the best answer to each question.

(1) Of all the students in the class, I wrote the answers to the first, second, and third questions correctly. (2) However, I got the low score on the fourth, fifth, and sixth questions. (3) I did manage to write the essay completely than the person next to me, at least!

(4) Ana got 100 percent, the good grade in the class! (5) I did good than Ana with 92 percent. (6) Daryl did good than me with a grade of 94 percent.

1. What is the correct way to write the adverb in sentence 1?

   A correctly
   B correct
   C most correctly
   D more correctly

2. What is the correct way to write sentence 2?

   F However, I got low the score on the fourth, fifth, and sixth questions.
   G However, I got the lowest score on the fourth, fifth, and sixth questions.
   H However, I got the most low score on the fourth, fifth, and sixth questions.
   J However, I got the lower score on the fourth, fifth, and sixth questions.

3. What is the correct way to write the adverb in sentence 3?

   A most complete
   B more completer
   C more completely
   D most completely

4. What is the correct way to write sentence 4?

   F Ana got 100 percent, the more good grade in the class!
   G Ana got 100 percent, the better grade in the class!
   H Ana got 100 percent, the worse grade in the class!
   J Ana got 100 percent, the best grade in the class!

5. What is the correct way to write the adverb in sentence 5?

   A worse
   B badder
   C better
   D more bad

6. What is the correct way to write the adverb in sentence 6?

   F better
   G best
   H worse
   J worst

Copyright © McGraw Hill. Permission is granted to reproduce for classroom use.

Name _____

Fold back the
paper along the
dotted line. Use
the blanks to
write each word
as it is read aloud.
When you finish
the test, unfold
the paper. Use the
list at the right
to correct any
spelling mistakes.

1. _____
2. _____
3. _____
4. _____
5. _____
6. _____
7. _____
8. _____
9. _____
10. _____
11. _____
12. _____
13. _____
14. _____
15. _____
16. _____
17. _____
18. _____
19. _____
20. _____

Review Words 21. _____
22. _____
23. _____

Challenge Words 24. _____
25. _____

1. root
2. route
3. tail
4. tale
5. wade
6. weighed
7. prince
8. prints
9. doe
10. dough
11. moose
12. mousse
13. we've
14. weave
15. who's
16. whose
17. bolder
18. boulder
19. patience
20. patients
21. cotton
22. muffin
23. eleven
24. straight
25. strait

Copyright © McGraw Hill. Permission is granted to reproduce for classroom use.

Name _____

> **Homophones** are words that sound alike, but they have different spellings and meanings, such as *heir* and *air*. While reading, use context clues in the piece to determine the meaning of a homophone.

SPELLING TIP

There is no spelling pattern to follow when determining the meaning of a homophone. Use a dictionary to help you.

Read aloud and write the ten pairs of spelling words that are homophones.

doe	dough	prints	route	weave
tale	wade	weighed	who's	patients
prince	tail	whose	bolder	root
moose	we've	mousse	patience	boulder

1. _____ _____

2. _____ _____

3. _____ _____

4. _____ _____

5. _____ _____

6. _____ _____

7. _____ _____

8. _____ _____

9. _____ _____

10. _____ _____

Work with a partner to find more word pairs that are homophones. Record the words you find in your writer's notebook.

Copyright © McGraw Hill. Permission is granted to reproduce for classroom use.

Name _____

> **Homophones** are words that sound alike, but they have different spellings and meanings, such as *heir* and *air*. While reading, use context clues in the piece to determine the meaning of a homophone.

Copyright © McGraw Hill. Permission is granted to reproduce for classroom use.

> **SPELLING TIP**
>
> There is no spelling pattern to follow when determining the meaning of a homophone. Use a dictionary to help you.

Read aloud and write the ten pairs of spelling words that are homophones.

root	prince	oar	route	dough
doe	who's	blue	peak	need
peek	whose	heard	herd	tale
tail	prints	knead	ore	blew

1. _____   _____

2. _____   _____

3. _____   _____

4. _____   _____

5. _____   _____

6. _____   _____

7. _____   _____

8. _____   _____

9. _____   _____

10. _____   _____

 **Work with a partner to find more word pairs that are homophones. Record the words you find in your writer's notebook.**

Name _____

A. Write the ten pairs of spelling words that are homophones.

mousse	principle	weather	taut	principal
presence	bolder	strait	boulder	patients
straight	doe	taught	dough	moose
patience	whose	who's	whether	presents

1. _____   _____

2. _____   _____

3. _____   _____

4. _____   _____

5. _____   _____

6. _____   _____

7. _____   _____

8. _____   _____

9. _____   _____

10. _____   _____

B. Compare the words *whose* and *who's*. How are they alike? How are they different?

_____

_____

_____

 **Work with a partner to find more word pairs that are homophones. Record the words you find in your writer's notebook.**

Copyright © McGraw Hill. Permission is granted to reproduce for classroom use.

Name _____

root	prince	we've	route	patience
tale	dough	weave	boulder	patients
wade	moose	whose	bolder	doe
tail	prints	who's	weighed	mousse

A. Write the spelling word that has the same meaning as each word or phrase below.

1. we have _____

2. more courage _____

3. a king's son _____

4. course _____

5. measured _____

6. writes _____

7. plant part _____

8. dessert _____

9. who is _____

10. blend _____

B. Write the spelling word that best completes each sentence.

11. The man had to _____ into the river to get the fish.

12. Roll the _____ before shaping it and putting it in the oven.

13. That large _____ can fall and roll down the mountain.

14. The doctor has a lot of _____ to see today.

15. That _____ has huge antlers and a big snout.

16. _____ sweatshirt is this?

17. The _____ protects her baby fawn.

18. That is quite a _____ you just told.

19. You must have _____ and wait for your turn.

20. The dog's _____ wagged happily when he saw me.

Copyright © McGraw Hill. Permission is granted to reproduce for classroom use.

Name _____

Underline the six misspelled words in the paragraphs below. Write the words correctly on the lines.

Once upon a time, there was a dou named Cinnamon. She lived in a great forest with all of her animal friends, including Printse Butternut. Cinnamon was very upset because her forest was in danger. Every year, humans would build another road or roote deeper into her home.

Then one day, Cinnamon shook her taile. She had an idea! She got all the other animals in the forest to help her build a wall. Bowlder upon rock, they built a barrier to protect themselves. It took pashence, but they finally finished it and made the forest safe again.

1. _____   4. _____

2. _____   5. _____

3. _____   6. _____

Writing Connection

Write a short story that takes place in a forest. Use four words from the spelling list.

_____
_____
_____
_____
_____
_____
_____
_____

Copyright © McGraw Hill. Permission is granted to reproduce for classroom use.

Name _____

Copyright © McGraw Hill. Permission is granted to reproduce for classroom use.

> **Remember**
>
> **Homophones** are words that sound alike, but they have different spellings and meanings, such as *heir* and *air*. While reading, use context clues in the piece to determine the meaning of a homophone.

A. Circle the spelling word in each row that rhymes with the word in bold type. Write the spelling word on the line.

1.	**lose**	hose	whose	toes	_____
2.	**show**	doe	new	shoe	_____
3.	**paid**	weighed	mad	claim	_____
4.	**male**	said	fame	tail	_____
5.	**shoot**	route	shop	pout	_____
6.	**juice**	flew	goes	moose	_____
7.	**leave**	reef	we've	pave	_____
8.	**stayed**	steed	wade	play	_____
9.	**shoulder**	butter	pusher	bolder	_____
10.	**clues**	who's	fuss	clips	_____
11.	**flute**	mutt	flume	root	_____
12.	**row**	cow	dough	comb	_____
13.	**goose**	mousse	room	nose	_____
14.	**sleeve**	weave	sleep	give	_____
15.	**colder**	cuter	boulder	milder	_____
16.	**fail**	tale	tall	game	_____

B. Write these words in alphabetical order: *patience, prince, patients, prints.*

17. _____   18. _____

19. _____   20. _____

Name _____

Copyright © McGraw Hill. Permission is granted to reproduce for classroom use.

Remember

Remember that **prefixes** are word parts added to the beginning of a base word to change its meaning. Knowing the meanings of common prefixes will help you define unfamiliar words. Take a look at these examples:

sub- : under   *mis-* : wrongly   *ex-* : out

im- : not   *tri-* : three   *co-* : together

Read the base words below. Add a prefix from above to each word and read the word aloud. Then write a definition for the word you have created. Consult a dictionary to make sure your words are correct.

1. _____ pilot   _____

2. _____ spell   _____

3. _____ zero   _____

4. _____ patient   _____

5. _____ standard   _____

6. _____ clude   _____

7. _____ exist   _____

8. _____ angle   _____

9. _____ inform   _____

10. _____ sect   _____

11. _____ hale   _____

12. _____ mature   _____

Name _____

Latin Prefix	Meaning	Greek Prefix	Meaning
non-	not	*hydro-*	water
pre-	before	*mega-*	large
dis-	opposite	*geo-*	earth

Read each sentence. Write the meaning of each word in bold on the line provided. Use the information about prefixes in the box above to help you.

1. The chapter **preview** in our book told us we would be studying marine life next week.

   _____

2. A **megawatt** is a greater unit of power than a watt.

   _____

3. Some ancient civilizations used rivers to create **hydropower**.

   _____

4. My friends looked at me in **disbelief** when I told them I met a movie star.

   _____

5. The **geothermal** temperature is hotter near Earth's core.

   _____

6. Some people used to think it was **nonsense** to say Earth was round!

   _____

Copyright © McGraw Hill. Permission is granted to reproduce for classroom use.

Name _____

- A **negative** is a statement that means "no," or the opposite of its regular meaning. Most statements can be changed to a negative form.
- If a sentence has a form of *be* or *have* as a main or helping verb, add *not* to make it negative. *Naomi is **not** coming to the party tonight.*

Rewrite each sentence by changing it to a negative form.

1. He does have dark hair.

   _____

2. I will go to bed early tonight.

   _____

3. I was glad that the day was over.

   _____

4. She does want to see the new action movie.

   _____

5. I have grown a lot in the past year.

   _____

Read this sentence from "The Game of Silence." Underline the negative. Then rewrite the sentence that doesn't contain a negative so that it contains a negative.

> It filled her mind with the sound of falling rain, which was easy. Outside, it was not just raining but *pouring* down a drenching, cold, miserable, early summer shower.

_____

_____

Copyright © McGraw Hill. Permission is granted to reproduce for classroom use.

Name _____

- A **negative** is a statement that means "no," or the opposite of its regular meaning.
- Many verbs with *not* can be made into contractions: *do not/don't.*
- There are other negative words that can be used in sentences, such as *never, no one,* and *nothing.*

A. Read each sentence. Underline the verb with *not*. Write the contraction for the words on the line.

1. I do not want to go to the carnival. _____

2. He will not see his friend all summer. _____

3. They tried, but they could not open the door. _____

4. The bear would not leave her cubs. _____

5. We have not gone on vacation in years. _____

B. Circle the negative word that correctly completes each sentence.

6. (Nothing/No one) is home right now.

7. The girls did (no/not) walk to school.

8. I wanted an apple, but there were (never/none) left.

9. She had (not/nothing) to do while she waited.

10. I have (no/never) been to Africa.

 In your writer's notebook, write a short paragraph about all the things you wish you could do in life. Underline each negative you include.

Copyright © McGraw Hill. Permission is granted to reproduce for classroom use.

Name _____

> - Do not use two negatives in the same sentence.
> - You can correct a sentence with two negatives by removing one negative.
> - You can correct a sentence with two negatives by changing one negative to a positive word.

Rewrite each sentence by dropping a negative or changing one negative to a positive word.

1. I do not know nothing about this book.

   _____

   _____

2. We didn't have no reason to complain.

   _____

   _____

3. She hasn't never tried to solve the puzzle.

   _____

   _____

4. There isn't no one here to help us.

   _____

   _____

5. We couldn't find the rare bird nowhere.

   _____

   _____

 **In your writer's notebook, write a short passage describing some things you don't like to do. Include at least three sentences containing negatives. Make sure to edit your passage for punctuation and capitalization.**

Copyright © McGraw Hill. Permission is granted to reproduce for classroom use.

Name _____

- A **negative** is a statement that means "no," or the opposite of its regular meaning.

- Many verbs with *not* can be made into contractions.

- Do not use two negatives in the same sentence. You can correct a sentence with two negatives by removing one negative or changing one negative to a positive word.

Rewrite the paragraphs below, correcting mistakes in negatives and contractions.

HANDWRITING CONNECTION

Be sure to write legibly. Use proper cursive and leave appropriate spaces between words.

1. There is no way that no one could have had a worse day. First, I did'nt have no money for lunch because I had left it at home. Then, I couldnt get to the bus on time after school, and it left without me. I probably won't never have a day like this again!

_____

_____

_____

_____

2. The wild horses couldn't find no water. They didn't not want to leave their grassy field, but they were thirsty. The stallion led the herd and wouldn't let the horses just go no where. He crossed the hill and found a stream where they wouldnt not be disappointed.

_____

_____

_____

_____

Copyright © McGraw Hill. Permission is granted to reproduce for classroom use.

Name _____

Read the paragraph. Then choose the best answer to each question.

(1) My family and I did _____ want to leave a single piece of trash on the beach. (2) When we were finished, _____ of the trash was left on the shore. (3) We will _____ forget how we felt when we saw the difference! (4) _____ can beat the feeling of seeing a clean beach!

(5) I wanted to go for a bike ride afterward, but my brother did not want to. (6) I <u>could not</u> believe he was tired already! (7) Since he <u>was not</u> in the mood for biking, I asked my friends instead. (8) I cannot remember having such an active day!

1. Which negative word fits best in sentence 1?

   A never

   B no

   C none

   D not

2. Which negative word fits best in sentence 2?

   A none

   B no

   C not

   D never

3. Which negative word fits best in sentence 3?

   F no

   G none

   H never

   J nothing

4. Which negative word fits best in sentence 4?

   A Never

   B Nothing

   C Not

   D No

5. Which two words in sentence 5 can make a contraction?

   F to go

   G for a

   H did not

   J not want

6. What is the correct contraction for the underlined words in sentence 6?

   A could't

   B could'not

   C couldn't

   D coun't

7. What is the correct contraction for the underlined words in sentence 7?

   F wan't

   G was't

   H was'not

   J wasn't

8. Which word in sentence 8 can make a contraction?

   A cannot

   B remember

   C having

   D an

Copyright © McGraw Hill. Permission is granted to reproduce for classroom use.

Name _____

Fold back the paper along the dotted line. Use the blanks to write each word as it is read aloud. When you finish the test, unfold the paper. Use the list at the right to correct any spelling mistakes.

1. _____
2. _____
3. _____
4. _____
5. _____
6. _____
7. _____
8. _____
9. _____
10. _____
11. _____
12. _____
13. _____
14. _____
15. _____
16. _____
17. _____
18. _____
19. _____
20. _____

Review Words 21. _____
22. _____
23. _____

Challenge Words 24. _____
25. _____

1. discourage
2. disappoint
3. disbelief
4. distrust
5. disloyal
6. misplace
7. mislabel
8. mislead
9. misstep
10. misnumber
11. nonfat
12. nonfiction
13. nonsense
14. nonstop
15. unable
16. unplug
17. uncertain
18. uncomfortable
19. uncover
20. unclean
21. prince
22. weighed
23. bolder
24. mishap
25. unravel

Copyright © McGraw Hill. Permission is granted to reproduce for classroom use.

Name _____

> A **prefix** is a group of letters added to the beginning of a word that changes the word's meaning. Knowing the meanings of the most common prefixes can help you to understand new words.

> **DECODING WORDS**
>
> In words that end in silent *e*, as in *misplace*, the *e* and the vowel before it must stay in the same syllable to decode it. Say the word aloud.

Read aloud and write the spelling words that contain the following prefixes.

unplug	disloyal	misstep	mislead	distrust
disappoint	misplace	nonfiction	disbelief	uncomfortable
nonstop	uncover	nonfat	unable	mislabel
uncertain	nonsense	misnumber	discourage	unclean

un-

1. _____
2. _____
3. _____
4. _____
5. _____
6. _____

mis-

7. _____
8. _____
9. _____
10. _____
11. _____

dis-

12. _____
13. _____
14. _____
15. _____
16. _____

non-

17. _____
18. _____
19. _____
20. _____

 **Work with a partner to find more words that contain prefixes. Read each word aloud. Record the words you find in your writer's notebook. Include words with the VCe pattern.**

Copyright © McGraw Hill. Permission is granted to reproduce for classroom use.

Name _____

> A **prefix** is a group of letters added to the beginning of a word that changes the word's meaning. Knowing the meanings of the most common prefixes can help you to understand new words.

DECODING WORDS

In words that end in silent *e*, as in *misplace*, the *e* and the vowel before it must stay in the same syllable to decode it. Say the word aloud.

Read aloud and write the spelling words that contain the following prefixes.

unable	disloyal	misstep	nonsense	unkind
displease	misplace	distaste	uncover	nonfat
misnumber	unplug	unfair	disorder	nonstop
distrust	mislead	nonfiction	mislabel	unclean

un-

1. _____
2. _____
3. _____
4. _____
5. _____
6. _____

mis-

7. _____
8. _____
9. _____
10. _____
11. _____

dis-

12. _____
13. _____
14. _____
15. _____
16. _____

non-

17. _____
18. _____
19. _____
20. _____

 **Work with a partner to find more words that contain prefixes. Read each word aloud. Record the words you find in your writer's notebook.**

Copyright © McGraw Hill. Permission is granted to reproduce for classroom use.

Name _____

Read aloud and write the spelling words that contain the following prefixes.

unpredictable	disloyal	disappear	misstep	nonsense
disappointment	unable	misnumber	nonspecific	uncomfortable
mismanage	disbelief	unofficial	misfortune	discourage
uncertain	misheard	nonfiction	unnecessary	nonessential

un-

1. _____

2. _____

3. _____

4. _____

5. _____

6. _____

mis-

7. _____

8. _____

9. _____

10. _____

11. _____

dis-

12. _____

13. _____

14. _____

15. _____

16. _____

non-

17. _____

18. _____

19. _____

20. _____

Work with a partner to find more words that contain prefixes. Read each word aloud. Record the words you find in your writer's notebook.

Copyright © McGraw Hill. Permission is granted to reproduce for classroom use.

Name _____

discourage	disloyal	misstep	nonsense	uncertain
disappoint	misplace	misnumber	nonstop	uncomfortable
disbelief	mislabel	nonfat	unable	uncover
distrust	mislead	nonfiction	unplug	unclean

A. Write the spelling word that matches each synonym below.

1. unsure _____

2. blunder _____

3. open _____

4. untrue _____

5. foolishness _____

6. lean _____

7. sadden _____

8. informational _____

B. Write the spelling word that best completes each sentence.

9. Do not _____ the pot while cooking.

10. There is no reason to _____ that what I say is true.

11. Did you _____ your hat the other day?

12. The directions are confusing and will _____ you.

13. He listened to music _____ for hours.

14. The seat is _____ and makes me ache.

15. Do not _____ the answers on the test.

16. The _____ room was filled with dirt and dust.

17. I tried but I could not _____ her from going.

18. I do not want to _____ this as mine if it is yours.

19. She was _____ to finish her homework before dinner.

20. I watched the amazing circus act with _____.

Copyright © McGraw Hill. Permission is granted to reproduce for classroom use.

Underline the six misspelled words in the paragraphs below. There are three errors in each paragraph. Write the words correctly on the lines.

The ocean is a wonderful and interesting place. In fact, there are many things about sea life that we are still incertain about. Studying the sea will not desappoint you, for there are many surprises in the water. There is nonnstop activity beneath the surface.

If you are unnable to see the ocean for yourself, you can look at pictures of it in books. They will not misslead you. You will stare in dusbelief when you see the number of amazing creatures in the sea. You might even find one or two animals that you want to learn more about.

1. _____ 4. _____

2. _____ 5. _____

3. _____ 6. _____

Writing Connection

Write about whether or not you like the ocean, and why. Use four words from the spelling list.

_____

_____

_____

_____

_____

_____

_____

Name _____

Remember

A **prefix** is a group of letters added to the beginning of a word that changes the word's meaning. Knowing the meanings of the most common prefixes can help you to understand new words.

discourage	disloyal	misstep	nonsense	uncertain
disappoint	misplace	misnumber	nonstop	uncomfortable
disbelief	mislabel	nonfat	unable	uncover
distrust	mislead	nonfiction	unplug	unclean

A. Fill in the missing letters of each word to form a spelling word. Then read the word aloud.

1. _____ _____ able
2. _____ _____ _____ place
3. _____ _____ _____ fat
4. _____ _____ _____ appoint
5. _____ _____ _____ sense
6. _____ _____ _____ lead
7. _____ _____ cover
8. _____ _____ _____ number
9. _____ _____ certain
10. _____ _____ _____ trust

11. _____ _____ _____ step
12. _____ _____ _____ belief
13. _____ _____ clean
14. _____ _____ _____ fiction
15. _____ _____ plug
16. _____ _____ loyal
17. _____ _____ _____ label
18. _____ _____ comfortable
19. _____ _____ _____ courage
20. _____ _____ _____ stop

B. Write these spelling words in alphabetical order. Alphabetize them to the fourth letter: *nonstop, misstep, misplace, nonfiction, mislead.*

21. _____
22. _____
23. _____
24. _____
25. _____

Copyright © McGraw Hill. Permission is granted to reproduce for classroom use.

Name _____

Remember that you can expand your vocabulary by adding inflectional endings, prefixes, and suffixes to a base word to create *related words* with similar meanings. Take a look at this example.

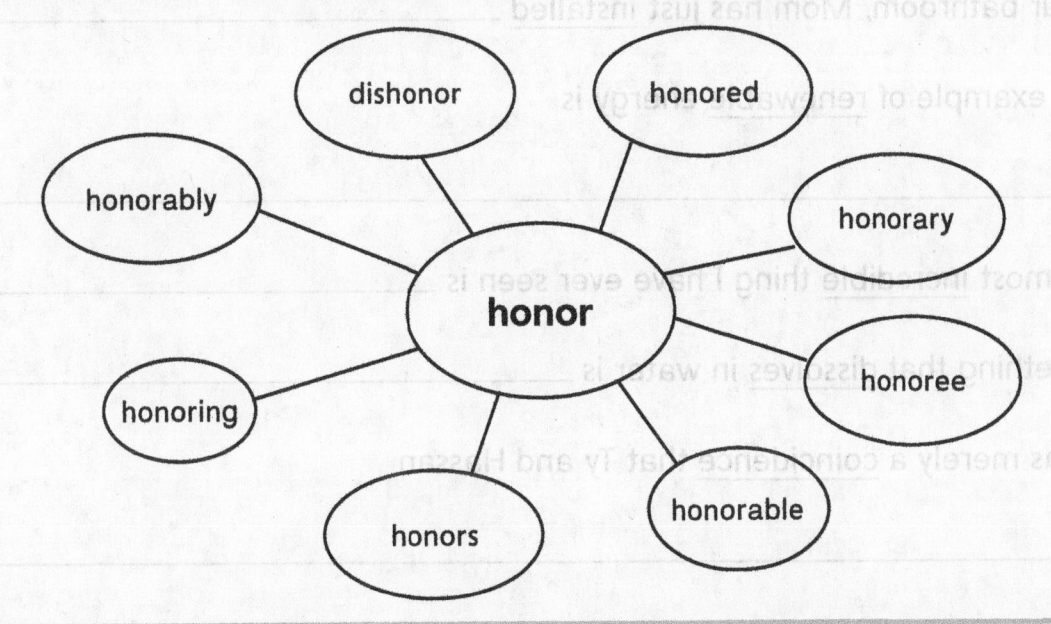

Choose a base word from "A Surprise Reunion." Write it above the illustration. Add prefixes, suffixes, and inflectional endings to write as many related words as you can. Use a dictionary to help you read the words aloud.

_____

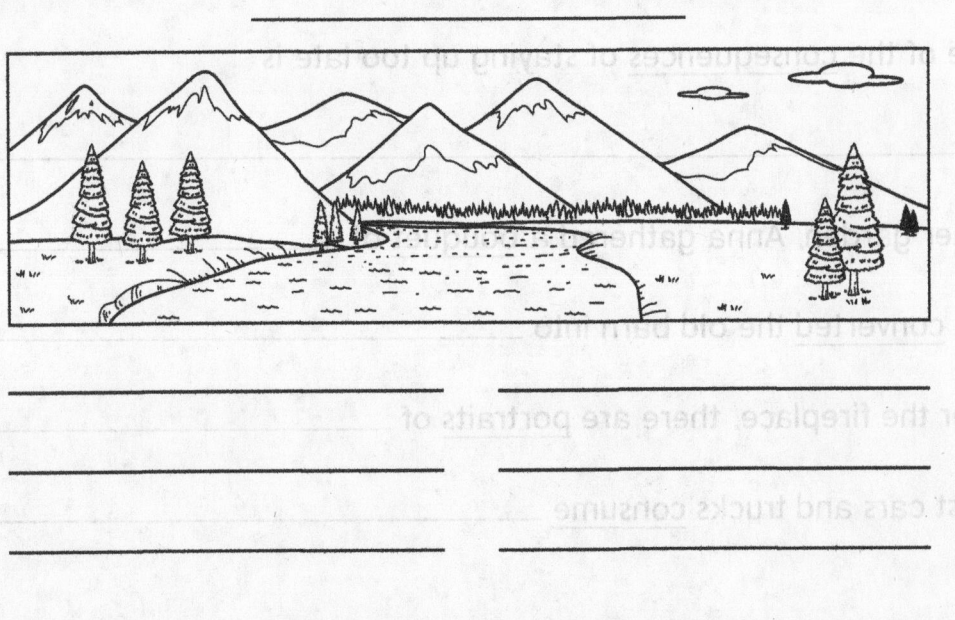

_____   _____

_____   _____

_____   _____

Copyright © McGraw Hill. Permission is granted to reproduce for classroom use.

Name _____

Complete each sentence below. Make sure your sentence shows the meaning of the underlined vocabulary word.

1. In our bathroom, Mom has just <u>installed</u> _____

2. One example of <u>renewable</u> energy is

    _____

3. The most <u>incredible</u> thing I have ever seen is _____

4. Something that <u>dissolves</u> in water is _____

5. It was merely a <u>coincidence</u> that Ty and Hassan

    _____

6. A more <u>efficient</u> way to write my report would be to

7. Dr. Carreras will <u>magnify</u> the cells with a _____

8. One of the <u>consequences</u> of staying up too late is

    _____

9. In her garden, Anna gathered a <u>bouquet</u> of _____

10. We <u>converted</u> the old barn into _____

11. Over the fireplace, there are <u>portraits</u> of _____

12. Most cars and trucks <u>consume</u> _____

Copyright © McGraw Hill. Permission is granted to reproduce for classroom use.

Name _____

> • A **preposition** is a word that shows the relationship between a noun or a pronoun and another word in a sentence, such as *in, on, under, to, for, with, by, of, after,* and *during.*
>
> • The noun or pronoun that follows a preposition is the **object of the preposition:** *into the* **forest**.
>
> • An **infinitive** is formed with the word *to* and the base form of a verb, such as *to make.*
>
> • Sometimes a verb can act as a noun in a sentence. This is called a **gerund.** *The talking grew louder.*
>
> • A **participial phrase** looks like a verb but actually acts as an adjective. It modifies a noun or pronoun. It consists of the past or present participle plus other words. *The man, smiling at us, gave us the puppy.*

A. Read each sentence. Underline the preposition and circle the object of the preposition. Write the preposition on the line.

1. The waitress placed the glasses on the table. _____

2. We decided to come home after the game. _____

3. Did you find your slippers under the bed? _____

4. The worker ran errands during his lunch break. _____

5. Put the dirty laundry in the washing machine. _____

B. Circle the gerund or participial phrase.

6. The waiting is the worst part!

7. The cow, mooing loudly, left the field.

Copyright © McGraw Hill. Permission is granted to reproduce for classroom use.

Name _____

- A **preposition** is a word that shows the relationship between a noun or a pronoun and another word in a sentence. The noun or pronoun that follows a preposition is the **object of the preposition**.

- A **prepositional phrase** is a group of words that includes a preposition, the object of the preposition, and any words in between: *on the table*.

- Prepositions and prepositional phrases tell about location, time, or direction, or they provide details.

- When a pronoun is the object of a preposition, it should be an object pronoun, such as *me, you, him, her, it, us,* and *them: after him.*

Underline the prepositional phrase in each sentence.

1. Do you think you will go on the Ferris wheel?

2. We carried the bag home from the market.

3. Let's meet this afternoon at the public library.

4. Did you drop a penny down the wishing well?

5. We came in from the cold and made some hot chocolate.

6. He put the quarters into his piggy bank.

Read this sentence from "Native Americans: Yesterday and Today." Circle the prepositions and underline the prepositional phrases. Then write a sentence about a trip you took. Check your work to make sure you used prepositions and prepositional phrases correctly.

The lands of the Ojibwe, also called Chippewa, spread across what are now the states of Michigan, Wisconsin, Minnesota, and North Dakota.

_____

_____

Copyright © McGraw Hill. Permission is granted to reproduce for classroom use.

Name _____

> - Use quotation marks at the beginning and end of a person's exact words. Capitalize the first word of each sentence within the quotation.
> - If a sentence begins before a quote, use a comma before the opening quotation mark. If a sentence continues after a quote, use a comma before the ending quotation mark.
> - Use quotation marks for the titles of short works.

Rewrite each sentence by punctuating and capitalizing quotations correctly.

1. I do not want to leave yet whined the young child.

   _____

2. The student asked, "when are the reports due?"

   _____

3. The Big Blue Sea is one of my favorite short stories.

   _____

4. I said softly I do not understand."

   _____

5. Come here, Jessie, and I will show you how to do it, he said.

   _____

6. Have you heard of the fable The Tortoise and the Hare"?

   _____

 **In your writer's notebook, finish the following conversation: "I never expected you to be here." Check to make sure you used quotation marks and prepositional phrases correctly.**

Copyright © McGraw Hill. Permission is granted to reproduce for classroom use.

Name _____

> • A **preposition** is a word that shows the relationship between a noun or a pronoun and another word in a sentence.
>
> • A **prepositional phrase** is a group of words that includes a preposition, the object of the preposition, and any words in between.
>
> • Use quotation marks at the beginning and end of a person's exact words and for the titles of short works. Use correct capitalization and punctuation in quotations.

Rewrite the sentences below, correcting mistakes in prepositions and quotations.

1. We walked slowly over the woods.

_____

2. The runner zoomed beside the finish line first.

_____

3. "how are you? my mother asked my teacher.

_____

4. She leaned down the wall to keep herself from falling.

_____

_____

5. I just read a short tale called Winter Rain.

_____

6. The dog jumped into the low backyard fence.

_____

Copyright © McGraw Hill. Permission is granted to reproduce for classroom use.

Name _____

Read the paragraph. Then choose the best answer to each question.

(1) The woman stepped _____ a puddle. (2) She looked into the beautiful forest scene that was spread out in front of her. (3) The bright green leaves on the tall trees shivered in the gentle breeze. (4) Squirrels scurried up the thick brown tree trunks. (5) Two raccoons chased each other in circles _____ the base of a large bush. (6) As she stepped onto the path, she watched a little rabbit hop in front of sight.

1. What word best fits in the blank in sentence 1?

   A inside

   B at

   C under

   D over

2. What change, if any, should be made in sentence 2?

   F Change *into* to **at**

   G Change *out* to **against**

   H Change *in front of* to **above**

   J Make no change.

3. What change, if any, should be made in sentence 3?

   A Change *on* to **onto**

   B Change *on* to **inside**

   C Change *in* to **into**

   D Make no change.

4. What is the complete prepositional phrase in sentence 4?

   F Squirrels scurried up

   G scurried up the thick

   H up the thick brown tree

   J up the thick brown tree trunks

5. What word best fits in the blank in sentence 5?

   A between

   B out

   C around

   D over

6. What is the correct way to write sentence 6?

   F As she stepped onto the path, she watched a little rabbit hop out of sight.

   G As she stepped outside the path, she watched a little rabbit hop in front of sight.

   H As she stepped under the path, she watched a little rabbit hop out of sight.

   J As she stepped over the path, she watched a little rabbit hop above sight.

Copyright © McGraw Hill. Permission is granted to reproduce for classroom use.

Name _____

Fold back the paper along the dotted line. Use the blanks to write each word as it is read aloud. When you finish the test, unfold the paper. Use the list at the right to correct any spelling mistakes.

1. _____
2. _____
3. _____
4. _____
5. _____
6. _____
7. _____
8. _____
9. _____
10. _____
11. _____
12. _____
13. _____
14. _____
15. _____
16. _____
17. _____
18. _____
19. _____
20. _____

Review Words 21. _____
22. _____
23. _____

Challenge Words 24. _____
25. _____

1. wireless
2. sunny
3. furry
4. really
5. hairy
6. barely
7. tasteless
8. handful
9. lifeless
10. fitness
11. hopefully
12. happiness
13. fullness
14. sorrowful
15. gently
16. sickness
17. joyfully
18. aimless
19. breathless
20. certainly
21. disappoint
22. nonfat
23. misnumber
24. superbly
25. successfully

Copyright © McGraw Hill. Permission is granted to reproduce for classroom use.

Name _____

A **suffix** is a group of letters added to the end of a word that changes the word's meaning. Knowing the meanings of the most common suffixes can help you to understand new words.

Copyright © McGraw Hill. Permission is granted to reproduce for classroom use.

DECODING WORDS

A suffix often forms the last syllable in a word, as in the word *life-less*. Use the suffix to divide the word into syllables to decode it and figure out its meaning.

Read aloud and write the spelling words that contain the following suffixes.

wireless	hairy	lifeless	fullness	joyfully
sunny	barely	fitness	sorrowful	aimless
furry	tasteless	hopefully	gently	breathless
really	handful	happiness	sickness	certainly

-y

1. _____
2. _____
3. _____

-less

4. _____
5. _____
6. _____
7. _____
8. _____

-ful

9. _____
10. _____

-ly

11. _____
12. _____
13. _____
14. _____

-ness

15. _____
16. _____
17. _____
18. _____

-fully

19. _____
20. _____

 **Use the suffixes above to write a short rhyming poem. Include four words from the spelling list. Check your work for errors.**

Name _____

> A **suffix** is a group of letters added to the end of a word that changes the word's meaning. Knowing the meanings of the most common suffixes can help you to understand new words.

DECODING WORDS

A suffix often forms the last syllable in a word, as in the word *life-less*. Use the suffix to divide the word into syllables to decode it and figure out its meaning.

Read aloud and write the spelling words that contain the following suffixes.

wireless	hairy	lifeless	fullness	joyful
sunny	barely	fitness	foggy	hopeless
furry	tasteless	hopeful	purely	cordless
really	handful	shortness	sickness	hardly

-y

1. _____
2. _____
3. _____
4. _____

-ness

5. _____
6. _____
7. _____
8. _____

-ful

9. _____
10. _____
11. _____

-ly

12. _____
13. _____
14. _____
15. _____

-less

16. _____
17. _____
18. _____
19. _____
20. _____

 Use the suffixes above to write a short rhyming poem. Include four words from the spelling list. Check your work for errors.

Copyright © McGraw Hill. Permission is granted to reproduce for classroom use.

Name _____

Read aloud and write the spelling words that contain the following suffixes. If a word has more than one suffix, place it under all the correct headings.

wireless	hurriedly	lifeless	truthfulness	annually
casually	barely	fitness	sorrowful	aimless
furry	tasteless	hopefully	assuredly	breathlessly
constantly	wonderful	happiness	foolishness	certainly

-y

1. _____

-less

2. _____

3. _____

4. _____

5. _____

6. _____

-fully

7. _____

-ly

8. _____

9. _____

10. _____

11. _____

12. _____

13. _____

14. _____

15. _____

-ness

16. _____

17. _____

18. _____

19. _____

-ful

20. _____

21. _____

22. _____

 **Use the suffixes above to write a short rhyming poem. Include four words from the spelling list. Check your work for errors.**

Copyright © McGraw Hill. Permission is granted to reproduce for classroom use.

Name _____

wireless	hairy	lifeless	fullness	joyfully
sunny	barely	fitness	sorrowful	aimless
furry	tasteless	hopefully	gently	breathless
really	handful	happiness	sickness	certainly

A. Write the spelling word that matches each antonym below.

1. health _____

2. tasty _____

3. sadly _____

4. mostly _____

5. wired _____

6. purposeful _____

7. hairless _____

8. lively _____

9. emptiness _____

10. doubtfully _____

B. Write the spelling word that best completes each sentence.

11. I picked up a _____ of sand at the beach.

12. The computer was _____ a great invention.

13. Is it _____ or cloudy outside today?

14. I was filled with _____ when I found my lost cat.

15. My team will _____ win today.

16. It was a _____ moment when we said goodbye.

17. I was _____ after running and could not speak.

18. _____ and proper diet are important for your health.

19. She _____ held the newborn baby.

20. The _____ dog was soft and cuddly.

Copyright © McGraw Hill. Permission is granted to reproduce for classroom use.

Name _____

Underline the six misspelled words in the paragraphs below. Each paragraph has three errors. Write the words correctly on the lines.

To many, winter seems like a sorrowfull time of year. There are certainley no flowers or birds singing in the trees. This lifeliss season may seem very dreary and depressing to some people.

In contrast, spring is usually suny and happy. All the furrey animals are out of their dens and searching for food. Birds are joyfuly flying above, and flowers are blooming. For these reasons, spring is often a popular season while winter is usually not.

1. _____   4. _____

2. _____   5. _____

3. _____   6. _____

Writing Connection

Write about your favorite season and why you like it. Use four words from the spelling list.

_____

_____

_____

_____

_____

_____

_____

_____

Copyright © McGraw Hill. Permission is granted to reproduce for classroom use.

Name _____

Remember

A **suffix** is a group of letters added to the end of a word that changes the word's meaning. Knowing the meanings of the most common suffixes can help you to understand new words.

wireless	hairy	lifeless	fullness	joyfully
sunny	barely	fitness	sorrowful	aimless
furry	tasteless	hopefully	gently	breathless
really	handful	happiness	sickness	certainly

Fill in the missing letters of each word to form a spelling word. Then write the spelling word on the line and read it aloud.

1. gent __ __   _____

2. hand __ __ __   _____

3. fur __ __   _____

4. life __ __ __ __   _____

5. certain __ __   _____

6. happi __ __ __ __   _____

7. wire __ __ __ __   _____

8. joy __ __ __ __ __   _____

9. breath __ __ __ __   _____

10. bare __ __   _____

11. full __ __ __ __   _____

12. sorrow __ __ __   _____

13. real __ __   _____

14. hair __   _____

15. sick __ __ __ __   _____

16. hope __ __ __ __ __ _____

17. taste __ __ __ __   _____

18. fit __ __ __ __   _____

19. sun __ __   _____

20. aim __ __ __ __   _____

Copyright © McGraw Hill. Permission is granted to reproduce for classroom use.

Name _____

Read each sentence from "The Generation Belt" below. For each word in bold, write the denotation on the line. Then write its connotation.

1. She could see her father's **sleek** canoe far off in the distance.

_____

2. Kanti's grandmother looked **dignified** sitting cross-legged in the center of their wigwam.

_____

_____

3. She held out an **elaborate** belt for Kanti to see.

_____

4. She looked at the loom with a **scant** five rows completed.

_____

_____

Copyright © McGraw Hill. Permission is granted to reproduce for classroom use.

Name _____

Many English words have roots from the ancient languages Greek and Latin. A few of these words are derived from the names of people and places in **Greek and Roman mythology**. If you know about these characters and stories, you can figure out the meanings of the words. The following mythical figures have inspired words we use today:

- **Odysseus** was a hero who went on a very long journey.
- The **Titans** were giant gods who ruled Earth.
- **Jove** lent his name to the planet Jupiter. People born under the influence of Jupiter were said to be joyful.
- **Echo** was cursed to only repeat words spoken by others.
- **Hercules** was a hero known for his great strength.
- The **Furies** were goddesses who cursed and tortured others.

Each sentence below contains a word derived from the names above. Use the explanations provided, your background knowledge, and context clues to write a definition for the underlined word.

1. Moving the heavy sofa seemed like a herculean task.

   _____

2. Everyone at the party was in a jovial mood.

   _____

3. The hurricane hit the town with a fury that had never been seen before.

   _____

4. Our trip home turned out to be a twelve-hour odyssey.

   _____

5. The explorers' voices echoed off the walls of the cave.

   _____

6. The skyscraper was a titanic structure that towered over us.

   _____

Copyright © McGraw Hill. Permission is granted to reproduce for classroom use.

Name _____

> • Prepositional phrases show location, time, and direction. They provide more details.
>
> • Two or more simple sentences that have **prepositional phrases** can sometimes be combined into one sentence. *The parrot was in the tree. The tree was at the park. The parrot was in the tree at the park.*

Combine the sentences with prepositional phrases.

1. We saw zebras at the zoo. The zoo was in the city.

   _____

2. Wally walked around the building. The building was on the hill.

   _____

3. The rabbit ran across the field. It ran to a low bush.

   _____

4. The car pulled into the driveway. It arrived before nightfall.

   _____

Writing Connection **Write a paragraph about all the activities that go on in the park. Include and underline at least three prepositions. Then check your work. Combine any sentences if you can.**

_____

_____

_____

_____

Copyright © McGraw Hill. Permission is granted to reproduce for classroom use.

Name _____

> • Two or more simple sentences that have **prepositional phrases** can sometimes be combined.
>
> • Prepositional phrases show location, time, and direction. They provide more details.
>
> • A prepositional phrase may be at the beginning, middle, or end of a sentence.
>
> • If the prepositional phrase begins the sentence, a comma is often inserted at the end of the phrase. *After school, I went home.*

A. Read each sentence and the prepositional phrase in parentheses. Add the prepositional phrase to the <u>beginning</u> of the sentence and rewrite the sentence on the line.

1. We all went back to the classroom. (after lunch)

   _____

2. You can see the little town. (past the mountain)

   _____

B. Read each sentence and the prepositional phrase in parentheses. Add the prepositional phrase to the <u>end</u> of the sentence and rewrite the sentence on the line.

3. I leaned tiredly. (against the gym wall)

   _____

4. Will you go to the supermarket? (with me)

   _____

 In your writer's notebook, write a paragraph about everything you have to do today. Include at least five prepositional phrases. Circle the preposition and underline the prepositional phrase.

Copyright © McGraw Hill. Permission is granted to reproduce for classroom use.

Name _____

- A prepositional phrase that begins a sentence is often followed by a comma.

- Appositives and appositive phrases giving extra information about a noun or pronoun are usually set off by commas. *The cat, a British shorthair, walked across the table.*

- When two adjectives modify a noun in the same way, there should be a comma between them: *the small, brown dog.*

Rewrite each sentence correctly by adding commas.

1. The tall thin man walked quickly across the room.

   _____

2. My pet lizard a sneaky creature escaped when I wasn't looking.

   _____

   _____

3. In the morning I like to have breakfast before getting dressed.

   _____

4. My grandfather a great man lives near the railroad tracks in town.

   _____

 In your writer's notebook, write a short passage describing your favorite after-school activity. Underline each prepositional phrase and circle each appositive that you include.

Copyright © McGraw Hill. Permission is granted to reproduce for classroom use.

Name _____

> • Two or more simple sentences can be combined by adding a **prepositional phrase**.
>
> • Prepositional phrases at the beginning of a sentence (and sometimes in the middle) have commas.
>
> • Appositives and appositive phrases are usually set off by commas.
>
> • When two adjectives modify a noun in the same way, there should be a comma between them.

Rewrite the paragraphs below, correcting mistakes in prepositional phrases and punctuation.

HANDWRITING CONNECTION

Be sure to write legibly. Use proper cursive and leave appropriate spaces between words.

1. Hannah my best friend, really went out of her way to help me today. On the bus this morning she helped me study for my math test. At lunch, she gave me half of her dessert. It was a sweet crunchy cookie. She also lent me a pencil when I lost mine. I couldn't ask for a better friend!

_____

_____

_____

_____

2. Growing a garden is harder than you might think. When you plant, the seeds they should be spaced evenly. Small shallow, holes are usually best. Then you must water the seeds and be patient. Waiting can be the hardest part.

_____

_____

_____

_____

Copyright © McGraw Hill. Permission is granted to reproduce for classroom use.

Name _____

Read the sentences. Then choose the best answer to each question.

(1) The people watched the ship sail. (2) It was sailing to the open sea. (3) The audience cheered. (4) They cheered for the ship. (5) I yelled out. (6) It was in an excited way.

(7) Then we walked to the park. (8) The park was down the block. (9) We pulled out our fishing rods. (10) We pulled them out of our bags. (11) I caught a fish from the lake. (12) It was a big bass.

1. What is the best way to combine sentences 1 and 2?
   A   The people watched the sailing ship the open sea.
   B   The people watched the ship sail to the open sea.
   C   The people watched the open ship sailing to the sea.
   D   The people to the open sea watched the ship sail.

2. What is the best way to combine sentences 3 and 4?
   F   The audience cheered the ship for.
   G   For the audience, the ship cheered.
   H   The audience cheered for the ship.
   J   The ship for the audience cheered.

3. What is the best way to combine sentences 5 and 6?
   A   I yelled out in a way.
   B   In an excited yell, I yelled out.
   C   In a way, I excited yelled out.
   D   In an excited way, I yelled out.

4. What is the best way to combine sentences 7 and 8?
   F   Then we walked to the park down the block.
   G   Then we walked down the block.
   H   Then we walked to the park was down the block.
   J   Down the block then we walked to the park.

5. What is the best way to combine sentences 9 and 10?
   A   We pulled our fishing rods out of our bags.
   B   We pulled our fishing rods and our bags out.
   C   We out of our bags pulled our fishing rods out.
   D   Out of our bags we pulled them out.

6. What is the best way to combine sentences 11 and 12?
   F   From the lake a big bass I caught.
   G   I caught a big bass from the lake.
   H   A big bass was pulled from the lake where I caught a fish.
   J   I caught a fish from the lake, it was a big bass.

Copyright © McGraw Hill. Permission is granted to reproduce for classroom use.

Name _____

Fold back the paper along the dotted line. Use the blanks to write each word as it is read aloud. When you finish the test, unfold the paper. Use the list at the right to correct any spelling mistakes.

1. _____
2. _____
3. _____
4. _____
5. _____
6. _____
7. _____
8. _____
9. _____
10. _____
11. _____
12. _____
13. _____
14. _____
15. _____
16. _____
17. _____
18. _____
19. _____
20. _____

Review Words 21. _____
22. _____
23. _____
Challenge Words 24. _____
25. _____

1. unchanged
2. unnamed
3. restate
4. reverse
5. infrequent
6. invisible
7. prepaid
8. displease
9. action
10. establishment
11. oversized
12. prejudge
13. interstate
14. intersect
15. deflate
16. semiweekly
17. happily
18. kindness
19. finally
20. fearful
21. really
22. handful
23. happiness
24. transplant
25. superhuman

Copyright © McGraw Hill. Permission is granted to reproduce for classroom use.

Name _____

> A **prefix** is a group of letters added to the *beginning* of a word that changes the word's meaning. A **suffix** is a group of letters added to the *end* of a word that changes the word's meaning. Knowing the meanings of the most common prefixes and suffixes can help you to understand new words.

SPELLING TIP

More than one prefix and suffix can be added to a word at once, such as *im·person·al·ly*. Each prefix and suffix changes the word's meaning slightly.

Read aloud and write the spelling words that contain the following prefixes or suffixes. If a word has more than one suffix or prefix, place it under all the correct headings.

deflate	infrequent	fearful	interstate	reverse
unnamed	intersect	establishment	invisible	kindness
restate	prepaid	oversized	unchanged	finally
happily	displease	prejudge	semiweekly	action

in-
1. _____
2. _____

over-
3. _____

un-
4. _____
5. _____

pre-
6. _____
7. _____

inter-
8. _____
9. _____

de-
10. _____

semi-
11. _____

re-
12. _____
13. _____

dis-
14. _____

-ness
15. _____

-ful
16. _____

-ion
17. _____

-ment
18. _____

-ly
19. _____
20. _____
21. _____

 **Work with a partner to find more words that contain the prefixes and suffixes listed above. Record the words you find in your writer's notebook.**

Copyright © McGraw Hill. Permission is granted to reproduce for classroom use.

Name _____

> A **prefix** is a group of letters added to the *beginning* of a word that changes the word's meaning. A **suffix** is a group of letters added to the *end* of a word that changes the word's meaning. Knowing the meanings of the most common prefixes and suffixes can help you to understand new words.

SPELLING TIP

More than one prefix and suffix can be added to a word at once, such as *im·person·al·ly*. Each prefix and suffix changes the word's meaning slightly.

Read aloud and write the spelling words that contain the following prefixes or suffixes. If a word has more than one suffix or prefix, place it under all the correct headings.

deplane	underdog	fearful	interstate	reverse
unnamed	intersect	establishment	invisible	kindness
restate	prepaid	oversized	unchanged	finally
happily	displease	prepack	semiweekly	action

under-

1. _____

in-

2. _____

over-

3. _____

un-

4. _____

5. _____

pre-

6. _____

7. _____

inter-

8. _____

9. _____

de-

10. _____

semi-

11. _____

re-

12. _____

13. _____

dis-

14. _____

-ness

15. _____

-ful

16. _____

-ion

17. _____

-ment

18. _____

-ly

19. _____

20. _____

21. _____

Work with a partner to find more words that contain the prefixes and suffixes listed above. Record the words you find in your writer's notebook.

Copyright © McGraw Hill. Permission is granted to reproduce for classroom use.

Name _____

Read aloud and write the spelling words that contain the following prefixes or suffixes. If a word has more than one suffix or prefix, place it under all the correct headings.

deflate	infrequently	fearful	interstate	reversible
unnamed	intersection	establishment	invisible	kindness
restated	prepaid	oversized	unchanged	finally
happily	displeased	prejudged	semiweekly	inaction

in-

1. _____

2. _____

3. _____

over-

4. _____

un-

5. _____

6. _____

pre-

7. _____

8. _____

inter-

9. _____

10. _____

de-

11. _____

semi-

12. _____

re-

13. _____

14. _____

dis-

15. _____

-ness

16. _____

-ful

17. _____

-ion

18. _____

19. _____

-ment

20. _____

-ly

21. _____

22. _____

23. _____

24. _____

 **Work with a partner to find more words that contain the prefixes and suffixes listed above. Record the words you find in your writer's notebook.**

Copyright © McGraw Hill. Permission is granted to reproduce for classroom use.

Name _____

unchanged	infrequent	action	interstate	happily
unnamed	invisible	establishment	intersect	kindness
restate	prepaid	oversized	deflate	finally
reverse	displease	prejudge	semiweekly	fearful

A. Write the spelling word that matches each definition below.

1. at last _____

2. the same _____

3. something created _____

4. something done _____

5. not often _____

6. highway _____

7. frightened _____

8. backward _____

9. remove air _____

10. cross over _____

B. Write the spelling word that best completes each sentence.

11. We _____ and excitedly got ready for the party.

12. Obey the rules so you will not _____ the teacher.

13. Air is _____, and you cannot see it.

14. Do not _____ me before you get to know me.

15. My mother goes to the gym _____.

16. The _____ sofa had lots of room for everyone.

17. An _____ person paid the patient's hospital bill.

18. Please _____ your name because I did not hear you.

19. _____ and generosity are good traits to have.

20. She owed no money for the _____ dress.

Copyright © McGraw Hill. Permission is granted to reproduce for classroom use.

Name _____

Underline the three misspelled words in each paragraph below. Write the words correctly on the lines.

Ali's mother drove the car down the inturstate. She saw Ali's face in the car mirror. It had remained unnchanged since she got home from school. It seemed as if an envisible weight was on Ali's shoulders, but she would not tell her mother what was wrong.

Finaly, Ali's mother turned into the overrsized driveway of the barn where Ali rode horses. Her mother checked the mirror and saw a smile on Ali's face. Her mother smiled back happilly. She knew that an afternoon with the horses would cheer Ali up.

1. _____   4. _____

2. _____   5. _____

3. _____   6. _____

Writing Connection   **Write about something that makes you happy. Use four words from the spelling list.**

_____

_____

_____

_____

_____

_____

_____

_____

Copyright © McGraw Hill. Permission is granted to reproduce for classroom use.

Name _____

Copyright © McGraw Hill. Permission is granted to reproduce for classroom use.

Remember

A **prefix** is a group of letters added to the *beginning* of a word that changes the word's meaning. A **suffix** is a group of letters added to the *end* of a word that changes the word's meaning. Knowing the meanings of the most common prefixes and suffixes can help you figure out the meaning of unfamiliar words.

unchanged	infrequent	action	interstate	happily
unnamed	invisible	establishment	intersect	kindness
restate	prepaid	oversized	deflate	finally
reverse	displease	prejudge	semiweekly	fearful

Fill in the missing prefix or suffix to form a spelling word. Then read aloud and write the spelling word on the line.

1. __ __ state _____

2. __ __ flate _____

3. fear __ __ __ _____

4. __ __ __ please _____

5. act __ __ __ _____

6. establish __ __ __ __ __ _____

7. __ __ changed _____

8. happi __ __ _____

9. __ __ verse _____

10. __ __ __ judge _____

11. __ __ visible _____

12. kind __ __ __ __ _____

13. __ __ __ __ __ weekly _____

14. __ __ __ __ __ __ state _____

15. final __ __ _____

16. __ __ __ paid _____

17. __ __ __ __ sized _____

18. __ __ __ __ __ __ sect _____

19. __ __ named _____

20. __ __ __ frequent _____

Name _____

> When you add prefixes, suffixes, and inflectional endings to the same base word, you create a group of **related words**. Examine the following related words with the base *individual* and think about their meanings.
>
> **individualize   individuality   individualism   individualist   individualistic**

Add the prefixes and suffixes in the box to write as many related words for the base word as you can. Read the words aloud. Use a dictionary to check words and spellings.

im-	-ed	-ine
re-	-ing	-ary
un-	-able	-ation

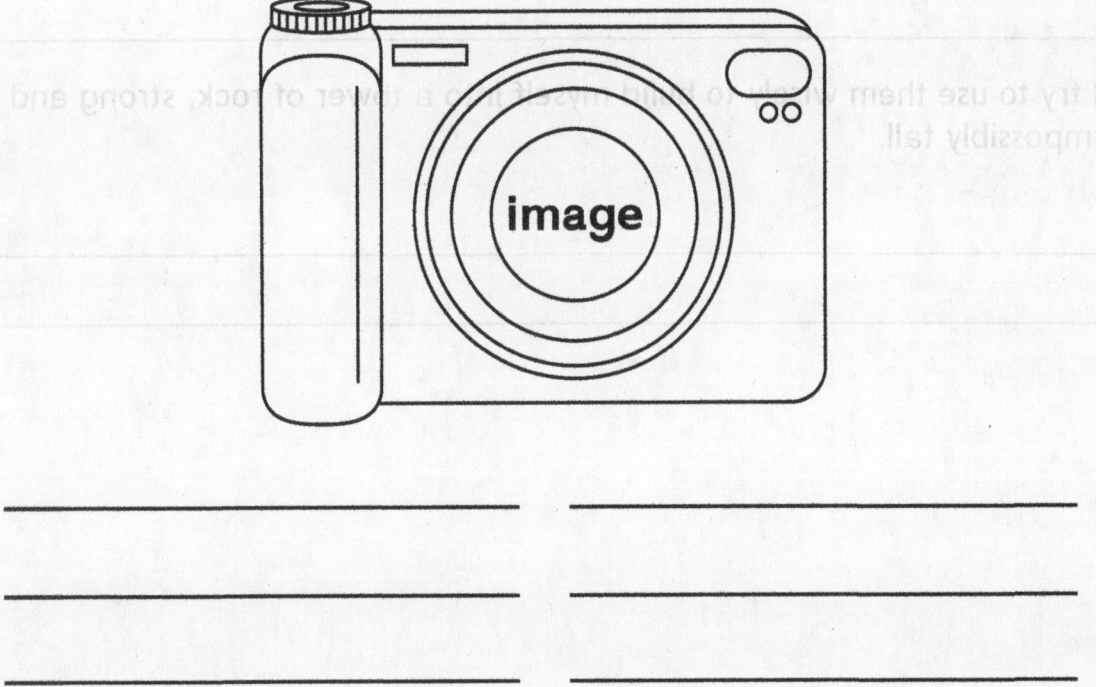

_____   _____

_____   _____

_____   _____

Copyright © McGraw Hill. Permission is granted to reproduce for classroom use.

Name _____

Read each passage. Underline the metaphor in the passage. Then write the two things that are being compared on the lines.

1. On the days I feel best, I am the Rocky Mountains . . .

    _____

    _____

2. On my worst day, I am Florida, the ocean tempting me away from the mainland . . .

    _____

    _____

3. I rise into the air, my hair a mist against the blue of the sky.

    _____

    _____

4. I try to use them wisely to build myself into a tower of rock, strong and impossibly tall.

    _____

    _____

Copyright © McGraw Hill. Permission is granted to reproduce for classroom use.

HANDWRITING

Table of Contents

Copyright © McGraw Hill. Permission is granted to reproduce for classroom use.

Cursive Writing Position

Left-Handed Writers

Sit tall. Place both arms on the table.

Keep your feet flat on the floor.

Slant your paper.

Hold your pencil with your first two fingers and your thumb.

Right-Handed Writers

Sit tall. Place both arms on the table.

Keep your feet flat on the floor.

Slant your paper.

Hold your pencil with your first two fingers and your thumb.

Copyright © McGraw Hill. Permission is granted to reproduce for classroom use.

The Cursive Alphabet

Aa Bb Cc Dd

Ee Ff Gg Hh

Ii Jj Kk Ll

Mm Nn Oo Pp

Qq Rr Ss Tt

Uu Vv Ww Xx

Yy Zz

Copyright © McGraw Hill. Permission is granted to reproduce for classroom use.

Size and Shape

Tall letters touch the top line.　　**Make your writing easy to read.**

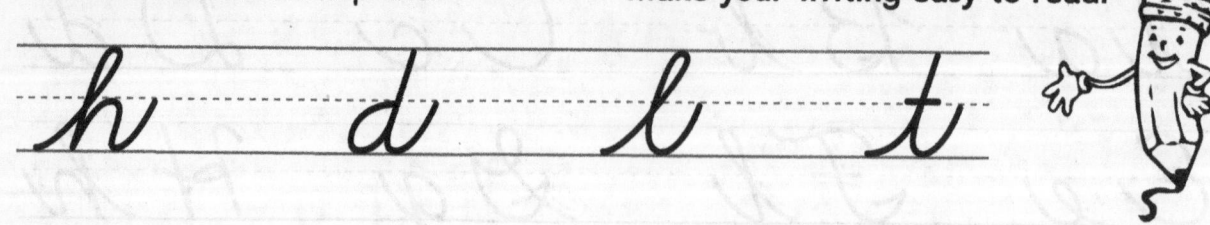

Short letters touch the middle line.

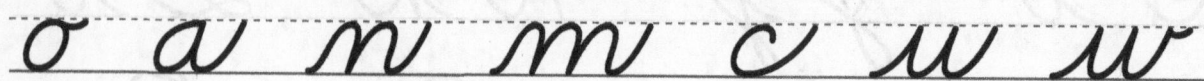

These letters go below the bottom line.

Circle the letters that are the right size and shape and sit on the bottom line.

Copyright © McGraw Hill. Permission is granted to reproduce for classroom use.

i t

Trace and write the letters. Then trace and write the word.

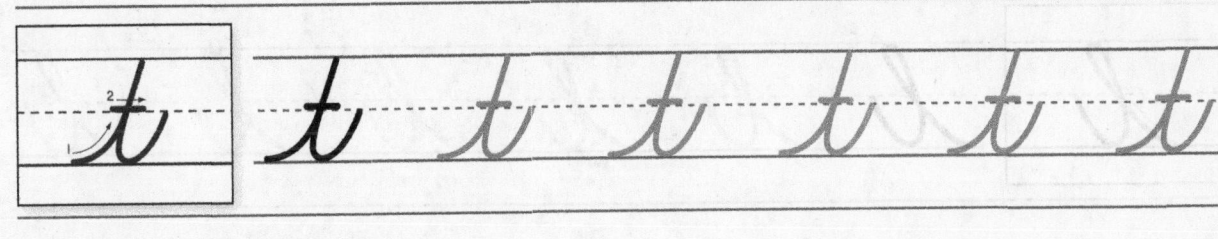

Copyright © McGraw Hill. Permission is granted to reproduce for classroom use.

e l

Trace and write the letters. Then write the words.

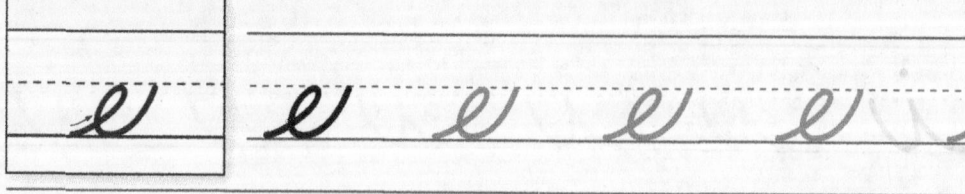

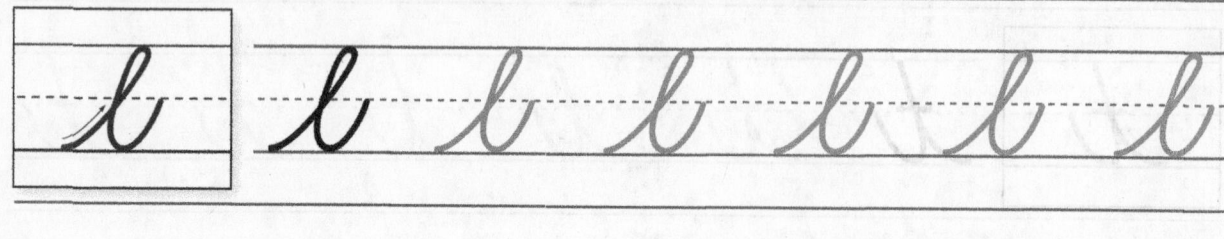

Copyright © McGraw Hill. Permission is granted to reproduce for classroom use.

o a

Trace and write the letters. Then write the words.

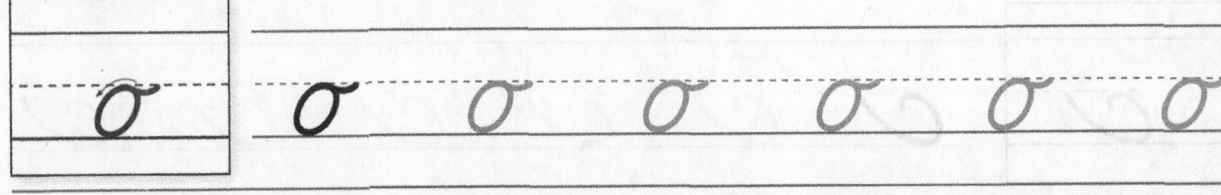

o o o o o o o o

a a a a a a a a

toe toll tail ate

tote oil oat lot

Copyright © McGraw Hill. Permission is granted to reproduce for classroom use.

c d

Trace and write the letters. Then write the words and the phrases.

c c c c c c c c c

d d d d d d d

coat deed code

dime dance time

Copyright © McGraw Hill. Permission is granted to reproduce for classroom use.

n m

Trace and write the letters. Then write the words.

n n n n n n

m m m m m m

name note moat

mitten tame nine

Copyright © McGraw Hill. Permission is granted to reproduce for classroom use.

Connectives

Trace the connectives.

air tie her like

an and end sand

glad just yell

zebra you yarn

gap lazy game

five pick jam

feel plan quite

Copyright © McGraw Hill. Permission is granted to reproduce for classroom use.

u w

Trace and write the letters. Then write the words.

u u u u u u

w w w w w w

wait wit would

undo uncle lute

Copyright © McGraw Hill. Permission is granted to reproduce for classroom use.

Name _____   Date _____

b f

Trace and write the letters. Then write the words and the phrases.

b b b b b b b

f f f f f f f

boat   fall   bubble

fine food bat ball

Copyright © McGraw Hill. Permission is granted to reproduce for classroom use.

h k

Trace and write the letters. Then write the words.

h   *h   h   h   h   h*

k   *k   k   k   k   k*

chick   hatch   hook

kilt   luck   kite

Copyright © McGraw Hill. Permission is granted to reproduce for classroom use.

Name _____ Date _____

g q

Trace and write the letters. Then write the phrases.

g g g g g g g

q q q q q q q

quacked good game

quite a fog

Copyright © McGraw Hill. Permission is granted to reproduce for classroom use.

j p

Trace and write the letters. Then write the phrases.

j j j j j j j

p p p p p p p

jump for joy

picture perfect

Copyright © McGraw Hill. Permission is granted to reproduce for classroom use.

r s

Trace and write the letters. Then write the phrases.

r r r r r r r r

s s s s s s s s

rose blossom

stars and stripes

Copyright © McGraw Hill. Permission is granted to reproduce for classroom use.

y z

Trace and write the letters. Then write the phrases.

y *y* *y* *y* *y* *y* *y* *y*

z *z* *z* *z* *z* *z* *z*

zip code zoom in

pretty azaleas

Copyright © McGraw Hill. Permission is granted to reproduce for classroom use.

v x

Trace and write the letters. Then write the phrases.

v v v v v v v v

x x x x x x x x

x marks the spot

vim and vigor

Copyright © McGraw Hill. Permission is granted to reproduce for classroom use.

Size and Shape

All uppercase letters are tall letters.
Tall letters should touch the top line.

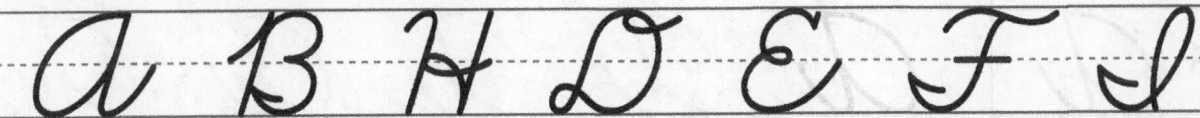

Letters with descenders go below the bottom line.

J   Z   Y

You can make your writing easy to read.

Look at the letters below. Circle the letters that are the correct size and shape.

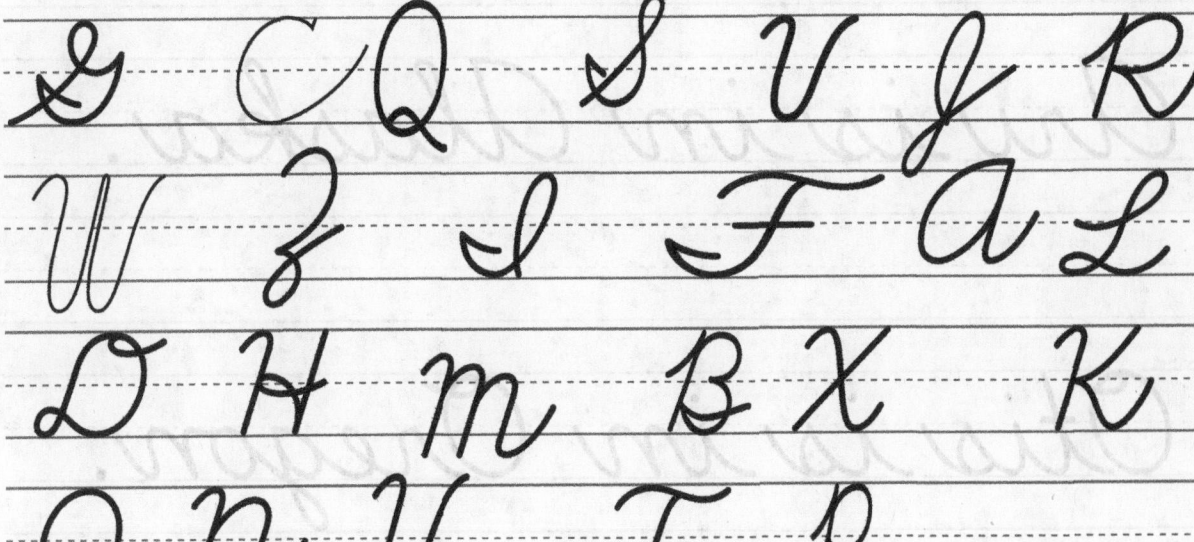

Copyright © McGraw Hill. Permission is granted to reproduce for classroom use.

A O

Trace and write the letters. Then write the sentences.

a   a   a   a   a   a

O   O   O   O   O   O

Ari is in Alaska.

Otis is in Oregon.

Copyright © McGraw Hill. Permission is granted to reproduce for classroom use.

C E

Trace and write the letters. Then write the sentences.

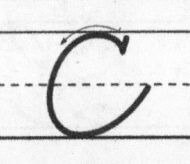 C C C C C C

 E E E E E E

Cece visits China.

Ed is in England.

Copyright © McGraw Hill. Permission is granted to reproduce for classroom use.

L D

Trace and write the letters. Then write the sentences.

L L L L L L

D D D D D D

Dad did a dance.

Leo dined at Del's.

Copyright © McGraw Hill. Permission is granted to reproduce for classroom use.

B R

Trace and write the letters. Then write the sentences.

B B B B B B

R R R R R R

Bill is in Brazil.

Rose is in Russia.

Copyright © McGraw Hill. Permission is granted to reproduce for classroom use.

T F

Trace and write the letters. Then write the sentences.

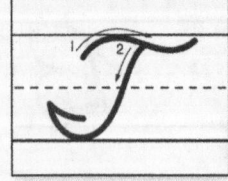 𝒯 𝒯 𝒯 𝒯 𝒯 𝒯

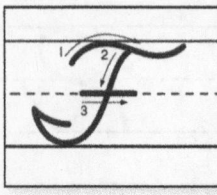 𝓕 𝓕 𝓕 𝓕 𝓕 𝓕

Theodore Roosevelt won. Friends cheer.

Copyright © McGraw Hill. Permission is granted to reproduce for classroom use.

S G

Trace and write the letters. Then write the sentences.

Sal Sr. met Gail.

Greg is our guest.

Copyright © McGraw Hill. Permission is granted to reproduce for classroom use.

I J

Trace and write the letters. Then write the sentences.

$\mathcal{I}$ $\mathcal{I}$ $\mathcal{I}$ $\mathcal{I}$ $\mathcal{I}$ $\mathcal{I}$ $\mathcal{I}$

$\mathcal{J}$ $\mathcal{J}$ $\mathcal{J}$ $\mathcal{J}$ $\mathcal{J}$ $\mathcal{J}$ $\mathcal{J}$

Ida is in India.

Jack is in Japan.

Copyright © McGraw Hill. Permission is granted to reproduce for classroom use.

Spacing Letters and Words

You can make your writing easy to read. Letters should not be too close or too far apart.

These letters are spaced just right.

Draw a slanted line between these words to check that the spacing is as wide as a small o. Then copy the sentences.

The flowers are in bloom.

Smell the flowers!

N M

Trace and write the letters. Then write the sentences.

n *n* *n* *n* *n* *n* *n*

m *m* *m* *m* *m* *m* *m*

Nebraska Nevada

Minnesota Maine

Copyright © McGraw Hill. Permission is granted to reproduce for classroom use.

H K

Trace and write the letters. Then write the sentences.

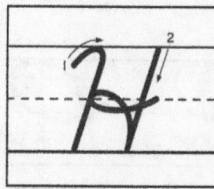  

H H H H H H H

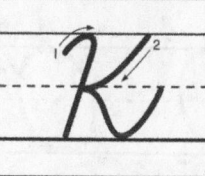

K K K K K K K

Hank likes Haiti.

Kai likes Kansas.

Copyright © McGraw Hill. Permission is granted to reproduce for classroom use.

P Q

Trace and write the letters. Then write the sentences.

P P P P P P P P P

Q Q Q Q Q Q Q Q Q

Quebec Quin Quito

Pittsburgh Plano

Copyright © McGraw Hill. Permission is granted to reproduce for classroom use.

Name _____ Date _____

V U

Trace and write the letters. Then write the sentences.

V V V V V V V

U U U U U U U

Viv is in Vermont.

Ute lives in Utah.

Copyright © McGraw Hill. Permission is granted to reproduce for classroom use.

W X

Trace and write the letters. Then write the words.

𝒲 𝒲 𝒲 𝒲 𝒲 𝒲

𝒳 𝒳 𝒳 𝒳 𝒳 𝒳

Will Waco Wales

Xavier Xia X-axis

Copyright © McGraw Hill. Permission is granted to reproduce for classroom use.

Y Z

Trace and write the letters. Then write the words.

Y Y Y Y Y Y Y

Z Z Z Z Z Z Z

Yolanda Yukon

Zena Zen Zachary

Copyright © McGraw Hill. Permission is granted to reproduce for classroom use.

Transition to Two Lines

Write the sentences. In the last two rows, write the sentences without the guidelines.

A robin has wings.

Ostriches run fast.

Parrots can talk.

Ducks lay eggs.

Copyright © McGraw Hill. Permission is granted to reproduce for classroom use.

Practice with Small Letters

This is your first complete lesson without a dotted control line. Write your letters and words the same way you have been writing them all year.

e u s r a

i w m n o

see rain mane

Sam was sure

he saw a fox.

Copyright © McGraw Hill. Permission is granted to reproduce for classroom use.

Practice with Tall Letters

Practice writing tall letters and words with tall letters. All tall letters should reach the top line.

t d l k h b f

fit tall doll kit

Tiff is the best.

Jill likes ducks.

Copyright © McGraw Hill. Permission is granted to reproduce for classroom use.